DISASTER MANAGEMENT
Approaches & Strategies

DISASTER MANAGEMENT
Approaches & Strategies

Tej Singh

AKANSHA PUBLISHING HOUSE
NEW DELHI • GUWAHATI • VISAKHAPATNAM

AKANSHA PUBLISHING HOUSE
4649-B/21, Ansari Road
Darya Ganj, New Delhi - 110 002
Ph.: 23263193 / 9811582579 / 09435116718
Fax: 011-23263193
Email: ektabooks@yahoo.com
www.akanshapublishinghouse.com

Disaster Management Approaches & Strategies

First Published 2006
First Reprint 2007
Second Reprint 2012

PRINTED IN INDIA

Published by Akansha Publishing House, New Delhi and Printed at Harmain Offset, Delhi.

Contents

Preface

The common view of disaster is due for a radical change. Though triggered of by natural events such as floods and earthquakes, disasters are increasingly man made. Some disasters (floods, droughts, famines) are caused more by environmental and resource mismanagement than by too much or too little rainfall. The impact of other disasters which are triggered by acts of nature (earthquake, volcano, tsumani, hurricane) are magnified by unwise human actions. Disasters are social and political events which can be and often are prevented. In the Developing countries, where the poor are forced to overuse their land and live on dangerous grounds, disasters are taking a rising toll. By emphasizing mitigation instead of development, current disaster relief is often inadequate to the task it sets itself.

We can only tackle the root causes if disaster prevention and response are designed so as to incorporate both developmental and environmental strategies. We must get at the root causes and reverse the trends of increasing poverty and environmental degradation before it is too late. A sustainable eco-system must be our aim, as one in which the global family can live in balanced harmony with the whole of nature. The rural poor, who are the principal victims of the three elements which between them make up the major part of the Third World disasters—deforestations, soil erosion and desertification should be central to the work of all disaster agencies. All the trends emphasize that ignorance and grinding poverty accelerate the onslaught of disasters and exacerbate the cruel impact they have, particularly on vulnerable groups of people. The poor, the handicapped, the infant and the aged are the first to lose their basic right to food, shelter and health. They need and deserve our help. The social development of people and their communities in disaster prone areas has been grossly ignored by governments and agencies alike. Such appalling human conditions can best be fought through the weapons of self-reliance, literacy, preventive health care and equitable pricing structures for rural food producers, that is, helping people to respond to their own basic needs, within their environment.

It has been a fundamental truth that disasters have been with us for as long as recorded history or even before that. Of late, it has been noticed that disasters (natural calamities) have become more frequent and diversified. It is also observed that poor—poor nations and poor people are more vulnerable to disasters. Due to inadequate infrastructure, poor communication facilities, and inadequate resource mobilization and lack of proper mechanism for rescue, relief and rehabilitation they suffer most. Though on any such eventuality the international agencies come forward with ready help, yet the time factor is most crucial at such moments. As such every nation must develop an efficient crisis management mechanism, forewarning system etc.

The present book addresses all crucial aspects of disaster management. The frequency, proneness, gravity, dimensions and magnitude, types, forewarning systems, rescue, relief and rehabilitation measures etc. In collating the readings, we have referred to and drawn much from the works of a number of leading experts in the field to whom we are highly indebted. In fact entire credit for this must go to all those leading scientists.

I am thankful to my colleagues and friends for their assistance and support while compiling the material. Finally Mr. M.P. Misra deserves all appreciation for materialising this venture.

We will feel amply rewarded if this could prove of some use to readers.

—Editor

1

Disaster: An Introduction

> To things, well considered, would prevent many quarrels: first, to have it well ascertained whether we are not disputing about terms rather than things and, second, to examine whether that on which we differ is worth contending about.
>
> —*Charles C. Colton*

> He who foresees calamaties, suffers them twice over.
>
> —*B. Porteus*

According to UNDHA (2001), "a disaster is a serious disruption of the functioning of society, causing widespread human, material or environmental losses which exceed the ability of affected society to cope on its own resources."

In fact, this clearly implies that the poor people/society are the most vulnerable to hazards/disasters as they possess fewer resources and have very poor capacity to prevent or cope with the impacts. No doubt, the sheer scope of the social and económic impacts of natural approach to dealing with the concept of risk and vulnerability in modern societies. Also, the social and economic costs of disasters unestimable and are difficult to estimate on a global basis. As far as international policy response is concerned, until the 1970s, the international community considered disasters as exceptional circumstances, when local coping capabilities were exhausted from external emergency relief was required. The term disaster management was considered equivalent to disaster response and tended to be within the exclusive competence of organizations such as IFCR or national civil societies defence institutions.

As per the Oxford English Dictionary states that the word 'disaster' derives from the 16th century French word 'disastre.' which is a combination of two terms. 'Des' meaning bad or evil and 'Astre,' means star, thus 'Desastre' signifying a 'Bad Star' or 'Evil Star.' (i.e. bad luck in spiritual terms) Disaster, therefore, was implying loss or damage occurring due to some unfavourable star.

Definitions

Turner (1977) has given a rather comprehensive definition of disaster:

> "An event, concentrated in time and space, which threaten a society or a relatively self-sufficient sub-division of a society which major unwanted consequences as a result of the collapse of precautions which had hitherto been culturally accepted as adequate."

Kreps (1984), elaborating upon an earlier attempt by Fritz, gave a more detailed of disaster in the following definition:

> 'Disasters are events, observable in time and space, in which societies or their larger such-units (e.g. communities, regions incur physical damages and losses and/or disruption of their routine functioning. Both the causes and consequences of those events are related to the social structures and processes of society or their sub-units.'

UNDRO (1984) has defined a disaster in more qualitative terms:

> "An event, concentrated in time and space, in which a community undergoes severe danger and incurs such losses to its members and physical *appurtenances* that the social structure is disrupted and the fulfillment of all or some of the essential functions of the society is prevented."

However, in terms of modern knowledge, the term

'disaster' denotes any odd event, whether natural or man-made, which can bring about sudden and great miseries to humanity in terms of loss of life or/and property. It also signifies misfortune at larger scale or a calamity of considerable amount for a section of humanity. Such calamitous event may have sudden destructive impact or may create distress over an extended period. The alternative meanings are similar to that of cataclysm, catastrophe, tragedy or devastation.

Factors which contribute to the construction of a rational definition of disaster are the following:

(a) multiple deaths or serious injuries occurring more or less simultaneously for which there is no one obvious human agent.

(b) severe, disruption of normal life pattern

(c) considerable loss of life, livelihood, hardship, resources crunch, property damage and adverse impact on health such as spread of disease or epidemics

(d) considerable adverse effect on social structure, such as destruction of or damage to infrastructure, buildings, communications and other essential services.

(e) considerable disruption of community needs such as shelter, food, clothing, medical assistance and social case.

(f) disasters by their nature are relative, contingent and often indeterminate.

(g) disasters usually involve high magnitude, low-probability events

(h) cause unpredicted and unexpected harm and are worthy of public attention.

The above types of definitions convey a better idea of the social stress created by a disaster, although no threshold or scale is given. It too concentrates on losses and implies a major incident requiring the mobilization of emergency services. So, a disaster can also be regarded as a particular type of an emergency, suggesting thereby an intense time-period and level of urgency.

Thus, the term, disaster, may be defined as an unexpected happening causing a huge loss of life and property. It may be both natural as well as man-made in the sense tnat in some parts of the country, floods occur due to the construction of check dams and embankments on the rivers. Disaster may come in the form of earthquakes, cyclones, floods, drought, fire etc. and ruin the life and property of the people. Though trigger-off by natural events such as floods and earthquakes, disasters are increasingly becoming man-made. Some disasters (floods, droughts, famines) are caused more by environmental and resource mismanagement than by too much or too little rainfall, the impact of other disasters which are triggered by acts of nature (earthquake, volcano, hurricane, tsumani) are magnified by unwise human actions. Disasters are social and political events which can be and often are prevented. In the developing countries where the poor are forced to overuse their land and live on dangerous grounds, disasters are taking a rising toll. By emphasizing mitigation instead of development, current disaster reliefs are often inadequate to the task they sets themselves. The common vector indentation of natural disaster is undergoing a radical change. A new term may even be needed, such as 'nature disaster' to distinguish calamities associated with the forces of nature from such tribulations as war and factory explosions. Today humans are playing too large a role in natural disasters. So a distinction must be made between the triggered events —too little rain, too much rain, earthshocks, hurricanes—which may be natural and the associated disasters which may be largely man-made. Despite the death, destruction and other effects of major natural disasters, researchers have received surprisingly little scientific attention. Science has not even had much success defining what is means by the term 'disaster.' Dictionaries use words such as 'misfortune' or 'calamity' implying, that a disaster implies suffering of the people. Thus, a cyclone or an earthquake is not a disaster unless it kills people or destroys property. However, in 1969 the Natural Hazard Research Group at the University of Colorado (US) defined disasters only in terms of their impact upon people. They came up with the following definition of a disaster: (i) more than $1 million in damage, or (ii) more than 100 people dead, or more than 100 people injured. This definition had the effect of separating the disaster event—destruction, death and injuries from the bigger mechanisms—high winds earth shocks lack of rain, excess of water, lava and high waves.

Causation

Human communities will always face natural hazards like floods, droughts, storms, earthquakes but today's disasters are sometimes man-made, and human action—or inaction-exacerbates virtually all of them. Poverty and population pressures increase the costs of natural hazards because more and more people have been forced to live on flood plains, earthquake-prone zones and unstable mountainous areas. Also, it is not accidental that more than 90% of all disaster victims worldwide live in developing countries. Unsustainable development practices also contribute to the ever greater impact of natural hazards. Massive logging operations reduce the soils capacity to absorb heavy rainfall, making erosion and flooding more likely. The destruction of wetlands reduces the ability of the land to soak-up run-off, which in turn increases the risk of flooding. While the earth has always experienced natural cycles of warming and cooling, the 14 hottest years since measurements first started in the 1860s have occurred in past two decades, and 1998 was the hottest year on record.

On the other hand, the causes of war the extreme form of man-made disasters, are inherently more difficult to explain than those of natural disasters. Social behaviour is not subject to physical laws in the same way as cyclones or earthquakes, people make their own history, often violently and sometimes inexplicably. The causal factors are therefore, complex and multidimensional, and it differs, often fundamentally, from war to war. Some conditions that increase the probability of war, include:

(i) Countries that are afflicted by war typically also suffer from inequality among the domestic social groups, based on ethnicity, religion, national identity or economic class. Thus tends to be reflected in the unequal access to political power which often forecloses the paths to peaceful changes.

(ii) Economic decline is also strongly associated with violent conflict, not least because the politics of a shrinking economy are inherently more conflictual than those of economic growth. In some instances, the impact of radical market-oriented economic reforms and structural adjustment programmes imposed without compensating social policies can undermine political stability. More generally, weak governments and, of course so called failed states have little capacity to stop the eruption and spread of violence that better organized and more legitimate governments could have prevented or contained.

(iii) The widespread rise of what is sometimes called identity politics, coupled with the fact that fewer than 20 per cent of all states are ethnically homogenous, means that political demagogues have little difficulty finding targets of opportunity and mobilizing support for chauvinist causes.

(iv) The pursuit of diamonds, drugs, timber concessions and other valuable commodities causes a number of internal wars in present times. In some countries, the capacity of the state to extract resources from society and to allocate patronage to cronies or political allies is the prize to be fought over.

(v) Lack of awareness and information about protective measures can also lead to disasters, such as, about measures that can be taken to build safe structures on safe locations; about safe evacuation routes and procedures; or about kind of assistance required at times of acute distress; and about specific steps that could be taken immediately to escape the disaster.

(vi) Serious environmental degradation can cause or exacerbate many disasters, such as, deforestation leading to extensive flooding and soil erosion; mangrove swamp's destruction increasing the destructive power of coastal cyclones, typhoons, and storm surges. Similarly prolonged drought conditions may be exacerbated by deforestation, overgrazing, loss of top soil, depletion of water resources, overpopulation of human being and domesticated animals.

(vii) Rapid transition in cultural practices, mostly descriptive and uneven ones, create gaps in social coping mechanisms and technologies. Rapid urbanization, is the most serious causal factor for disasters, such as landslides, floods in hilly and flood-prone urban areas. Similarly unchecked population growth can create havoc in unsafe, habitats.

(viii) Poverty inculcates extreme vulnerability towards disasters, such as landslides, floods, droughts, epidemics, famine, etc.

Approaches

These approaches differ from each other due to the different viewpoints they project regarding the conceptual evolution of the understanding of disasters and disaster management process. Many approaches have specified proponents, however, others have come into popularity with the development of the specified subject area itself, such as, anthropology, medicine and epidemiology, and technical studies. The focus of each approach differ from one another and thereby help the approach to the said subject in various ways.

1. *Geographical approach.* Focus on chronological distribution of disasters, their impact and vulnerability. Based on this understanding of spatio-temporal factors, choices are made among various kinds of adjusting to such disasters.

2. *Anthropological approach.* A community oriented approach with focus on role of disasters guides the socio-economic evolution of population of civilization. They also search for threshold points for local communities beyond which they no longer provide the basic requirements for survival of their members.

3. *Sociological approach.* Focus is on vulnerability and its impact on human behaviour and psychologically determined defensive reaction pattern.

4. *Developmental studies approach.* Major area of interest are aid, relief measures, refugee management, health care and avoidance of starvation. Line of thinking holds developing countries as most disaster prone and poverty responsible for increased human vulnerability.

5. *Disaster medicine and epidemiology approach.* Focus is on mass casualty management, trauma treatment and epidemiological surveillance of communicable diseases.

6. *Technical approach.* Focus is on scientific and technical aspects of disasters. Major areas of interest are seismology, volcanology, geomorphology and geophysical approaches to disasters.

7. *Human ecology approach.* Focus is on determinants of human behaviour and the process that facilitates human adjustments to disasters through social organizations.

TYPES OF DISASTERS

Disasters are often classified according to their speed of onset i.e. sudden or slow.

1. *Sudden Onset Disasters/(Rapid Onset Disasters)* e.g. earthquakes, tsunamis, floods, tropical storms, volcanic eruptions, landslides, etc. (which are mostly geological and climatic disasters).

2. *Slow Onset Disasters* e.g. drought, famine, land-depredation, climate change, desertification, deforestation, pest infestation.

1. Categorization

For better understanding of disasters and for evolving better management practices, it is necessary to categorise various kinds of disasters. Homogeneity with respect to elements and causing particular disaster is the major basis for such classification and categorization. Such categorization/ classification go a long way in evolving models of disaster management applicable to one category of disasters whether natural, man-made or of hybrid nature. While some prefer to categorise on the basis of framework of disaster management applicable. While others do it as per the degree of anthropogenic factors involved. Some others categorize on the basis of understanding of risks involved, while some categorization are suggested based on potentially hazardous environmental processes involved. The following details briefly describe the aforementioned categories of disasters from the point of view of existing framework for disaster management:

1. Elemental Disasters

(a) Earthquake
(b) Tsunami
(c) Tidal waves
(d) Floods

(e) Volcanic eruptions
(f) Landslides

2. *Foreseeable Disasters*

(a) Famines
(b) Epidemics

3. *Deliberate Disasters*

(a) Wars
(b) Civil wars
(c) Guerrilla warfare
(d) Insurgency activities
(e) Terrorism

4. *Accidental Disasters*

(a) Industrial catastrophes
(b) Nuclear catastrophes.

Elemental disasters are distinguished from other disasters because they are instantaneous and prompted, by climatic or geological forces. Their destructive capability depends more on the number of vulnerable people in a given area than on their inherent severity. In many parts of the world, manmade errors exacerbate the damage such elemental disasters cause.

Foreseeable disasters have complex root causes in which climatic and human activity interact over extended periods, leaving large numbers of people vulnerable. Such an interaction creates a vicious circle whose recurrence is often predictable.

Deliberate disasters have roots in social, economic and political inequity. This can result in both high intensity hostile enemy actions in forms of declared battles or wars or low intensity conflicts such as guerrilla warfare, terrorism, sabotage, riots, communal discord or riots, civil strife, internal disturbance, arson or crowd violence.

Accidental disasters are a biproduct of negligence of risk-assessment while making scientific and technological advances. Recent incidents of Bhopal, Chernobyl, Three Mile Island, etc. attest to the grave threat posed by such disasters.

Yet another classification based on predominant agent, disasters could be categorized as of three types, i.e. first the natural, secondly the man-made, and lastly as hybrid disasters.

Natural disasters are the result of natural phenomena, for instance, earthquake, tsunami, volcanic eruption, hurricane, tornado, avalanche or flood.

Man-made disasters are of an anthropogenic origin, and exemplifies some of the terrible accidents that have resulted from human beings interaction with artificial environment, which they themselves have created. Sinking of Titanic, crash of Turkish Airlines DC-10 outside Paris, capsizing of Herald of Free Enterprise ferry at Zeebrugge in 1957, Chernobyl accident in Russia, Three Mile Island in USA, Windscale in UK, Union Carbide in (Bhopal) India, are examples of such disasters.

Hybrid Disasters arise from a linkage of anthropogenic events and natural events. For example, spread of disease from a community in which the disease is endemic to a community which has no natural immunity, destruction of forests and resulting increased floods; large scale deaths due to smog, etc. Hybrid disasters can also be categorised and termed complex disasters or compound disasters. Increasingly throughout many parts of the world, one kind of disaster can trigger another type of disaster which in turn triggers subsequent kinds of disasters. For example, a drought in Ethiopia, Sudan, Somalia (storm of African countries) in early 1990s led to a famine which in turns lead to a civil conflict that resulted in the mass displacement of people. Such compound disasters need to happen sequentially; they can also happen simultaneously. Thus, people caught between contending forces in a civil war find that in the midst of a major drought they have no means either to grow food or to receive outside assistance. Essentially, any complex/hybrid/compound disaster is a form of human-made emergency in which the cause of the emergency as well as the assistances to the afflicted are bound by intense levels of political considerations. In fact, many affected people live in areas outside the government control. They are often the persons who are most in need and they are often the most difficult to reach with aid. The disaster becomes 'complex' because either the collapse or diffusion of political control makes assistance highly problematic. Solutions ultimately depend upon agreements with all parties involved in the conflict to permit assistance to be provided to recognized civilian noncombatants. These solutions may be agreements that are seen essentially as compromising fundamental aspects of sovereignty for what have been labeled as "new mechanisms of humanitarian assistance" (for example, corridors of tranquility).

Categorization of disasters based on comprehending and assessing risk perception, risk management, disaster prevention, civil protection in legal terms such as employment status (as between the driver of a train and its passengers, for example), relational matters (as between parent, child, or spouse following accidental death, for example) and jurisdictional divisions (as between Scotland and England and Wales, for example).

1. *Environmental*—including hurricanes, earthquakes, floods;

2. *Ordinary*—including rail accidents, where there is a low risk perception by passengers;

3. *Technological*—including radiation escapes such as Three Mile Island and Chernobyl, where high technology.

4. *Industrial*—for instance, oil installations and mining, where workers know that their job is hazardous;

5. *Crowd violence*—such as that of Hillsborough and Heysel.

Categorization has also been suggested based on potentially hazardous environmental agencies or processes which may affect society. Since these hazards have such different origins and impacts that a more focused and manageable definition is required.

1. *Atmospheric*

(a) *Single Element Atmospheric Hazards:* Such as, rain, freezing rain (glaze) , hail, snow, wind, lightening, temperature (heatwave, whiteout, cold spell, frost), fog, etc.

(b) *Compound Atmospheric Hazards:* Such as, rain and windstorms, 'glaze' storms, thunderstorms, tornados storms, tornados, hurricanes, blizzards, droughts.

2. *Hydrologic hazards:* Such as, flooding (riverine due to rain, snowmelt, natural dam-burst floods), lake and sea-shore wave action, waterlogging sea-ice and ice-bergs, runoff drought, glacier advancement.

3. *Geologic Hazards:* Such as, mass-movements (landslides, avalanches, mudflows, subsidence, etc.), erosion (foundations, soils, etc.), sitting (dikes, rivers harbours, farmland), earthquakes, volcanic eruptions, shifting sands, etc.

4. *Biologic Hazards:* Such as, severe epidemics in humans, severe epidemic in plants, severe epidemics in domestic and wild animals, animal and plant invasions (e.g. locusts), forest and grassland fires, etc.

5. *Technologic Hazards:* Such as, transport accidents, industrial explosions and fires, accidental releases of toxic gas, nuclear power plant failures, failure of public buildings or other structures, germ or nuclear warfare, etc.

Another kind of categorization, of environmental hazards partly based on valued environmental components (VECs), propounded by Beanlands and Duinker (1983), and after much refinement in terms of their causal structure and their likelihood of occurrence as most hazardous problems gives a triparticle structure i.e. pollution-based hazards, resource-depletion hazards and natural hazards.

1. Typology

The following typology has been evolved to incorporate most kinds of disasters, human-history has experienced. Broadly, three categories have been prepared, such as, natural disasters, man-made disasters, and epidemics (invertent through inadequate quarantine. While 6 categories of natural disasters have been identified such as climate and wind related, climate and water related, earth related, ocean related, space related and temperature related. Certain amount of overlap do occur while we attempt to make such a typology. As many as forty-five kinds of man-made disasters have been identified. The epidemics have been categorized in 5 groups. Such a typology, it is hoped, will go a long-way in suggesting disaster prevention, control and mitigation measures in times to come.

(A) Natural Disasters

1. Climate and Wind Related

(a) Wind storm (tropical storms)/storm surges/hailstorm/snowstorm
(b) Cyclone/Tropical cyclones
(c) Tornadoes
(d) Hurricane
(e) Tidal waves
(f) Typhoons
(g) Blizzard
(h) Fog

2. Climate and Water Related

(a) Floods/drainage/river bank erosion/dam-bursting/

levee failure
- (b) Cloud bursts
- (c) Flash flood
- (d) Heavy (excessive) rains/glaze (freezing rain) storms
- (e) Drought
- (f) Snowfall/cold spell waves/bitter winters/hail/frost

3. *Earth Related (Geological)*
- (a) Earthquakes/severe tremors
- (b) Tsunamis
- (c) Avalanches/snow avalanches
- (d) Landslides
- (e) Volcanic eruptions
- (f) Rockfalls
- (g) Mudslides
- (h) Subsidence
- (i) Shifting sands

4. *Ocean Related*
- (a) Ocean currents El Niño/La Niña

5. *Space Related*
- (a) Asteroid collisions
- (b) Lightnings

6. *Temperature related*
- (a) Heat wave
- (b) Whiteout
- (c) Forest fires/Bush fire

(B) Man-Made Disasters

1. War/battle/hostile enemy actions
2. Arson/sabotage/internal disturbance/riots crowd violence
3. Accidents of vehicles/trains/aircrafts/ships/traffic

accidents/transport accidents

4. Industrial accidents disaster/explosion of boilers/gas cylinders/gas chambers/gas leak technological disasters/industrial explosions/fires.
5. Fire/forest fires/scrub fires/wildfires/bushfire/grassland fires.
6. Nuclear explosion disaster/accidents/radioactive fallout/leakages/commercial nuclear power/radiation: Non-radon plant failure/accidents
7. Ecological disasters like deforestation/desertification/environmental pollution/social erosion/air pollution/water pollution.
8. Famine/food crises/food contamination/food security/food additives
9. Epidemics/pest infestations epidemics/insect infestations infections diseases proliferation/destitution refugee cities.
10. Urbanization/mega-cities.
11. Land degradation/salinization/alkalinization.
12. Toxic chemicals and hazardous wastes/release/dumping/carriage/chemical time bombs/chemical accidents.
13. Chemicals in workplace.
14. Indoor air/radon/non-radon.
15. Toxic air pollutants.
16. Stratospheric ozone depletion/ground-level ozone formation.
17. Acid rain/acidification.
18. Thermal radiation.
19. Ocean water intrusion/sea-level rise/coastal flooding/marine pollution.
20. Groundwater contamination/depletion.
21. Wildlife extinction.

22. Fish deaths
23. Freshwater contamination/biological/metal and toxic/eutrophication/sedimentation.
24. Pollution climate change/global warming/greenhouse effect.
25. Renewable resource depletion.
26. HIV/AIDS
27. Demographic disaster/population bombs.
28. Biotechnological hazards threats/GMOs (Genetically modifying organisms)
29. Refugee crises/settler migration.
30. Slums/shanty habitats/shelter problems war victims/war deaths/civil war/riot.
31. Sanctions.
32. Plastic panics.
33. Apartheid forced removals.
34. Poverty.
35. Smoking.
36. Mountaineering.
37. Germ (Biological) and chemical warfare.
38. Nuclear warfare
39. Failures of public buildings or other structures.
40. Animal and plant invasions (locusts).
41. Oil spills.
42. Mining disasters.
43. Radio-active dumping at sea
44. Terrorism.

(B) (i) *Epidemics* (Invertent through inadequate quarantine)

1. Vector-born diseases.

(a) Plague.

2. Water-born diseases.

3. Food-born diseases.
4. Person-to-person diseases (contact and respiratory spread).
5. Complications from wounds.
6. Veterinary epidemics (within and across species)

Conclusion

In sum it could be said that multiplicity of viewpoints exist as far as defining disasters and identification of their causal factors are concerned. Such as diversity of ideas has indeed enriched the subject area of disaster management. Various major approaches present the varying perspectives on disaster management in all their possible dimensions. The exhaustive classification/initiatives provided hereby further compliment in finding sustainable policy options in terms of existing disaster management practices. Viewing the probable unavoidable overlaps into account, an attempt has been made to see the subject area of disasters and disaster management from major existing prevalent practices and views.

REFERENCES

Annan, K.A. (1999), Preventing War and Disaster: A Growing Global Challenge, 1999 Annual Report on the Work of the Organization, UN, Department of Public Information, New York, pp. 1-61.

Beanland, G.E., and Duinker, P.N. (1983), An ecological framework for environmental impact assessment, In *RES*, Dalhousie University, Canada.

Cohen, D. (1991), *Aftershock: The Psychological and Political Consequences of Disaster*, Paladin.

Kreps (1984), Sociological Inquiry and Disaster Research, *Annual Review of Sociology*, 10, pp. 309-312.

Turner, B.A. and Nick F. Pidgeon (1977), *Man-made Disasters,* Butterworth-Heineman, Oxford.

Wells, C. (1995), *Negotiating Tragedy: Law and Disasters*, Sweet and Maxwell, London.

2

Disaster-prone World: A Survey

> If you have nothing else to do, look about you and see if there isn't something close at hand that you can improve! It may make you wealthy, though it is more likely that will make you happy.
>
> —*George Matthew Adams*

Infact, the 1990s can be termed as the "Decade of Environmental Disasters." The tally of cataclysms includes the northern Iran earthquake; volcanic eruptions in the Philippines (Pinatubo) and Alaska (Redoubt Volcano); flooding along the Trinity, Red, and Arkansas rivers in Texas, and the perennial flood in Bangladesh. These were soon followed by the Persian Gulf War, the Oakland-Berkeley Hills fire in California, the cholera epidemics in Peru, the continuing droughts in California and in Eastern Africa. We also saw the first glimpses of the widespread environmental degradation in the erstwhile Soviet Union and Eastern and Central Europe, not to mention the depletion of the ozone layer and toxic contamination of military sites. As 1992 came to a close, Hurricane Andrew struck south Florida (USA) leaving 125,000 people homeless and billions of dollars worth of damage, making it the largest disaster in America's history. Within weeks, another storm, Hurricane Iniki, devastated the Hawaiian island of Kauai.

Are these extreme events becoming more frequent? More severe? Or is the frequency of events remaining the same, but is society becoming more vulnerable to them? These are just a few of the questions hazard researchers attempt to answer.

DISASTER TRENDS

Natural Events

In a review of natural disaster trends from 1945 through 1986, Glickman, Golding, and Silverman (1992) make a number of very thoughtful observations. Worldwide there was an increase in the number of small (those with 25 or fewer fatalities) natural disaster events during this forty-year period. At the same time, the number of large events (more than 1,000 fatalities) has remained relatively steady. What has prompted the concern of hazard researchers is the uneven distribution of these disasters. Not only is the developing world bearing the brunt of fatalities from natural disasters, it is also having more disaster events. Most of the natural disasters were meteorological in origin—riverine flooding, coastal inundation from hurricanes and typhoons—accounting for more than a third of all disasters during this time period. Earthquakes, although far fewer in number, are more fatal. More than half of all deaths attributed to natural disasters result from earthquakes.

TABLE 1

Top Ten Natural Disasters, 1945-1990

Year	Location	Type	Deaths#
1976	China	Earthquake	700,000
1970	Bangladesh	Tropical cyclone	500,000
1948	Soviet Union	Earthquake	110,000
1970	Peru	Earthquake	66,794
1949	China	Flood	57,000
1990	Iran	Earthquake	50,000
1965	Bangladesh	Tropical cyclone	36,000
1954	China	Flood	30,000
1965	Bangladesh	Tropical cyclone	30,000
1968	Iran	Earthquake	30,000
1971	India	Tropical cyclone	30,000

#Based on number of estimated fatalities

Source: Glickman, Golding, and Silverman 1992; UNEP 1991.

The 1987-1989 show similar patterns (UNEP 1991). More than 90 percent of the natural disasters occurred outside North America, with slightly more than half occurring in developing countries. While the number of events may be holding steady, unlike the earlier time period, clearly the magnitude of their impacts is increasing. The "hit rate" (the tendency for natural events to adversely affect society) of disasters is greater now than in the past (UNEP 1991). The hit rate can be explained by the sheer increase in the world's population, thus increasing the likelihood that human beings will be affected by these natural events. It is also a function of population movements into more concentrated and higher density settlements, including cities, as well as movement into marginal lands with known seismic, flood, or coastal storm risks. Because of extraordinary population pressures, many parts of the world are extremely vulnerable to natural disasters such as earthquakes and tropical storms, even though the frequency and magnitude of these events have not changed radically in the last forty years. Population growth and distribution do not diminish the impact of these large-magnitude disasters (Table 1); they simply mean that we might anticipate greater fatalities in the future from both earthquakes and tropical storms.

North America suffers much less severely than the rest of the world from fatalities caused by natural disasters. Storms, including floods, are the most frequent event, but hurricanes are more deadly. Property damages, not fatalities, are more significant in North America, as the costs associated with Hurricane Hugo, the Loma Prieta earthquake, and the Oakland-Berkeley Hills fire attest.

Industrial and Chemical Accidents

Two recent reviews of the historical trends in industrial accidents and chemical accidents reveal some interesting global patterns. Since 1945, the frequency of industrial accidents has increased steadily, peaking in 1979 (a result of better reporting) and then declining thereafter (Glickman, Golding, and Silverman 1992). Fatalities from industrial accidents are far fewer when compared to natural disasters (excluding the methyl isocyanate gas leak in Bhopal, India). Industrial accidents have a smaller catastrophic potential. The most fatal (Bhopal) resulted in 4,000 deaths compared to the fatalities associated with the worst natural disasters, such as the 1970 tropical cyclone that killed 500,000 people in Bangladesh or the 1976 Chinese earthquake that claimed an estimated 700,000 lives (Table 2). Regionally, the United States and Canada have the greatest frequency of industrial accidents.

TABLE 2

Top Ten Industrial Disasters. 1945-1990"

Year	*Location*	*Type/Agent*	*# Deaths*[b]
1984	Bhopal, India	Toxic vapor/methyl isocyanate	2,750-3,849
1982	Salang Pass, Afghanistan	Toxic vapor/carbon monoxide	1,550-2,700
1956	Cali, Colombia	Explosion/ammunitions	1,200
1958	Kyshtym, USSR	Radioactive leak	1,118[c]
1947	Texas City, TX	Explosion/ammonium nitrate	576
1989	Acha Ufa, USSR	Explosion/natural gas	500-574
1984	Cubatao, Brazil	Explosion/gasoline	508
1984	St. Juan Ixhautepec, Mexico	Explosion/natural gas	478-503
1983	Nile River, Egypt	Explosion/natural gas	317
1986	Chernobyl, USSR	Explosion/radioactivity	31-300[c]

a. Based on fatality estimates

b. Estimates vary depending on the source(s) used, therefore ranges are provided where there are differences in the total.

c. Total number of deaths are hard to gauge since the reported fatality figures only reflect immediate deaths, not the longer term deaths associated with radioactive exposures.

Sources: Glickman, Golding, and Silverman 1992; Cutter 1991. 1993.

Equally interesting patterns emerge with regard to toxic clouds from industrial accidents. Using a longer time frame (1900-1990), Cutter (1991) found a dramatic increase in accidents in the 1970s and 1980s as the use of chemicals intensified in all areas of society. While most of the accidents occurred in the industrialized world, nearly 36 percent of all incidents during the twentieth century occurred in developing countries, especially those in Latin America and Asia. While the frequency of accidents increased, their severity in terms of immediate fatalities has decreased. However, the hazard potential of chemical accidents has actually increased as more incidents involving acutely toxic materials are recorded. Worldwide, about a third of the incidents involve vapor releases of acutely toxic substances—those that cause immediate physical harm and possibly death to exposed populations within minutes to hours (Cutter 1993). In the last twenty years, around 40 percent of all chemical accidents involved acutely toxic releases.

In the United States, the pattern is quite different. During the last 90 years, slightly less than half (48%) of the releases involved acute toxics. During the last twenty years, more than half (53%) of the incidents involved these deadly substances.

While the United States may be less at risk than many parts of the world from natural disasters such as earthquakes, floods, and hurricanes, the country does have more than its share of industrial disasters. As with natural disasters, the human impact (measured by deaths) of these industrial disasters is often much less than in other world regions. Why is the United States seemingly less vulnerable to these extreme events? What about chronic risks and hazards affecting modern living that have delayed or cumulative effects, such as drought or pollution? Are we becoming more or less vulnerable to these as well?

Risk and Hazards: Changing Nature

Traditionally, hazards research has been based oh questions relevant to decision makers. What can be done to reduce the impacts of flooding? What types of policies are needed for longer term recovery from natural disasters? How effective is emergency preparedness, including warning systems in protecting the public from nuclear power plant accidents? Today these questions are still as relevant as they were fifty years ago. What has changed is the way we think about hazards.

During the last few years, two significant changes have occurred in our thinking about hazards (Mitchell 1989). The first is in the very nature of hazards. New risks and hazards are constantly identified and old ones rediscovered. The simple exercise of categorizing hazards as the consequence of extreme natural events (acts of God) or technological failures (acts of people) no longer works well. Is global warming a natural hazard, a technological hazard, or some combination of the two? Also, hazards are no longer viewed as singular events, but as complex interactions between natural, social, and technological systems. Even the basic textbooks in hazards now acknowledge this interrelatedness and increased complexity of the phenomena we study (Smith 1992, Burton, Kates, and White 1993).

A second major change is in how we respond to hazardous events. Researchers are no longer simply interested in the event itself, but are dwelling more and more on the context within which the event occurs. *Hazard, or some* in larger political, social, economic, and technological structures, and it is often impossible to separate these influences from the impacts of the event. In assessing societal vulnerability to hazards, it is impossible to divorce the context from the event (Cuny 1983, Cutter 1993). Similarly, it is virtually impossible to separate hazards from broader based environmental or social problems. As a consequence, the management of risks and hazards has also become quite complex, entailing new management systems at the local, regional, and global scale. More often than not, management alternatives no longer rely solely on technical solutions; as risks and risk reduction becomes increasingly politicized, and management options are debated in the court of public opinion.

The increasingly complex nature of hazards means that geography matters now more than ever. Scale is a crucial element in understanding the distribution, impact, and reduction of risks and hazards. While there is still a concern for hazards with localized impacts, more and more attention is directed at those risks and hazards that alter planetary systems and produce global environmental changes (Turner et al. 1990a). The effects of global hazards are more dispersed and cumulative and require the globalization of management systems.

The changes in the hazards themselves have forced us to alter and adjust local, national, and international management systems (Mitchell 1990). For example, better scientific understanding of and data gathering techniques on the causes and consequences of hazards are needed. We also need more informed theoretical explanations on the processes by which hazards are produced, and the social options for recovery from them.

How do local risks and hazards become the driving forces for global environmental change (Turner et al 1990b)? How does sustainable development increase or decrease vulnerability to natural hazards? These are two questions that will occupy hazard researchers throughout the 1990s. Given these changes and trends in disasters, it is not coincidental that the United Nations has named the decade of 1990-2000 as the International Decade for Natural Disaster Reduction. This multinational effort acknowledges the importance of natural disasters in the decline of the human condition and is designed to reduce losses from sudden-impact events. Its intention is to reduce our vulnerability to natural disasters.

LESSON FROM THE PAST

While we are constantly reminded of the precarious nature of environmental risks and hazards and how they often dominate our everyday lives in the 1990s, formalized social science research in this area did not begin until the mid-twentieth century. Hazards coevolved along parallel paths in the social sciences under such diverse names as natural hazards, technological hazards, disaster research, and risk assessment and management.

Since our collective and institutional view of hazards is rapidly changing, it is important that we reflect on previous work in hazards research. We learn from past experiences and past mistakes. Hazards are complex phenomena, and it is important to understand all social science perspectives in order to bridge artificial intellectual boundaries between hazards, disasters, and risk communities. Our intention here is to acquaint with some seminal works in the fields of hazards, disasters, and risk management.

To conclude, it may be admitted that everything we do involves some risk. Since we all have different perceptions of risk, our responses to it are equally varied. Some risks and hazards are so highly politicized that it impedes their management. Others are unevenly distributed, and their effects are more severe in some places and on some people than others. Still others are completely ignored. The acceptability of risks and hazards and the social choices made as to their management is the real problem. The task forces for disaster management must keep this in mind and to must be ready to meet any eventuality.

REFERENCES

Burton, I., R.W. Kates, and G.F. White, (1993), *The Environment As Hazard*. New York: Guilford.

Cuny, F.C. (1983), *Disasters and Development*. New York: Oxford University Press.

Glickman, T.S., D. Golding, and E. D. Silverman (1992), "Acts of God and acts of man: Recent trends in natural disasters and major industrial accidents," Center for Risk Management Discussion Paper CRM 92-02, Washington D.C.: Resources for the Future.

Mitchell, J.K., (1989), "Hazards research," in Gary L. Gaile and Cort J. Willmott (Eds.), *Geography in America*. Columbus: Merrill, pp. 410-24.

Smith, K., (1992), *Environmental Hazards: Assessing Risk and Reducing Disaster*. London: Routledge.

Turner, B.L., R.E. Kasperson, W.B. Meyer, K.M. Dow, D. Golding, J.X. Kasperson, R.C. Mitchell, and S.J. Ratick, (1990a), "Two types of global environmental change: Definitional and spatial-scale issues in their human dimensions," *Global Environmental Change* 1(1): 14-22.

Turner, B.L., W.C. Clark, R.W. Kates, J.F. Richard, J.T. Mathews, and W.B. Meyer, (1990b), *The Earth as Transformed by Human Action*. Cambridge: Cambridge University Press.

UNEP (United Nations Environment Programme), (1991), *Environmental Data Report*. Oxford: Basil Blackwell.

3

Natural Hazards Research

> Those who have finished by making all others think with them, have usually been those who began by daring to think with themselves.
>
> —*Charles C. Colton*

To a remarkable degree during the 1960's, geographers turned away from certain environment problems at the same time that colleagues in neighboring fields discovered those issues. This cluster of problems relates to the relationship between man and his natural environment, with particular reference to the kinds of transactions into which man enters with biological and physical systems, and to the capacity of the earth to support him in the face of growing population and of expanding technological alteration of landscape. In their self-conscious concern for developing the theoretical lineaments of a discipline, geographers tended to overlook those problems with which they, by tradition, had been concerned and which do not fall readily into allotted provinces of other scientific enterprises.

By neglecting the theory of man-environment relationships and its applications to public policy, the geographer loses an opportunity to apply his knowledge, skills, and insights to fundamental questions of the survival and quality of human life. He also fails to sharpen and advance theoretical thinking by testing it in a challenging arena of action. Any critical examination of man's activities as a dominant species in an ecosystem draws upon and invites refreshing appraisal by workers in other fields.

This argument is demonstrated by the line of natural hazard research as it has taken shape over the past many years. It is presented here as an instance in which pursuit of a public policy issue led to a simple research paradigm and a model of decision-making dealing with how man copes with risk and uncertainty in the occurrence of natural events. The approach was refined and extended in a variety of situations, served to stimulate new methods of analyzing other geographical problems, and fostered a few changes in methods of environmental management by national and international agencies.

The study and policy activities related in this direction of research represent an attempt to deepen understanding of the decision-making process accounting for particular human activities at particular places and times. The research seeks application of new techniques to one of the old and recurring traditions of geographical enterprise—the ecology of human choice. The results are slim yet promising. The experience may point more to errors to be avoided than to procedures to be emulated. However, the approach deserves appraisal as a possibly fruitful way of orienting new research and teaching of an old problem. Application of this model and paradigm does not require any drastic changes in institutionalized teaching and research. Nor does it claim to establish a new sector of geographical inquiry. Rather, it offers one device for bridging some of the divergent lines of current investigation.

THE PROBLEM

How does man adjust to risk and uncertainty in natural systems, and what does understanding of that process imply for public policy? This problem, raised initially with respect to one uncertain and hazardous parameter of a geophysical system—floods—in one country—the United States—provides a central theme for investigation on a global scale the whole range of uncertain and risky events in nature.

GENESIS OF THE RESEARCH

Definition of the problem had its genesis in observation of the results of a massive national effort in the United States to deal with the rising toll of flood losses. In 1927 the Corps of Engineers was authorized to conduct a series of comprehensive investigations to find means of managing the river basins of the United States for purposes of irrigation, navigation, flood control, and hydroelectric power. The legislative authorization called for the presentation to the Congress of plans specifying the needs of each area, the types of engineering construction work which could be undertaken, and projects proposed for Federal or State investment, giving the estimated cost and benefit. In the years following 1933 the so-called "308 reports" submitted to the Congress contained explicit benefit-cost analysis of possible construction projects.

In theory, to present a benefit-cost appraisal of a proposed project for a river basin required an analysis of the possible actions which man would take in managing the water and associated land resources of the area, and it also called for a systematic canvass of what, from the standpoint of society, would be the flows of social gains and losses to whomsoever they might accrue arising from any one of those interventions in the ecosystem. This was a monumental and presumptuous task.

Even in his most naive periods of technological mastery, man could not expect to understand the full set of consequences of any major interventions such as the channelization of the lower Mississippi River or the construction of a dam on the Upper Ohio or the building of a system of levees along the Sacramento. The investigator could make educated and hopefully intelligent guesses as to certian outcomes, e.g., alteration of stream regimen. He could not hope to identify all possible consequences. Measuring them would be still more difficult. Moreover, to complete a genuinely competent appraisal of possible lines of action would require canvass of the full range of possible activities which might be undertaken. A proposed dam then could be compared with other steps such as a levee, upstream management of vegetation, or downstream management of the flood plain. Yet, the practical engineering and administrative imperative was to go ahead with such investigations, using the best knowledge then available and applying an elementary kind of economic analysis in order to show for those items which could be readily quantified an estimate of prospective benefits and costs.

Thus, a program of planning took shape which was to have major consequences for resources planning and scientific work in other parts of the world as well as in the United States. Benefit-cost analysis of water projects in the United States became the most sophisticated piece of social impact investigation for several decades. There were more careful and detailed methodologies for computing water benefits and costs than for any other type of public investment. The procedures as first developed by the Corps of Engineers were later revised and embodied in rules and regulations issued by the Bureau of the Budget and approved by the Congress in two separate stages, and were the basis for extensive literature of economic analysis. The analysis was of a normative sort: it was designed to suggest ways by which estimates could be made as to the most effective investments to achieve specified public aims. Almost no time was given to finding out what in fact resulted from such investment. It was assumed that what was proposed—as, for example, the reduction of flood losses or the increase in waterway traffic—would in fact be realized if only the proper combination of technical means, discount rates, and time horizons could be found.

The 308 reports found their way into concrete action in a remarkably short period of time because they first appeared in the midst of the great economic depression of the 1930's and provided individual projects which could be used in mounting public works programs intended to relieve unemployment and stir economic recovery in the nation. The Tennessee Valley Authority was established with the intent, soon discarded, of using part of the Corps of Engineers 308 plan for that area. Large projects such as Grand Coulee Dam and the reservoirs in the Upper Ohio were authorized in the interest of revising a depressed economy.

Geographers early took an interest in this new line of planning but their more lively efforts either proved abortive or dwindled over a long period of time. They were active in the National Resources Planning Board—the first Federal agency in the United States to attempt to draw together the plans of independent state and national agencies into single, comprehensive river basin plans—and they joined in analysis of area economic and employment problems.

This interest stirred an investigation of the range of alternatives with respect to flood loss reduction (White 1942) It also stimulated the first comprehensive attempt to anticipate the full social impacts of a large impoundment. The impact study was carried out by the Bureau of Reclamation and associated agenices on the effects of the Grand Coulee Dam on the Columbia Basin (U.S. 1941). The latter work under the leadership of Harlan H. Barrows was not only a pioneer piece of interdisciplinary research, but defined in broad outlines and with notable gaps the problem of ecological impact which, while studied with considerable care for Grand Coulee, was not to be investigated again with similar energy or breadth until the late 1960's.

In 1936, following a series of disastrous floods affecting urban areas in the Mississippi system, the Congress authorized a national flood control policy which declared it to be the intent of the Federal government to contribute to the cost of flood control works wherever the anticipated benefits from such works would exceed the anticipated cost. In 1938 a supplemental act provided that where reservoirs were selected as a means of flood control no local contribution should be required to the cost of projects inasmuch as the allocation of benefits among the several state beneficiaries was so complicated that it seemed best to change it all on the Federal account.

Twenty years passed, more than five billion dollars were expended on new Federal flood control works, and in 1956 a geographic investigation was begun on what had happened in the urban flood plains of the nation as a result of the investments during the two intervening decades. That investigation was to be followed by more thoughtful and searching studies through which ran the common thread of a relatively consistent research paradigm.

RESEARCH PARADIGM

In carrying out the 1956 appraisal of changes in land use in selected flood plains following the Flood Control Act of 1936, the geographic research group asked the following questions:

1. What is the nature of the physical hazard involved in extreme fluctuations in stream flow?
2. What types of adjustments has man made to those fluctuations?
3. What is the total range of possible adjustments which man theoretically could make to those fluctuations?
4. What accounts for the differences in adoption of adjustments from place to place and time to time?
5. What would be the effect of changing the public policy insofar as it constitutes a social guide to the conditions in which individuals or groups choose among the possible adjustments?

These questions were addressed to seven sites, chosen to give a diversity of conditions of floods, urban land use, and flood loss abatement measure (White, et al. 1958). A review also was made of the record for flood control expenditures and flood damages for the nation as a whole.

From that view any human response to an extreme event in a natural system had the effect of (a) modifying the cause, (b) modifying the losses, or (c) distributing the losses.

A number of conclusions emerging from the field studies had an unsettling effect upon those who were responsible for Federal flood control programs, and triggered new investigations to probe unresolved questions. In brief, it was found that while flood-control expenditures had multiplied, the level of flood damages had risen, and that the national purpose of reducing the toll of flood losses by building flood-control projects had not been realized. Parts of valley bottoms were protected from floods, but increasing encroachment on the flood plain increased the damage potential from a smaller flood. One part of a city was protected by a levee, but new urban growth took place outside the levee. Works which controlled flood with a recurrence interval of 500 years were certain to fail with catastrophic consequences when the 1,000 year flood took place. The findings also indicated that because of the Federal government's concentration upon flood-control works and upstream water-management activities to the exclusion of other obvious but relatively unpracticed types of adjustments, the situation was becoming progressively worse and showed no promise of being improved by a continuation of the prevailing policies. It was recognized that a rising flood toll might be beneficial if accompanied by larger benefits from flood plain use. However, the increased losses were contrary to the public expectation.

At that stage the study had (1) demonstrated that geographic research could have a direct bearing upon the formation of public policy in one country; and (2) posed a set of problems requiring further investigation if satisfactory policy readjustment was to be obtained. These problems centered on how to account for the differential behavior of individuals and groups in dealing with flood problems from one place to another. It had been shown that people did not behave as it had been expected that they would when the benefit-cost ratios for several thousand flood control projects had been drawn up. It was not equally clear why people had chosen the particular solutions they did and, therefore, what sorts of changes in public action would lead to genuine improvement in the character of their choices over a period of time. The effort to deal with this problem sastisfactorily demanded further inquiry.

TABLE 1

Types of Adjustments to Floods

Modifying the Cause	*Modifying the Loss*	*Distributing the Loss*
Upstream land treatment	Flood protection works	Bearing the loss
	Dams	Public relief
	Levees	
	Channelization	Insurance
	Emergency measures	
	Flood warning	
	Flood	Evacuation
Proofing	Structural changes in buildings	
	Land elevation	

MODELS OF DECISION-MAKING

In all of the benefit-cost analysis and in the earlier work on changes in flood plain use, it was postulated that the choice made by people living on flood plains was essentially economic optimization. This was in the tradition of economic analysis, and conformed to the normative judgments on which the projects had been initiated. In essence, it assumed that individuals living in places of hazard would have relatively complete knowledge of the hazard and its occurrence, would be aware in some degree of the consequences, and would seek to make those adjustments which would represent an optimal resolution of the costs and benefits from each of the adjustments open to them. The ideal of the completely optimizing man was viewed as one rarely achieved in action, but as the framework within which a modified model, namely a model of subjective expected utility, might be explanatory. The subjective utility model held that man would seek to optimize but his judgement would be based on incomplete knowledge and upon his subjective view of the possible consequences. It would be expected that if the view people had of the expected effects of using a particular piece of flood plain could be ascertained, it would be possible to judge their probable response by selecting those solutions which would give them the maximum net utility.

Neither the optimizing model nor the subjective utility model seemed to explain much of the behavior observed in the study areas. For example, it was found that although people seemed to recognize distinct differences in hazard from one part of the flood plain to another, they did not readily translate that recognition into differentials in assigned valuation of the property. People oftentimes returned to the use of land which had been severely damaged by floods being aware of the consequences of a recurrence and facing probable disaster of either a personal or financial character from such recurrence. Adequately to describe behavior for purposes of predicting responses to changes in public policy required the use of some other kind of model. Experimentation began with other possibilities. The obvious direction in which to move was the model of bounded rationality as described by Simon and others (Simon 1959). It was proposed in a general sense for a variety of resource management decisions, and was developed in a more rigorous fashion by Kates in his study of Lafollette, Tennessee (Kates 1962). In examining the behavior and expressed perceptions of residents of a flood plain in the Tennessee Valley, Kates attempted to find out how people perceive the hazard, how they perceive the range of adjustments open to them, and what factors accounted for differences in their perceptions. This required measurement of clearly economic gains and losses as perceived by them, but also consideration of a number of other factors such as the information available to the individual, his personal experience, and the physical nature of the event.

In the following years additional efforts were made to refine a model of bounded rationality, the most recent being that developed by Kates in connection with the collaborative research on natural hazards (1970). It will be noted from a simplified version as presented, that a resource-management decision may be hypothesized to involve the interaction of human systems and physical systems in terms of adjustment to a particular hazard. The interaction is represented as a choice-searching process as affected by personality, information, decision situation and managerial role. The result is a much more complicated model of how people make their choices in dealing with uncertainty and risk in the environment, one that did not lend itself as readily to careful field investigation, but that promised more revealing explanations of individual and group behavior.

THE ROLE OF PERCEPTION

As it was recognized that the judgment of the resource manager could be more important than the judgment of the scientific observer, other types of investigations were stimulated. It was clear in the most elementary way that the definition of a flood hydrograph as developed by the meteorologists and hydrologists would be important in the decisions by individuals only to the extent that the described flood parameters were meaningful to the user. This resulted in suggestions of different modes of describing floods and different modes of presenting the results of scientific analysis to flood plain occupants. For example, the question was raised as to what sort of graphic display of a flood hazard would be meaningful to a person considering building a house on an area in which he had a choice between land above and below the maximum flood. To investigate this sub-problem required knowledge of the occupant's perception—that process by which individuals organize exterior stimuli in order to form some concept of an event or situation— and as to the relationship between such perceptions, verbalized expressions of attitudes, and behavior. Here was encountered one of the truly difficult problems of social science: the relationship, if any, between verbalized attitudes and actual behavior.

In dealing with perception, it was recognized that psychological studies had been largely within the laboratory and had dealt with very limited physical phenomena. There was doubt as to their applicability to observations of more complex and gross phenomena. Hewitt investigated the theoretical ground for expressing extreme events in probabilistic terms (1969). At this point the interest of geographers in problems of perception and attitude formation converged with those of psychologists, sociologists, city planners and architects who also were trying to specify perception and its implications (Burton and Kates 1964). Out of the concern for perception of floods came the first AAG symposium on problems of perception (Lowenthal 1967), a series of investigations dealing with perception of differing facets of the environment such as drought, recreational water, reservoirs, water supply alternatives, water recycling, and the like (Saarinen 1966; Baumann 1969), and Saarinen's geographic review of the perception literature (Saarinen 1969).

Out of the concern for attitudes developed a joint seminar between sociologists and geographers on problems of attitude formation, a joint investigation of attitudes toward water (White 1966), and a number of investigations bearing upon decision-making and public participation in such decisions (MacIver 1970; Johnson 1971).

INTERDISCIPLINARY COOPERATION

Much of the research could not have taken place without strong cooperation with workers in other disciplines. Engineers were essential to appraisal of the effects of physical structures, and they often were the key professional group in applying geographic findings. Part of the field investigations were supported by the Tennessee Valley Authority's division of Local Flood Relations, and its engineering personnel were a chronic source of critical encouragement. Members of the Corps of Engineers engineering staff participated in a few studies (Cook and White 1962), and the agency later invited and used the results of appraisals of operating experience in flood plain management. Hydrologists from the U.S. Geological Survey shared in the design and assessment of flood plain mapping and its presentation to public agencies.

Wherever an urban area was studied there usually was collaboration with responsible city planning officials. Their critiques were illuminating, and in some cases produced interesting new ventures such as the combination of geographic planning and engineering skills in devising an urban redevelopment scheme for Waterloo, Iowa. However, it was necessary for geographic investigators to resist the temptation to become heavily involved in consulting activities. The pressures were to give time to applying the meager research findings rather than to expanding them.

Economists were drawn into the investigation, and contributed fresh insights into the process of optimal decisions. Unconventional views of flood losses as nature's rental for flood plains were developed by two of them (Renshaw 1961; Krutilla 1966). A refined method of assessing losses and benefits from land-use regulation was devised by Lind (1966). A more rigorous analysis of the economics of natural hazards was carried out by Russell (1970). An investigation of rural use of flood plains in the early 1960's was supported by the Agricultural Research Service of the Department of Agriculture, and brought geographers into working relations with agricultural economists (Burton 1962). However, it did not yield the anticipated refinements in economic aspects of flood hazard, and that sector of study awaits more intensive investigation.

Psychologists were drawn into examination of the personality traits affecting resource decisions. A simple sentence-completion test was devised by Sims (Natural Hazards Working Paper No. 16, 1970) and he collaborated in using thematic apperception tests (Saarinen and Sims 1969). A psychologist joined the research staff at the Department of Geography of the University of Toronto (Schiff 1971), and Kates collaborated with a psychology colleague in editing a review of hazard experience (Kates and Wohlwill 1966).

Interdisciplinary research in which workers in several fields genuinely interact is far more difficult to carry out than is research which draws from other fields at the pleasure of the investigator. In the latter case it is a readily manageable, sometimes gayly ostentatious, sometimes humbling exercise but always in the command of the investigator. When it is required by common commitment to solution of a problem, collaboration is not easily abandoned without persona] hurt as well as cost to the whole enterprise.

APPLICATIONS TO PUBLIC POLICY

It may help to briefly note a number of applications of this research paradigm and these models of decision-making to specific public policy issues. The interest in each case is twofold: (1) what was its use in forming public policy and (2) what feedbacks, if any, did it have upon geographic theory?

At the outset of the flood plain occupance studies in 1957 an attempt was made to enlist the collaboration of people who were directly concerned in drawing up and carrying out such plans, and it was recognized that a principal alternative to the construction of flood control works was the regulation of land use. A representative of the Corps of Engineers took a year for a study leave to work with the Chicago geographic group and to produce a critical appraisal of experience with flood plain regulations (Murphy 1958). This led to tentative hypotheses as to community response to regulations and it also stimulated a legal investigation of the constitutional and statutory grounds for such regulation (Dunham 1959). The latter became the standard legal work on the subject.

Discussions of how people perceive the range of adjustments contributed to the establishment by the Corps of Engineers of a system of "flood plain information reports" which since have become operating practice. Early appraisals of providing flood plain information to residents of such areas showed the importance of individual perception in contrast to that of the scientific observer (Roder 1961), and fostered detailed experiments with modes of mapping sponsored by the U.S. Geological Survey (Shaeffer 1964). The Chicago metropolitan area became the first metropolitan area in the world to be completely mapped in terms of flood hazard. In the course of promoting and carrying out flood plain mapping through the Northeastern Illinois Metropolitan Planning Commission, further inquiries were made into the decision process. It became apparent that merely publishing the maps would be unlikely to have any significant effect upon decisions made by individuals or public agencies whereas if specific and favorable situations could be found in which the maps would be made available, the decision making might be changed. Thus, Sheaffer arranged for the organized group of land appraisers to make systematic use of the maps so that they in turn could attach a judgment about flood hazard to each land value assessment submitted to financial and mortgage agencies in connection with the purchase of buildings or property.

TABLE 2

Action Recommended by The Task Force on Federal Flood Control Policy

To improve basic knowledge about flood hazard

The immediate listing of all urban areas with flood problems to alert the responsible agencies.

Preparation on maps and aerial photographs by the U.S. Geological Survey of reconnaissance delimitation of hazard areas.

More floodplain information reports from the Corps of Engineers and Tenessee Valley Authority.

Agreement by federal agencies on a set of techniques to be used in determining flood frequencies.

A national program by the Corps of Engineers and Department of Agriculture for collecting more useful data on flood damages, using decennial appraisals, continuing records on sample reaches and special surveys after unusual floods.

Research by Department of Housing and Urban Development and USDA to gain greater knowledge on problems of floodplain occupance and on urban hydrology under the U.S. Geological Survey and HUD.

To coordinate and plan new developments on the floodplain

Specification by the Water Resources Council of criteria for regulation of floodplains and for treatment of floodplain problems.

Steps to assure that state and local planning would take proper and consistent account of flood hazard in:

Federal mortgage insurance (Federal Housing Authority and Veterans Administration)

Comprehensive local planning (HUD)

Urban transport planning (Bureau of Public Roads)

Recreational open space and development planning (Bureau of Outdoor Recreation)

Urban open space acquisition (HUD)

Urban renewal (Urban Renewal Administration and Corps of Engineers)

Sewer and water facilities (HUD, USDA, Department of Health, Education and Welfare, and Economic Development Administration)

Consideration by Office of Emergency Planning, Small Business Administration, and Treasury Department of relocation and flood-proofing in rebuilding flooded areas.

A directive to all federal agencies to consider flood hazard in locating new facilities.

To provide technical services to managers of floodplain property

Collection and dissemination of information by Corps of Engineers in collaboration with USDA and HUD on alternative methods of reducing flood losses.

An improved system of flood forecasting under Environmental Sciences Service Administration.

To move toward a practical national program for flood insurance

A brief study by HUD on the feasibility of insurance.

To adjust federal flood control policy to sound criteria and changing needs

Broadened survey authorizations for Corps of Engineers and USDA.

Provision by the Congress for more suitable cost sharing by state and local groups.

Reporting of flood control benefits to distinguish protection of existing improvements from development of new property.

Authorization by the Congress to include land acquisition as part of flood control plans.

Authorization by the Congress of broadened authority to make loans to local interests for their contributions.

In addition, Sheaffer carried the first academic study of the possibilities of flood proofing, working jointly with personnel of the Tennessee Valley Authority (Sheaffer 1960). In time, that experience was the groundwork for preparing for the Corps of Engineers the preliminary manual of procedures for flood proofing for use of engineers, architects, and other technicians concerned with those alternative adjustments to floods (Sheaffer 1967). Geographers joined in the studies of receptivity that lay the foundation for the first fully operative national program of flood insurance in the United States (Czamanske 1967). They also helped sharpen the method of estimating flood losses (Kates 1965).

The eventual upshot of these investigations and their application in sample areas was the formulation of a new Federal flood policy under a task force in which geographers had a hand, established by the Executive Office of the President (U.S., 1966). The new policy involved basic changes in approaches and collaboration among nineteen different agencies, outlined a comprehensive effort by all interested agencies to deal with flood loss management, and inspired new lines of research and of data collection on their part (see Table 2). An Executive Order (Number 11296) at the same time required all government agencies responsible, directly or indirectly, for locating new buildings on flood plains to take account of flood hazard in the location decision.

It would be a mistake to suggest that the resulting policy has been fully or effectively translated into action in all responsible agencies. Any basic change in bureaucratic outlook is slow at best. Yet, part of the geographic view of flood plain adjustments had been adopted within four years. A geographer had been appointed to head the flood plain study section of the Corps of Engineers. While reasonable progress was made by most units of government, several agencies dragged their heels against revisions in their procedures, as when the Department of Agriculture committed itself to building flow regulation and land treatment structures to the virtual exclusion of other types of adjustments (White 1970a).

In a number of states such as Iowa, Nebraska, and Ohio, geographers played a part in instigating and carrying out state efforts to apply the same comprehensive approach to flood problems in their respective areas. Under the leadership of geographers the Center for Urban Studies at the University of Chicago initiated several appraisals of experience with flood plain management which assisted in revision of Federal operating policies.

Certain of the activities recommended by the Task Force found interested response in other countries. Thus, the preparation of maps of flood prone areas was undertaken in France under the sponsorship of the Ministere de I'Equipement et du Logement (France, n.d.; 1968). Studies of flood problems were sponsored by government agencies in Canada (Sewell 1965).

At the international level, the Department of Economic and Social Affairs of the United Nations joined with the Ministry of Reclamation and Water Management and other agencies in the USSR in sponsoring in 1969 a Seminar on Methods of Flood Loss Management. The Seminar brought together specialists, primarily engineers, from 28 developing countries and a number of consultants, including one geographer each from Canada, Japan, the United Kingdom, and the United States (White. 1970b). They gave careful thought to the approaches initiated in the United States, and in some countries the effects are now observable in national study activity. The United Nations report on the Seminar gives the Seminar findings, points out the implications of geographic research, and suggests new flood loss reduction policies for informal guidance of officials coping with flood losses in developing countries.

The approach which seemed to be yielding results in the realm of flood losses was given application in several other sectors. The Office of Science and Technology established a special Task Force on Earthquake Problems which was patterned after the experience of the Task Force on Federal Flood Control Policy and which benefitted from the geographic contribution to the National Academy of Sciences report on the Alaska earthquake. Russell, Kates, and Arey pursued the problem of optimization in dealing with drought hazard as related to municipal water supply following the New England drought of 1965 (1970).

COLLABORATIVE STUDIES ON NATURAL HAZARD

The various threads of inquiry were drawn together again in 1968 by a collaborative investigation of natural hazards supported by the National Science Foundation. Burton of Toronto and Kates of Clark joined with the author in examining the experience with a large array of hazards—drought, earthquake, flood, frost, landslide, hurricane, snow, tornado, and volcano—in a variety of settings (Burton et al. 1968).

Scientific as well as public policy response to these activities was sufficiently promising so that the International

Geographical Union Commission on Man and Environment decided in 1969 to adopt as one of its two principal thrusts in the succeeding three-year period a program for international collaboration in the study of problems of environmental hazards. These joint investigations now comprise a number of comparative field observations and national studies as outlined in Table 3.

The selection of study areas and collaborators was in many instances fortuitous: areas were chosen in terms of the inherent interest of the occupance and environmental problems but with a practical eye to the availability of competent personnel to carry out the work. It is hoped that from them will come a more rigorous and searching testing of a number of the hypotheses that slowly have emerged over the years since the first office analysis was made of the range of adjustments to floods. Some of the early findings no doubt will be reversed or discarded. The principal hypotheses are new under examination by the collaborators at Clark, Colorado and Toronto.

TABLE 3

Field Studies as Part of Collaborative Research on Natural Hazards, 1971

Comparative Observations of Small Areas	
Coastal Erosion	Scotland
	United States
	Wales
Drought	Australia
	Brazil
	Mexico
	Tanzania
	United States
Earthquake	Peru
	Sicily
	United States

Flood	Canada
	Ceylon
	France
	India
	Japan
	United Kingdom
United States	
Frost	United States
Hurricane	Pakistan
	United States
Landslide	Japan
	United States
Snow	United States
National Studies of One Hazard	
Drought	Australia
	Tanzania
Hurricane	East Pakistan
	United States
Flood	Ceylon
Air Pollution	United Kingdom

Perhaps the most fundamental of those hypotheses is that rational explanations can be found for the persistence of human occupance in areas of high hazard by examining the perception of the occupants of such areas and searching out their views of the alternative adjustments and the likely consequences of adopting any one of those opportunities.

In general, we suspect that there are three major types of response to natural hazards. Tentatively, we characterize these as follows: (1) Folk, or pre-industrial response, involving a wide range of adjustments requiring more modifications in behavior and harmony with nature than control of nature and being essentially flexible, easily abandoned, and low in capital requirements. (2) Modern technological, or industrial response involving a much more limited range of technological actions which tend to be inflexible, difficult to change, high in capital requirement, and to require interdependent social organization. (3) Comprehensive, or post-industrial, response combining features of both of the other types, and involving a larger range of adjustments, greater flexibility, and greater variety of capital and organizational requirements. We hypothesize that the United States currently is passing the peak of the modern technological type and is beginning to catch glimpses of the comprehensive type as it emerges here and elsewhere, but we do not suggest that there is a necessary sequence in the types of response.

It is also hypothesized that variations from place to place in hazard perception and estimation can be accounted for in considerable measure by a combination of factors embracing (1) certain physical characteristics of the hazard, (2) the recency and severity of personal experience with the hazard, (3) the situational characteristics of decisions regarding adjustment to the hazard, and (4) personality traits.

We have been inclined to try to describe choice of adjustment in terms of a perception model dealing with the individual manager's subjective recognition of the hazard, of the range of choice open to him, the availability of technology, the relative economic efficiency of the alternatives, and the likely linkages of his action with other people.

We further hypothesize that there are significant differences in the way in which these factors interact in relation to community action in contrast to individual action.

THE ALTERNATIVES APPROACH

Another spinoff from the early flood plain investigations was application of the idea of range of alternative adjustment to other aspects of natural resources management. In elementary terms the alternatives approach in flood losses could be adopted to any other purposeful intervention in the environment. For example, in combatting stream pollution, the building of waste treatment works or of storage for diluting stream flow are only two of a much larger range of adjustments (Davis 1968). Alternatives would include such measures as controlling waste at the source, use of waste in agriculture, oxygenating streams, constructing special channels for waste transport, and the like.

This view was expressed in two reports from the National Academy of Sciences Committee on Water, with geographic participation (NAS 1966, 1968); that had a significant effect on national water policy in the late sixties. Attention to the full range of practicable adadjustments converged with concern for systems analysis to produce water planning methods found in the North Atlantic Regional Water Study. In the North Atlantic study all interested Federal agencies and twelve states join in preparing river basin reports showing for each of three alternative aims (national economic efficiency, regional development, and environmental preservation) the range of possible activities, including non-structural devices, which might be undertaken to meet perceived needs.

The same approach was embodied in part of the High School Geography Project. Its unit on environmental study introduces the student to analysis of alternative ways of dealing with flood losses in an industrial area. The treatment there coincides with increasing emphasis in the social scene on consideration of the range of possible social action in contrast to dependence upon simple technological solutions.

APPRAISAL

It is too early to venture an appraisal of how influential this direction of natural hazards research has been upon either public policy or geographic thinking; nor are we well equipped to try. In the short run it clearly has been linked to changes in methods of managing water and associated land resources in one nation, and to a smaller degree in several others. What effect those changes will have in the long run is impossible to predict. As of 1971 they pointed to more searching examination of the range of choice available to man in coming to terms with his environment. Although the research has made only modest contributions to a theory of man-environment relations, it supported new efforts to specify the nature of environmental perception, to recognize the process of decision making for resource management, and to identify the landscape consequences of alternative public policies.

In essence, the activity was problem oriented and interdisciplinary. Such work is often tiresome and sometimes exhilarating. It requires research findings in a form highly intelligible to workers in other fields. It ignores conventional divisions of art academic field.

One lesson emerges from this history of investigation of a single environmental problem, using a rather unsophisticated research paradigm. It is that if environmental problems are pursued rigorously enough and with sufficient attention to likely contributions from other disciplines they may foster constructive alternations in public policy but at the same time may stimulate new research and refinement of research methodology to the benefit of geographic discipline. Both may serve to advance man's painful, faltering, and crucial struggle to find his harmonious place in the global systems of which he is a part.

REFERENCES

Burton, I. (1962), Types of agricultural occupance of flood plains in the United States; University of Chicago, *Department of Geography Research Paper No. 75.*

Burton, I. (1965), Rood damage reduction in Canada; *Geophysical Bulletin* 7, 161-85.

Burton, I. and Kates, R.W. (1964), Perception of natural hazards in resources management; *Natural Resources Journal* 3, 412-41.

Burton, I., Kates, R.W. and Snead, R.E. (1969), The human ecology of coastal flood hazard in megalopolis; *University of Chicago, Department of Geography Research Paper No. 115.*

Burton, I., Kates, R.W. and White, G.F. (1968), The human ecology of extreme geophysical events; *Natural Hazard Research, Working Paper No. 1, Department of Geography, University of Toronto.*

Cook, H.L. and White, G.F. (1962), Making wise use of flood plains; In *United Nations Conference on Applications of Science and Technology,* (Government Printing Office, Washington), Vol. 1, 343-59.

Czamanske, D.V. (1967), *Receptivity to Flood Insurance;* (Master's Dissertation, University of Chicago).

Davis, R.K. (1968), *The Range of Choice in Water Management: A Study of Dissolved Oxygen in the Polomac Basin;* (Johns Hopkins Press, Baltimore).

Dunham, A. (1959), Flood control via the police power; *University of Pennsylvania Law Review* 107, 1098-132.

France, Ministere de l'Equipment et du Logement, *Inventaire des Zones Incndables;* (Paris: BCEOM, n.d.).

France, Ministere de l'Equipment et du Logement (1968), *Etats-Unis: Recherches Methodologiques sur la Rentabilite Economique des Mesures de la Controle des (rues a L'Etranger;* (Paris, BCEOM).

Goddard, J.E. (1971), Flood plain management must be ecologically and economically sound; *Civil Engineering* September, 81-5.

Hewitt, K. (1969), Probabilistic approaches to discrete natural events: A review and theoretical discussion; *Natural Hazard Research Working Paper No. 8, Department of Geography,* University of Toronto.

Johnson, J.F. (1971), Renovated waste water; *University of Chicago, Department of Geography Research Paper No. 135.*

Kates, R.W. (1964), Variation in flood hazard perception: Implications for rational flood plain use; In *Spatial Organization of Land Uses: The Willamette Valley,* (Oregon State University, Corvallis).

Kates, R.W. (1962), Hazard and choice perception in flood plain management; *University of Chicago, Department of Geography Research Paper No. 78.*

Kates, R.W. (1965), Industrial flood losses: Damage estimation in the Lehigh Valley; *University of Chicago, Department of Geography Research Paper No. 98.*

Kates, R.W. (1971), Natural hazard in human ecological perspective: Hypotheses and models; *Natural Hazard Research Working Paper No. 14,* Department of Geography, University of Toronto.

Kates, R.W. and Wohlwill, J.F. (Eds.) (1966), Man's response to the physical environment; *Journal of Social Issues* 22, 1-140.

Lind, R.C. (1966), *The Nature of Flood Control Benefits and the Economics of Flood Protection;* (Stanford University Institute for Mathematical Studies in the Social Sciences).

Lowenthal, D. (Ed.) (1967), Environmental perception and behavior; *University of Chicago, Department of Geography Research Paper No. 109.*

MacIver, I. (1970), Urban water supply alternatives: Perception and choice in the Grand Basin, Ontario; *University of Chicago, Department of Geography Research Paper No. 126.*

Miller, D.H. (1966), Cultural hydrology: A review; *Economic Geography* 42, 85-9.

Murphy, F.C. (1958), Regulating flood plain development; *University of Chicago, Department of Geography Research Paper No. 56.*

National Academy of Sciences Committee on Water (1966), *Alternatives in Water Management;* Publication 1408, (Washington, D.C.).

National Academy of Sciences Committee on Water (1968), *Water and Choice in the Colorado Basin: An Example of Alternatives in Water Management:* Publication 1689, (Washington, D.C.).

National Hazard Research (1970), Suggestions for comparative field observations of natural hazards; *Natural Hazard Research Working Paper No. 16, Department of Geography,* University of Toronto.

Roder, W. (1961), Attitudes and knowledge in the Topeka flood plain; In 'Papers on Flood Problems', *University of Chicago,* Department of Geography Research Paper No. 70.

Russell, C.S. (1970), Losses from natural hazards; *Journal of Land Economics,* Vol. 46, p. 38-00.

Saarinen. T.F. (1969), Perception of environment; *Association of American Geographers. Commission on College Geography,* (Washington, D.C.).

Saarinen, T.F. (1966), Perception of the drought hazard; *American Geographers, Commission on College Geography,* (Washington, D.C.).

Schiff, M.R, (1971), Psychological factors relating to the adoption of adjustments for natural hazards in London, Ontario; *Paper presented to Association of American Geographers,* Boston, April 1971.

Sewell, W.R.D. (1965), Water management and floods in the Fraser River Basin; *University of Chicago,* Department of Geography Research Paper No. 100.

Sheaffer, J.R. (1960), Flood proofing: An element in a flood damage reduction program: University of Chieago. Department of Geography Research Paper No. 65,

Sheaffer, J.R. (1964), Economic feasibility and use of flood maps; *Highway Research Record* 58, 44-6.

Sheaffer, J.R. (1967), *Introduction to Flood Proofing: An outline of principles and methods;* (University of Chicago, Center for Urban Studies).

Sims, J. and Saarinen, T.F. (1969), Coping with environmental threat: Great Plains farmers and the sudden storm; *Annals of the Association of American Geographers* 59, 677-86.

United States Bureau of Reclamation (1941), *Columbia Basin Joint investigations-Character and Scope;* (Government Printing Office, Washington, D.C.).

United States, Eighty-ninth Congress, Second Session (1966), 4 *Unified National Program for Managing Flood Losses;* House Document 465, (Washington, D.C.).

White, G.F. (1942), Human adjustment to floods; *University of Chicago, Department of Geography Research Paper No. 29.*

White, G.F., Calef, W.C., Hudson, J.W., Mayer, H.M., Scheaffer, J.R. and Volk, D.J. (1958), Changes in urban occupance of flood plains in the United States; *University of Chicago, Department of Geography Research Paper No. 57.*

White, G.F. (1969), *Strategies of American Water Management;* (University of Michigan Press, Ann Arbor).

White, G.F. (1970a), Flood loss reduction: The integrated approach; *Journal of Soil and Water Conservation* 25 172-6.

[This chapter is substaintially based on the work of GIlbert F. White. We owe a deep sense of gratitude to him for sharing his views.—Ed.]

4

Disaster: Dimensions and Implications

> Men often oppose a thing merely because they have had no agency in planning it, or because it may have been planned by those whom they dislike.
>
> —*Alexander Hamilton, The Federalist*

This is also a fundamental truth that 'Disasters' has been with us as long as recorded history, and presumably even longer. Generations of people have had to withstand disaster. There are certain factors which need to be considered in relation to the modern challenges facing disaster management.

1. Traditional Disaster Threats

In tradition disaster threat there has not been very much reduction. Natural hazards—including avalanches, cyclones and other wind storms, floods, wildfire, drought and locust infestations—occur throughout much of the world. Most of the problems remain as threatening as ever. Same is the case with man-made disasters such as major accidents which cause loss of harm on lives, loss of property, social loss and damage to the environment. The fact remains that we have learned to live with these problems to some extent. But we have neither eliminated nor contained them. On the contrary, some of the traditional disaster threats have grown both in intensity and frequency. The human-induced factors in recent past have in fact added to these threats such as, unchecked population growth, human-settlements on ecosensitive and fragile areas, etc. These changes have induced such chain reactions which are indeed detrimental to human survival and development. Ignoring traditional wisdom's use in coping with such disasters and implementing new architectural designs and resource management systems without having conducted sustained risk assessment, process have started giving new lethal dimension to these traditional threats.

2. New Disaster Threats

'New Disaster Threats,' since World War II, may be grouped as under:

(a) increase in social conflicts and violence, such as hijacking, terrorism, civil-strife.

(b) increase in use of light weapons/traditional weapon systems/conventional arms and its serious negative impact on economy.

(c) increased production, trade and trafficking in hazardous chemical and toxic materials, including accidents involved during transportation.

(d) hazardous wastes dumping in areas of future importance.

(e) nuclear material dumping and use, causing accidents, radiological impacts.

(f) possible nuclear holocaust as worst stage scenario in case of nuclear war.

(g) terrorist's capture and use of nuclear weapon system.

(h) wrong-use (abuse/misuse) of biotechnology/genetic engineering in causing environmental hazards.

3. Geographical Distribution of Various Disasters

"Geographical distribution of Disaster" is another vital factor which need to be taken into account. Primarily it falls between Tropic of Cancer and Tropic of Capricorn. Coincidently, it represents the area where most of the developing countries harbouring majority of world population live. Economic underdevelopment combined with severe natural and man-made disasters/epidemics create a situation where the impact in terms of deaths, injuries, homelessness etc. increase many fold.

4. Modern Loss Factors

This include the following:

(i) inappropriate cost-benefit analysis of disaster mitigation efforts.

(ii) ineffective disaster management capability in terms of its spread and intensity.

(iii) absence of well-coordinated international assistance and action and lack of appropriate national interface.

As such, in contemporary global, regional, national and local disaster scenario, taking proactive initiatives is very important. Similarly, developing site-oriented and issue-oriented optimum disaster management is of utmost importance. These plans need to be complementary in nature towards issues like social justice and equity, environmental restoration, poverty alleviation, food security and sustainable development of natural and anthropocentric systems. The urgent need is to focus on the following:

(a) disaster mitigation,

(b) disaster containment, and

(c) disaster assistance.

The goals at national level, especially, during post-disaster threats, should be:

(a) restoration of existing assets

(b) satisfactory prompt and recovery plan

(c) actions to be taken under a comprehensive approach to disaster management covering all major possibilities.

The following elements must be incorporated in an effective national disaster management cycle:

(a) prevention;
(b) mitigation;
(c) preparedness;
(d) awareness;
(e) response;
(f) recovery;
(g) rehabilitation; and
(h) other miscellaneous disaster related developments.

Major Trends and Implications

Obviously, the contemporary world and its inhabitants are becoming increasingly vulnerable to disasters and hazards, both environmental and man-made. From tsunamis and earthquakes to floods and famines, from technological and industrial disasters to epidemics humankind is never threatened by the forces of nature and their alterations by anthropogenic factors. With almost a billion people now living in unplanned urban shanty towns, with deforestation, wrecking natural ecological defences against catastrophic natural events, and with global climatic changes making the forces of wind, rain, ocean and sun ever harden to predict and counter, the world is at risk as never before. For instance, world-wide epidemics of disease, droughts, forest fires and floods that accompanied the meteorological phenomena of El Niño and La Niña make climatologists believe that these will only intensify and become more and more frequent and aggressive as climatic changes take hold. So, both the severity and diversity of environmental and man-made disasters have become a matter of great concern.

The recent Tsunami (2004) has devastating impact in south and south east Asia, when millions of people lost the life and immeasurable assets were lost. Contemporary analyses of major trends and implications of natural man-made and hybrid disasters suggest while on one hand all kinds of disasters have grown in terms of loss of life there is a significant shift. More people got killed in 2004 than in the 1980s or in the 1990s. In terms of disaster affected people however, about 50% more people were impacted upon by some kind of disaster in the 1990s than the cases in the 1980s. Disasters caused by climate/weather and water experienced a growth in the 1990s while the number of geophysical disasters have remained rather steady during 1980s and 1990s. In 1990s, disasters such as droughts, windstorms and floods alone shared about 90% of total people killed during the decade from all kinds of disasters. Floods emerged as most widespread natural disaster covering two thirds of total people affected, but in terms of causing death, they share only 15 per cent of all deaths due to natural disasters.

As far as socio-economic implications of various natural disasters are concerned, there is no clear picture emerging at the global level. Even the estimates made based on insurance claims are rather misleading. Similarly, the assessment of environmental impacts both in short-term and long-term remains highly unreliable as availability of coherent and reliable data still elusive. Besides, the current disaster statistics focus on local disasters such as wildfire, small floods, droughts, pest-infestations etc. are completely missing, thereby, putting the developing countries on a loosing footage. While droughts and famines have emerged as more devastating in terms of human-life and sufferings, disasters such as floods, earthquakes, and windstorms are proven to be more damaging in economic/financial terms.

Economic Impact of Disasters

As per the Munich Report (2001) while the numbers of major catastrophic events over the past decade has increased three fold in comparison with the 1960s, the rate of economic losses has increased by a factor of almost 9 times over the same period. However, one of the facts which has emerged conclusively as a major implication of contemporary natural disasters globally is the trend that while less developed countries must not rely mostly on external relief if a disaster happen as their economies need more time to recover. In developing countries, there exist greater capability and capacity to cope with such disasters, as the resultant economic losses are to a considerable extent absorbed by the national/regional economy and most assets are insured. Fifty percent of the total number of least developed countries are at great risk due to such disasters with major negative consequences as far as their human development index is concerned. Ironically, more than 50% of all natural disasters during the last decade occurred in developing countries with medium level of "Human Development Index." While more than 75% of all killed hailed from least developed countries, only 2% was shared by the highly developed countries. As per the International Federation of the Red Cross (2001), on an average, for every 22.5 persons death in highly developed countries, due to natural disasters, there is a figure of 145 deaths in developing countries and as high as 1052 deaths in the least developed countries.

Notably, global warming as the main reason for extreme weather conditions. Climate change can alter global precipitation pattern, wind-velocities, soil-moisture content, vegetation cover, etc. to a great extent thus not only influencing the occurrences of storms, hurricanes, floods, drought, landsliding etc. but also their intensity to do great damage. El-Nino, ozone layer depletion, biodiversity extinction, sea-level rise, greenhouse effect, etc. will slowly and surely make this world more unsafe and unpredictable to live-in. For example, El-Nino related death globally reached more than 24,000 during 1997-98 due to high winds, floods, storm and surges. More than 110 million people were affected globally and as many as 6 million were displaced. Again, due to extensive logging and inappropriate land-uses for short term economic gain inside the country and in neighbouring countries, countries like Venezuela and India have been prone to serious floodings in recent past. As another case study, migration of people from rural to urban and coastal areas has created a great imbalance. As a result in coastal and urban areas now, natural disasters kill and affect more people. Even the economic loss has increased. The fact remains that although the seismic activity has remained rather constant over recent years, the damages due to earthquake on the urban population appear to be increasing.

As far as major trends and implications of human-induced disasters are concerned a number of major accidents involving chemicals and nuclear materials have drawn attention worldwide to the dangers of accidents due to mismanagement. Mining accidents in industrial sectors, accidents during transport of radioactive and hazardous chemical and nuclear wastes, nuclear accidents, technological accidents etc. made the world rather more unsafe today than any time in the history. The trans-boundary implication of such human-induced disasters have created a doubt regarding the whole development paradigm which the humans have been following and the necessity of exhaustive risk-assessment before launching any such technology with wider implications. Nuclear safety, safe disposal of toxic chemicals, hazardous wastes, nuclear wastes, safe energy sources, in particular, renewable ones, clear environmental practices, raised environmental safety standards, etc. have gained attention today. As a result of international policy responses, mainly due to the 1990s declared as International Decade for Natural Disaster Reduction, risk reduction has been placed on a higher political agenda.

The risk reduction strategy includes:

(a) the identification of areas that are safe for settlement and development;
(b) the vulnerability mapping activity;
(c) the adoption of building codes based on disaster resilient engineering and on local hazard risk assessments; and

(d) the proper enforcement of these plans and codes with the help of economic, market-based, and other incentives.

As a result, the United Nations has established an International Strategy for Disaster Reduction, a global platform aimed at helping all communities to become resilient to the effects of natural disasters and to proceed from protection against hazards to the management of risk through the integration of risk prevention into sustainable development.

Year 2001 Disasters: An Overview

- In mid- to late January, heavy rains over Zambezia Province caused the Licungo River to flood in Mozambique. Nearly 500000 people were affected by the floods.
- In March, floods devastated a wide area of northeastern Hungary, northwestern Romania and western Ukraine. Tens of thousands of people were forced to move.
- Flash floods unexpectedly struck parts of Pakistan on 23 July. The cities of Islamabad and Rawalpindi were the worst affected. 132 people were killed.
- In mid-November, as many as 576 Vietnamese had been killed by natural disasters, mainly floods and typhoons. Material losses amounted to more than US$200 million.
- A persistent multi-year drought in Central and Southwest Asia had affected about 60 million people by November 2001.
- After several months of drought, devastating floods tore through the Algerian capital Algiers on 10 November, killing 751 people. Thousands were injured, and about 40000 people were left homeless.

[*Source:* Relief Web (2002), Munich Re 2001.]

The resources in the world are limited; hence it may be

wise to give priority attention to those pollutants and problems that pose the greatest risk to human society. Therefore, it is all the more important to systematically understand why and how the severity and nature of environmental hazards vary from place to place world-wide. Besides, for setting priorities for future action plan in this regard, those chorological and chronological indicators need to be assessed in comparative terms. No doubt, these indicators vary from country to country and their focus is also varied, such as on sources of environmental degradation, effects of environmental disturbance, state of environment *per se*, etc.

The models suggested by Hosenemser, Kasperson, and Kates (1985) called 'causal model' and 'causal taxanomy' of environmental hazards tries to mitigate the aforementioned shortcomings in current practice. This proposed methodological framework is helpful in both defining the data most relevant for priority setting and global comparative assessment of environmental hazards and in structuring those data in a way that makes them usable in policy-making, thus constituting essential foundations for long-term in improvements in management performance (Hutchison 1977). In early 1980s, scholars at Clark University's Center for Technology, Environment, and Development (CENTED) began a seminal research on the characterization of health and environmental hazards arising from the use of technology (Hohenemser, Kates, and Slovic, 1985; Kates, Hohenemser, and Kasperson, 1985). Other attempts on shedding more light on the establishing priorities in this regard were also made. However, none of these approaches are directly applicable for comparative assessment of environmental hazards in developing countries where the needs for priority setting are most urgently required in light of the fact that the scarcity of data and its authenticity is most problematique. The 'causal taxonomy approach' has many advantages over other simpler approaches to hazard assessment. The simple linear model of hazard causation is anchored a one end by the human activities or natural events that perturb the environment and at the other by consequence of those perturbations for people and things they value. It provides the backbone against which number of key characteristics of environmental hazard is defined, such as; persistence of a pollutant in the environment, the population exposed and health consequences. For each of these characteristics, specific measurable descriptors as many as 8 are defined and normalized on the scale of 1 to 9. The same model structure and descriptor definitions are applied to all hazards. Next, the specific set of potential environmental problems are identified and characterized. Three criteria were applied to select these:

(1) that they be understandable and meaningful to policy makers and other non-specialists;

(2) that they be comprehensive, so as to include virtually all the potentially significant environmental problems faced by any nation; and

(3) that they be defined at a level of resolution yielding a list of neither too general nor too complex for practical utility.

A group of 28 problems was selected for the said characterization.

1. *Pollution-based Hazards*

(a) *Water Quality*

(i) Fresh water: Biological contamination.

(ii) Fresh water: Metals and toxic contamination

(iii) Fresh water: Eutrophication

(iv) Fresh water: Sedimentation

(v) Marine water

(b) *Atmospheric Quality*

(vi) Stratospheric Ozone depletion

(vii) Climate change

(viii) Acidification

(ix) Ground-level ozone formation

(x) Hazardous and toxic air pollution

(c) *Quality of the human environment*

(xi) Indoor air pollutants: Radon

(xii) Indoor air pollutants: Non-radon

(xiii) Radiation: Non-radon

(xiv) Chemical in workplace

(xv) Accidental chemical releases

(xvi) Food contaminants

2. Resource-depletion Hazards

(d) *Land-water resources*

(xvii) Agricultural land: Salinization, Alkalizatic

(xviii) Agricultural land: Soil erosion

(xix) Agricultural land: Urbanization

(xx) Groundwater

(e) *Biological Stocks*

(xxi) Wildlife

(xxii) Fish

(xxiii) Forests

3. Natural Hazards

(xxiv) Floods

(xxv) Droughts

(xxvi) Cyclones

(xxvii) Earthquakes

(xxviii) Pest epidemics.

However, learning what our environmental values are and ought to be requires a means of examining and reflecting upon their implications for the ordering of specific real-world priorities (Wildavsky, 1979). Also for a majority of 28 hazard, a normalized score of 9 will imply a more hazardous problem that a score of 1, but this is not necessary the case. This is particularly true for recurrence (Material Flux Descriptor) and Delay (Exposure Descriptor). For this aggregation scheme total Ecosystem consequences, the high, medium and low ranked problem are defined by the break points in the scoring: a score of 14 or above indicates a high hazard, a score of 6 or 10 is a medium hazard, and a score of 2 is a low hazard. No doubt, despite its many shortcomings, the use of a causal taxonomy for comparative-hazard assessment permits a full characterization of environmental hazard. This allows for hazards to be ranked on the basis both of their consequences and of other important characteristics like disruption to the environment, pervasiveness, and manageability. By focusing on aggregation schemes that are chosen by the uses and can be clearly communicated to others, the method makes transparent the value judgments inherent in any scheme for comparing and ranking hazards. This is of particular importance when ranking hazards that cause different types of consequences, that occur over different time-frames, and that appear in very different perspectives in different parts of the world.

II

DISASTER DATA: KEY TRENDS AND STATISTICS

World Disasters Report 2001 features more data and analysis than before. Natural disasters are now subdivided into hydro-meteorological and geophysical categories, to emphasize the effect on the decades disasters of global warming.

Disaster data is analysed not only by continent and type of phenomenon, but for the first time by disasters' impact on countries categorized by the United Nations as being of high, medium and low human development. In addition, a new wall map included in the report presents the effect of disasters on nations by expressing the total numbers of people killed or affected as a percentage of each nation's total population. This analysis presents a clearer picture of the impact of disasters on the world's most vulnerable nations.

Another new set of data for *World Disasters Report 2001* is the combination of disaster and conflict data. These statistics combine the totals of those killed and affected by armed conflict and by natural or technological disasters — in effect, those people whose development is denied, either temporarily or permanently, by conflict and disaster. Along with data on refugees, internally displaced people and financial flows, this chapter provides a fuller picture than before for those responding to disasters.

An Overview

More disasters were reported for 2000 than in any year over the last decade. Fortunately these disasters proved less fatal than in previous years: around 20,000 people lost their lives worldwide, compared to the decade's average of 75,250 deaths per year. However, last year 256 million people were reported affected by disasters, well above the decade's average of 210 million.

Natural disasters killed a reported 665,598 people from 1991-2000. This figure is probably an underestimate. Famine reportedly killed 280,000, but well-placed sources estimate that those who died just in the Democratic People's Republic of Korea's famine from 1995-98 may have numbered between 800,000 and 1.5 million. Of all those killed by natural disasters, 83 per cent were Asians. On average, natural disasters accounted for 88 per cent of all deaths from disasters over the last decade.

While the number of geophysical disasters reported over the last decade has remained fairly steady, the number of hydro-meteorological disasters since 1996 has more than doubled During the past decade, over 90 per cent of those killed by natural disasters lost their lives in hydro-meteorological events such as droughts, wind storms and floods.

Floods accounted for over two-thirds of the annual average of 211 million people affected by natural disasters, while famine affected nearly one-fifth. Yet floods proved less deadly, accounting for 15 per cent of deaths from natural disasters, compared to famine's 42 per cent.

The cost of damage inflicted by disasters is notoriously difficult to estimate. Statistics adjusted for inflation reveal that natural disasters worldwide inflict an average of US$ 78 billion per year in damage. The most expensive disasters are floods, earthquakes and wind storms. While earthquakes accounted for 30 per cent of estimated damage, they killed just 9 per cent of all those killed by natural disasters.

Analysing disasters by their impact on nations ranked by the United Nations Development Programme (UNDP) according to their level of human development reveals some unexpected trends. Of the 2,557 natural disasters reported over the last ten years, more than half were in countries of medium human development (MHD). However, two-thirds of those killed came from countries of low human development (LHD), while just 2 per cent came from highly developed nations. By comparing the totals reported killed with the total number of disasters, the effect of development on disasters becomes stark. On average, 22.5 people die per reported disaster in highly developed nations, 145 die per disaster in nations of medium human development, while each disaster in LHD countries claims an average of 1,052 people.

Coming to those affected by natural disaster, 88 per cent are from MHD nations, while just one-tenth are from countries of low human development. This may be explained by the fact that the UN categorizes China and India, home to some of the world's biggest natural catastrophes, as nations of medium human development. Estimated cost of damage tells a different story: 58 per cent of the direct costs of natural disasters is borne by highly developed countries, although these nations account for just ?. per cent of deaths. Meanwhile, LHD countries, which account for 67 per cent of deaths, bear just 4 per cent of the costs. Comparing estimated costs of natural disasters with the numbers reported, the average disaster costs highly developed nations US$ 636 million, medium developed nations US$ 209 million, and nations of low human development US$ 79 million.

Looking back over two decades, 1991-2000 proved less deadly than 1981-1990. The average number of those killed by natural and non-natural disasters fell from 86,328 to 75,252. The high mortality figures of the 1980s were largely due to major catastrophes in Ethiopia, Sudan and Mozambique. However more people were affected by disasters over the last decade - up from an average of 147 million per year (1981-1990) to 211 million per year (1991-2000). During 2000, Asia, Africa and Europe all reported statistics for those affected higher than the decade's average.

For the first time, the *World Disasters Report* has totalled the annual average (from 1991- 2000) of those reported as killed and affected by natural and technological disasters, and expressed this figure as a percentage of each nation's total population (see wall map). This analysis of the 'proportional effect of disasters on nations' populations creates some surprising results. The most affected nation is the Solomon Islands — exposed, as are many small island states, to recurrent natural hazards. The three hardest-hit nations (Solomon Islands, Malawi and Cambodia) are all classified as least developed countries (LDCs).

Combined Effects of Conflict and Disaster

One amazing reality is that over the last decade, conflicts reportedly killed nearly 2.3 million people - over three times the 665,600 killed by natural disasters. Nations of low human development account for 76 per cent of the deaths reported due to conflicts. Of the 2.3 million people reported as killed by conflict from 1991-2000, over three-quarters were from nations of low human development. Of the 665,600 reported killed by natural disasters over the same period, two-thirds were from LHD nations. Meanwhile, of the 86,923 deaths reported over the decade from technological disasters, 64 per cent were in nations of medium human development.

Combining the above figures, just over 3 million people reportedly lost their lives to conflict and both natural and technological disasters over the last decade. Conflict claimed the lion's share — killing over three times the number killed by natural disasters.

However, natural disasters reportedly affected on average 211 million people per year from 1991-2000. This is seven times more than the average of 31 million people annually affected by conflict.

On totalling over the last decades statistics, an average of 242 million people per year are killed and affected by disasters and conflicts. For all three categories of nation— low, medium and high human development—the total killed and affected by natural disasters is higher than the total killed and affected by conflict. Many of these millions - whether refugees fleeing the fighting in Afghanistan and Angola, or Chinese and Bangladeshis fleeing annual floods — are affected by conflict and disaster year after year. For them, development hardly has a chance to take hold — it is denied by disaster.

Financial Flows

For the second successive year, official development assistance (ODA) from members of the Organisation for Economic Cooperation and Development's Development Assistance Committee (DAC) has risen, reaching US$ 55 billion in 1999, the latest year for which statistics are available.

This represents a rise of US$ 3 billion from 1998 — in real terms, an increase of 5.6 per cent. Most of this increase is accounted for by Japan's increase of US$ 2.8 billion between 1998 and 1999. Japan, the largest donor of ODA, has increased its giving 70 per cent in real terms since 1996. This is all the more remarkable considering the other big four donors (US, France, Germany, UK) have all reduced their giving by an average of nearly 10 per cent over the same period. Since 1991, ODA has fallen from US$ 61.6 billion - a drop in real terms of 11 per cent. Over this period the US, which started the decade as the world's biggest giver, has reduced aid flows by 30 per cent. Expressed as a percentage of donor nations' gross national product (GNP), ODA has remained static at an average of 0.39 per cent - well below the UN's target of 0.7 per cent, and down from 1991's average of 0.48 per cent. Only four nations out of the 22 DAC members make the UN target: Sweden (0.7), Netherlands (0.79), Norway (0.91), and Denmark (1.01). However, eight nations managed to increase their giving from 1998-1999 as a proportion of GNP.

Bilateral ODA to the 48 least developed countries continues to fall. At constant 1998 prices, its value was US$ 16.8 billion in 1991 compared to just under US$ 11 billion in 1999. As a share of 1999's bilateral ODA cake, the LDC slice was a little over one-quarter. Emergency relief from DAC donors shot up 56 per cent in real terms, from US$ 2.8 billion in 1998 to US$ 4.4 billion in 1999. Roughly one-third of this leap is accounted for by spending in the Balkans, which increased US$ 572 million between 1998 and 1999. All DAC donors, except Denmark, increased emergency spending. The US, notably, increased its relief donations by 76 per cent from US$ 898 million in 1998 to US$ 1,579 million in 1999 (at 1998 prices). However, the share of total bilateral emergency relief which goes to the LDCs has shrunk from 46 per cent in 1995 to just 28 per cent in 1999.

Data on disaster occurrence, its effect upon people and its cost to countries remain, at best, patchy. No single institution has taken on the role of prime providers of verified data, so the *World Disasters Report* draws upon two main sources (described in more detail below): the Centre for Research on the Epidemiology of Disasters (CRED) and the US Committee for Refugees (USCR). CRED has used the OECD's DAC database for ODA and emergency/distress relief

Key problems today with disaster data include the lack of standardized collection methodologies and definitions. Problems exist over such loose categories as 'internally displaced' people or even people 'affected' by disaster. Much of the data in this chapter, except that on DAC spending, is culled from a variety of public sources: newspapers, insurance reports, aid agencies, etc. The original information is not specifically gathered for statistical purposes and so, inevitably, even where the compiling organization applies strict definitions for disaster events and parameters, the original suppliers of the information may not. The figures therefore should be regarded as indicative.

Information systems have improved vastly in the last 25 years and statistical data is now more easily available. However, the lack of systematic and standardized data collection from disasters in the past is now revealing itself as a major weakness for any long-term planning. Despite efforts to verify and review data, the quality of disaster databases can only be as good as the reporting system. Fortunately, due to increased pressures for accountability from various sources, many donor and development agencies have started placing priority on data collection and its methodologies, but this has yet to result in any recognized and acceptable international system for disaster-data gathering, verification and storage.

Dates can be a source of ambiguity. For example, the declared date for a famine is both necessary and meaningless — famines do not occur on a single day. In such cases, the date the appropriate body declares an official emergency has been used. Changes in national boundaries also cause ambiguities in the data, most notably the break-up of the Soviet Union and Yugoslavia, and the unification of Germany. Data can be skewed because of the rationale behind data gathering. Reinsurance companies, for instance, systematically gather data on disaster occurrence in order to assess insurance risk, but only in areas of the world where disaster insurance is widespread. Their data may therefore miss out poorer disaster-affected regions where insurance is unaffordable or unavailable.

Data on the numbers of people affected by a disaster can provide some of the most potentially useful figures, for planning both disaster preparedness and response, yet these are also some of the most loosely reported figures. The definition of 'affected' is open to interpretation, political or otherwise. In conflict, warring parties may wish to maximize sympathy for their causes and exaggerate the numbers of people under their control who are said to be affected. Even if political manipulation is absent, data is often extrapolated from old census information, with assumptions being made about percentages of an area's population affected.

The *World Disasters Report* divides disasters into the following types:

Natural Disasters

- *Hydro-meteorological:* avalanches/landslides; droughts/famines; extreme temperatures; floods; forest/scrub fires; wind storms; and other (insect infestation and waves/surges).
- Geophysical: earthquakes; volcanic eruptions.

Non-natural Disasters

- *Industrial:* chemical spill, collapse of industrial structures, explosion, fire, gas leak, poisoning, radiation.

- *Miscellaneous:* collapse of domestic/non-industrial structures, explosion, fire.
- *Transport:* air, rail, road and water-borne accidents.

GLOSSARY

Disaster

A situation or event, which overwhelms local capacity, necessitating a request to national or international level for external assistance. In order for a disaster to be entered in EM-DAT and least one of the following criteria has to be fulfilled:

- 10 or more people reported killed;
- 100 people reported affected;
- a call for international assistance; and/or
- declaration of a state of emergency.

Killed: People confirmed dead, or missing and presumed dead.

Affected: People requiring immediate assistance during a period of emergency, i.e., requiring basic survival needs such as food, water, shelter, sanitation and immediate medical assistance In EM-DAT, the total number of people affected include people reported injured, homeless, and affected.

Estimated damage: The economic impact of a disaster usually consists of direct damage (e.g., to infrastructure, crops, housing) and indirect damage (e.g., loss of revenues, unemployment, market destabilization). EM-DAT's estimates relate only to direct damage.

Conflict

The use of armed force between the military forces of two or more governments, or of government and at least one organized armed group, resulting in the battle-related deaths of at least 10 deaths or 100 affected in one year.

International conflict: includes border disputes, foreign invasion and other cross-border attacks.

Intrastate conflict or civil conflict: includes state control, state formation and state failure.

Refugees, asylum seekers and internally displaced people.

5

Relief, Rehabilitation, Damage Assessment

Disaster relief require a lot of steps to be followed and measures to be undertaken. Any integrated framework for disaster relief will necessitate proper planning and its enforcement in practical terms, as and when needs. Items which attain centre-stage while planning and preparing for disaster relief measures include the following:

(i) Search
(ii) Rescue
(iii) Evacuation
(iv) Shelter
(v) Resettlement/ relocation camps (Temporary)
(vi) Livestock relief measures
(vii) Debris removal/clearance
(viii) Disposal of the dead bodies
(ix) Fire-control
(x) Food
(xi) Communication
(xii) Access
(xiii) Water supply
(xiv) Power supply
(xv) Subsidized supply (Temporary)
(xvi) Health and sanitation
(xvii) Public information
(xviii) Security

(xix) Contribution requirements
(xx) Safety and welfare inquiry.

The post-disaster phase, the foremost relief operations which are undertaken are Search and Rescue (SAR). The untraced disaster victims are searched and rescued with the help of local communities, specialist group of people and sniffe dogs. Heavy machine tools such as cranes, earthmovers, bulldozers, cutters, boat rafts, vehicle helicopters. Generally a sector is demarcated for each SAR team and in the case of predictable slow one-set disasters they are geared up and placed in a standby position to get into action as and when required. Trained rescuers. SAR is followed by the process of evacuation which primarily involves the relocation of the disaster affected population from areas of risk to a safer destination. For successful evacuation to happen, an early and accurate warning system is required, besides marking of safe escape routes, a consistent policy towards evacuation and long-term public education on various aspects of evacuation.

In the contemporary modern world, the tools, the techniques and the methods of search rescue and evacuation have advanced considerable, thus bringing down the relative rate of mortality and morbidity quite remarkably. Scientific and technological advancement has played an important role. Geographical information system (GIS), remote sensing techniques, satellite imagery and other geographical technique have emerged as major tool in SART and evacuation process. Modern fete-Communication and advanced transportation system fitted with much required medical facilities have improved the SAR and evacuation scenario to a great extent. All kinds of networking have become very vital to achieve best possible results, so has been the role of early warning system (EWS) and skilled manpower in these areas.

Another important aspect of disaster relief, measure is shelter for disaster victims for the purpose of temporary rehabilitation. However, the shelter camp being established should be disaster specific, site specific, culture specific and time-duration specific. Any proper mechanism of shelter provision needs following elements for incorporation.

A shelter strategy depends on factor like level and extent of short and long-term intervention design options, resources required, frequency and intensity of disaster etc. Based on the aforementioned factors and may other details a disaster strategy has to be weighted in favour of either large shelter space, temporary relief camps, rehabilitation settlements, smount of repair and restoration, reporting and strengthening. In situations of collapse of disasters shelters itself, immediate relief measures enroute creation of alternative shelter either at the same place or at different ones.

The principal shelter relief materials required for distribution by relief camps include roofing item, camping gears, plastic sheets, food, water, medicines etc. Disaster prone structures in disaster-prone areas may also be erected regularly or in a phased manner so as to house the affected population in times of need. Similar structures could also be made for the animal population. Such facilities could also be otherwise allowed to be used for educational, medical (health) training or other purpose, as desired by the local community in normal disaster free time. Shelter relocation with first construction of homes on a new site may also be adopted in areas where large scale devastation may have taken place. Retrofitting may also serve as a strategy to reduce the vulnerability of the structure against future disasters. Appropriate disaster resistant construction features, if incorporated properly, can prove itself to be a very potent relief measure. The most important relief measure, in terms of psychological support, however, may be the provisions made for securing the property (i.e. valuables, cash, household items, etc). Timely and full evacuation, protection of anti-social elements and proper handling of situation can help secure the property of disaster affected people.

Livestock related relief measures need to focus at:

1. reducing the loss of animal life
2. reducing the amount of injury to animals
3. reducing animal disability
4. preventing epidemics due to animals
5. preventing epidemics among animals
6. preventing animals from starvation
7. preventing ongoing neglect of livestock problems during disaster
8. active animal husbandry services during post-disaster period with proper stock of medicines related facilities and availability of doctors.

Quick erection of livestock shelters, sustainable fodder stock; special training to veterinary staff and local community contingency plan for relocating affected animals, including infrastructure facilities required; provision for drinking water, protection against beasts of prey and poisonous insects, snakes and reptiles, maintenance of proper hygiene, damage assessment by veterinary and paraveterinary staff, disposal of dead animals, involving NGOs and local community in relief activities and animal care, and reconstruction of damaged veterinary and artificial examination centres, etc. are some of the most required relief measures as far as livestocks are concerned during and post-disaster period.

So far as removal of debris and disposal of the dead human beings / animals are concerned during the post-disaster phase, they constitute vital aspect of emergency relief measures. Debris clearance is done to protect both the trapped life and valuable items. Rescue operations can be done most successfully when debris clearance is undertaken in a systematic way. With the use of proper technology and skilled trained man-power, debris clearance can finally pave way for a very successful rescue and relief operations. It involved following steps in order of general priority.

(i) search for trapped survivors and related debris removal

(ii) tracing people buried under rubble and related debris clearance, carefully and scientific

(iii) cordoning of the most affected areas and allowing technical, trained people to undertake such operations

(iv) Bystanders to be allowed only when left with no other options

(v) organising technological and monetary support such as cranes, lifts, earth moving equipments, buldozers cutters, drills, trucks etc.

(vi) demolition of irreparable heavily damaged buildings

(vii) structural geophysical survey of whole built-up area.

Main debris types include concrete buildings, flyovers, bridges, uprooted trees, electric and telephone boardings, damaged vehicles/goods, accumulated solid waste. With the use of electrone devices, flash lights, snuffer dogs, the trappled lives need to be rescued first, before initiating major efforts for debris clearance. However, caution should be exercised not to temper with any infrastructure and service networks.

Disposal of Dead Bodies

Disposal of dead bodies, of both human and animal, is a major relief operation work during post-disaster period. This particular assignment has to be undertaken with the sense of urgency as decomposing dead bodies can not only spread highly unpleasant odour but can also lead to various epidemics.

Human bodies, once identified need to be disposed with dignity keeping the social, religious and cultural ethos in mind.

Proper fuel for mass cremation or proper mass burial facilities need to be created for unidentified bodies, after carefully selecting the disposal site.

Animal bodies, particularly that of stray animals, are accorded low priority, as the rescuers are generally unwilling to handle animal carcasses. Taking the health and environment threats into account, extraction of hides or bones or other recoverable materials should be completely banned. Local volunteer need to be motivated to undertake the aforementioned tasks even before the official action comes into action for such purposes.

Fire Control and Protection

Control of fire in post-disaster period is another amount rescue measure which needs proper consideration. Natural fires, such as forest fire, and man-made ones should be taken up seriously. While forest fires can happen due to volcano eruptions, forests, lighting in the sky or by human carelessness. Deforestation, unscientifically planted forests without open patches, monoculture, absence of regular pruning and non-clearance of fallen materials on the ground are few factors which promote forest fire to convert itself into a catastrophic fire disaster. Land clearing by fire, illicit felling of trees, shifting cultivation, and corruption on the part of forest officials are other deliberate reasons. However, carelessness on the part of human beings is perhaps the biggest reason for forest fires. Factors which need to be taken into account while controlling forest-fires include, fuel power; vulnerable southern slopes, topography, rain, and when conditions. An effective wild fire control measure includes early prevention, planing and management and incident management techniques. Fore fighting can be undertaken principally by three methods i.e. direct method, indirect method (i.e. by using natural breaks) and a combination of both. Fireline procedures while working at the fire edge should be properly understood and followed. Education and training should be provided to vulnerable communities, volunteers, NGOs. Expert group for particular five fighting should be prepared with all infrastructure support. Rapid detection and flashing the message instantaneously can go a long way. Fire brodge force both at group and in the air, should be created fire contingency plan should incorporate early warning systems, setting-up of the control rooms, depot services for service squads and safe transportation facilities. Action plan should incorporate stages like making alert, taking preparatory measures and integrated operational works.

Man-made fires, both intentional (i.e. riots terrorism, suicides, rivalry etc.) and un-intention (i.e. human carelessness accident, violation of safety norms while constructing buildings and non-buildings activities, causes have to be understood and cared for Non-buildings include slums, temporary structures, camps, road vehicles, railway repair yards etc.

Major fire protection and contrôl measures include the following:

(i) Creation of elaborate safety norms.

(ii) adherence to related building bye-laws.

(iii) use fire-proft /fire resistant materials, structures and design.

(iv) qualified and trained force protection and control engines.

(v) public awareness of preventive techniques and prescribed guidelines.

(vi) punishment for defaulters, both capital and jaiterm.

(vii) fire-fighting capability built-up in terms of human capacity building, equipment facilities and water resources.

(viii) up-dating on prevention, detection and fire-fighting technique and changes adopted accordingly.

(ix) regular mock exercises / drills.

(x) printed evacuation plans appearing clearly at required places, such as lifts, staircases, gathering places, etc. and exist signs permanently illuminated independently.

(xi) placing push button fire alarms.

(xii) placing fire-extinguishers.

(xiii) unobstructed staircases/doors/routes.

(xiv) clearly printed evacuation instructions placed properly.

Disaster Damage Assessment

Rapid disaster damage assessments are done both for emergency relief measures (e.g. for food, water, cloth, shelter medicines, etc.) and for long-term restoration and rehabilitation measures, requiring therefore a detailed technical analysis. The later however, also reflects on the type of failure which led to the disaster i.e. disaster causation. In sum disaster damage assessment is a vital tool to assimilate the extent of impact of a disaster, both short-term and long-term, and forms the basis for any disaster management and mitigation process and action plan.

Disaster damage-assessments consists of following elements:

(i) Identification of type of information needed and sources of data-collection

(ii) Data collection through primary and secondary sources.

(iii) Analysis of data

(iv) Data interpretation

(v) Report-writing

(vi) Drawing conclusion

(vii) Making forecasts

(viii) Recommendations and measures suggested for decision-makers, planners, implementors community groups, NGOs etc.

While 'Rehabilitation relates to the work undertaken in weeks and months after a disaster occurs aimed at the restoration of basic services to enable the human population, return to normalcy. Disaster Relief' relates to the immediate days and weeks in post-disaster phase when all-round attempts are made to fulfill the basic needs like food, clothing, shelter, medicines, etc. to the victims. So in a way the main of any disaster management policy is to first provide for proper relief and rehabilitation to the target population in an organised way. In addition it also aims at limiting the damage to the affected community, in the form of saving lives and property, so as to prevent the possible situation of further deterioration in groups and communities are asked to network and channelise their efforts and shape the required infrastructure of society such that recurrence of scarcities and other related calamities, such as epidemics, are minimised.

Whereas disaster relief involves adequate infrastructure setup and quick response on the part of the entire system, primarily dealt with by governments and institutions. On the other hand, disaster preparedness is a continuous process which had to involve all sections of society. In a way, this preempts that there is an important role of local communities and local institutions which need to create and sustain disaster preparedness.

The Socio-economic Aspects of Rehabilitation

It is to be noted that the *social rehabilitation* package consists of the following items:

(A) *Health care facilities and infrastructure* restrengthening is very important at the time of emergency period during disaster or during spread of epidemic in post-disaster phase. For aforementioned purpose and for proper information exchange and co-ordination of medical support during fact emergencies *Control centres* must be established in vital locations. State level information exchange and networking among various health departments, directorates of health services, medical education centres hospitals etc., should take place. Control centres may also be used for collection and storage of immediate medical supplies received from various sources including international relief agencies / Groups / common unflinching commitment of the available health machinery remains the key element for better results.

Also, for making the health related disaster preparedness plan efficient and workable, additional facilities within the existing hospital and required. Putting the objectives of such plan for future health sector infrastructure and creation of additional facilities, thereby, becomes the main tasks.

(B) *Resurrection of Educational Facilities* in the affected areas is another immediate task. Besides constant counselling of both teachers and students, necessary educational equipments books, writing materials and transport facilities need to be provided in time. For better results, however, adherence to a partice patony mode of education is recommended. Proper orientation sessions need to be held so as to train the group members in identification of target groups choice of methodology, typology and time schedules.

(C) *Rehabilitation of Women and Children*, the most vulnerable groups during disaster, is the matter of utmost priority.

Economic Aspects of Rehabilitation

(A) *Agricultural Rehabilitation*, both short-term and long-term, of the affected areas; while short term measures mainly concerns with sowing of seeds for the next crop or / and harvesting of the remaining portion of crops, provisions should also be made with respect to availability and distribution of fertilizers, insecticides or pesticides. On the other hand, the long-term measures include the following:

(i) making provision for large number of agriculture equipments and implements, in tradition to other agricultural inputs.

(ii) a revival of irrigation wells and pump-sets.

(iii) a proper and scientific study to assess the actual

situation / condition of required system and their urgent rehabilitation.

(a) With respect to housing, elements such as location of rehabilitation and reconstruction is of utmost important depending. On the kind of disaster is generally strikes that region. The vital sub-components here are acquisition of land for resettlement with required compensation, land-use and reconstruction of the houses.

(b) With respect to infrastructure and related facilities, components, such as, improvement of transit shelters infrastructure and amenities in relocated areas, roads, and bridges, public buildings, repair and strengthen of historical monuments, etc.

(c) *Artisans' and Small Businessmen' Rehabilitation:* A plan which takes care of necessities such as work sheds, tool kits, soft loans and setting up of small industrial units. Other inputs which need to be taken care of include interval roads, electricity supply, water supply, etc.

(d) *Livestocks' Rehabilitation:* It will include replacement of lost / disabled livestocks, making provisions for fooder, cattle sheds, and services related to animals husbandry including preventive medication for survival livestock epidemics.

(e) *Reconstruction and rehabilitation,* besides being priority disaster management activity, should also be viewed as a development oriented one. This will help integrate the rehabilitation process with the overall development process, besides seeking out opportunities even in threat situations. In sum a timely launch of long-term rehabilitation strategy is what one needs to look for in such situations. Also, it is important to focus on the building construction details, elements systems, technologies, etc. Planning and architectural designs guidelines which involve the participation of local artisans and households should be preferred.

Affordable and specialising building structures that can withstand the destabilising forces of related disasters need to be erected. No doubt, while devising both structure and non-structural disaster mitigation strategies, it is necessary to recognise and assimilate integrate the useful elements of indigenous technology wisdom, and locally available materials and the cost-effective traditional coping mechanisms practical locally in the said disaster-prone area.

(ii) As far as economic rehabilitation is concerned, both economic-loss-assessment and fund-raising-initiative, attain importance. The subcomponents which need to be taken into account include replacement of farm implement and related minor equipment; replacement of cattle stock; advancement of skilled man-power and small-scale-entrepreneurs as to create more job opportunities repair/ reconstruction of dug wells/tube-well / irrigation systems; etc.

(iii) As far as ecological restoration activities are concerned, priority needs to be given to afforestation, restoration of aquifers, etc.

(iv) As far as agricultural and irrigation are concerned, reconstruction and rehabilitation may be provided through food-supply, improvement of irrigation systems, crop and soil conservation practices, water-shed management canal irrigation, etc. Damage caused, both in physical and economic terms, to the agriculture and irrigation by natural disasters are considered interms actual damage to agriculture and related infrastructure, impacts on cropping pattern and crop-varied. Assessment of crop damage may be done with the help of following crop-wise information on:

(a) Completely damaged, partially damaged and reason areas, and

(b) Yield under normal, partially damage and reason conditions.

For accurate assessment, selection of particular aging to undertake such job and the motive/purpose behind such assessments, are very significant. Assessment of damage to the irrigation system can also be done both in physical terms and interms of loss of infrastructure and the recurrent loss caused thereby.

Notable measures to combat the losses caused to agriculture and irrigation include the following.

(a) Adoption of alternative cropping pattern, involving techniques like Crop Life Saving Technique, Compensatory Cropping Programme, Intermixed cropping etc.

(b) Sustainable watershed management by construction of check-dams, contour binding, nala plugging, etc. supports with required vegetative cover.

(c) Undertaking wager harvesting in small catchments, at micro-scale.

Finally, development of pasture lands, livestock, farm forestry and other relief measures are also of considerable importance as far as rehabilitation and reconstruction is concerned in disaster-let areas. Suspension and remission of land revenue, provision of temporary employment to affected people, strengthening of public distribution system and development of village industries are also vital in this regard.

(v) Proper housing is concerned, it is a major tool to resist disasters including relocation. The impact of disasters like earth quakes cyclones, floods etc. can be greatly reduced by sustainable planing and designing of housing as per the nature of the specific disaster prone areas. From the earthquake point of view, where building and associated infrastructures are worst threatened the suggested building types could be of engineered type or non-engineered one. The former consists of RCC frame and shear wall buildings steel buildings with rigid joints, etc. while the area i.e. engineered buildings. It is mostly the non-engineered buildings, made with local materials, contractors, masons, etc. that suffer maximum devastation during earthquakes. The worst performance is by stone masonary buildings, followed by earthen buildings, brick buildings depending upon type of roof, mortar used and overall quality). The performance of wooden buildings is much better. Earthquake resistant house construction is, therefore, most in demand in earthquake-prone areas. The location and siting of such earthquake resistant housing projects depend upon factors such as stability of slope, loose sands or sensitive clays, etc. The layout of such houses depend upon their symmetry, rectangularity, separation of blocks, simplicity and overall enclosed area. The design aspects suitable for being disaster resistant vary for earthen houses. brick building, and stone buildings. Similarly, the priorities for cyclone resistant house construction and flood resistant house construction depend largely on factors as mentioned above, however with few remarkable differences in location and siting, layout, and design aspects in particular w.r.t. roofs, projection, wall and supporting frames door and window openings in walls. Flood prone area planing involves proper reevaluation of urban and rural land-use and flood plain zoning.

Another area of concern regarding housing issue in disaster struck area is related to retrofitting repairing and strengthening of houses. Only the modern techniques of construction of buildings prescribe the required construction materials and techniques which are helpful in providing buildings which can considerable reduced the damage supposed to be inflicted by a particular disaster.

Problems Resulting from the Lack of a Well-Defined Veterinary Disaster Management Plan during Huricane Andrew (1992, USA)

(a) Waste of precious time in trying to locate names and phone numbers because no list had been prepared in advance of individuals, organisations and groups to assist in collecting. sheltering and providing badly needed medical care for pets and livestock alike.

(b) Delay in donation of cages, food, mobile phones, and fax machines, transportation and medical supplies because donors did not know where to send them.

(c) Disappearance of supplies with no one certain of how they had been used, because ownership, authority and proper methods to document their use were unclear.

(d) Development of rivalries between various groups contributing to relief efforts with no one clearly in charge to settle disputes.

(e) Inadequate communication particularly a shortage of telephone lies to the control centre for animal aid set up in the central control area.

(f) Lack of clear identification and thearly lack of a central clearing house for animals transported to other areas for shelter prevented many animals from being returned to their owners.

(g) Rumours such as a story that all horses and stray dogs were being shot on site flourished and frightened victims in an environment so chaotic that the normally unbelievable was easily believed.

II

MANAGEMENT OF DISASTER AND REHABILITATION

The term disaster may be defined as an unexpected happening causing a huge loss of life and property. It may be both natural as well as man made in the sense that in some parts of the country, floods are coming due to the construction of check dams and embankments on the rivers. Disaster may come in the forms of earthquakes, tsumanis, cyclones, floods, drought, fire, etc. and ruin the life and property of the people.

Anthropology is mainly concerned with through how to prevent, predict and initigate major disasters? So far, scientific and technological development the prevention of earthquakes, cyclones, floods, droughts, fires, etc. may be prevented and predicted to some extent, but there is no doubt that proper planning and effective management can reduce the after-effects and hazards of disasters, since it is not the earthquake itself but the defective buildings which cause loss of life and property.

To prevent disaster, there should be pre-planning of all the available resources, communication facilities, manpower, etc. Experience has shown that before starting the rescue work administration has to clean the roads and bridges which are badly damaged. For this not only an inventory of local resource should be prepared but also bypasses and alternative routes should be identified in the plan itself. Since disaster is a state subject, the state government is responsible for rescue, relief and rehabilitation. However, at the national level ministry of agriculture, Government of India, is the nodal agency and there is one Crisis Management Committee in which all departments are represented along with Planning Commission. Recently the Finance Commission recommended for sharing of relief between the centre and state on 50:50 basis. Further there should be an emergency plan for each and every district in which response mechanism should be clearly spelt out. For instance what, how and when the relief is to be given, is to be specified. The allocation of work—who will do what; and clarification of organisation into: public, NGOs, army or civil administration should be properly undertaken otherwise the natural disaster results into chaos, anarchy and destruction due to confounded confusion. The price to pay for the demands imposed by mankind on our environment, extravagant to the point of profligacy, is increasing with time. It is the poorest who suffer the most, but all of us are caught up in the same syndrome. Humankind inherit but one earth, which they conspire against while destroying the gifts of nature by reducing the water-table, deforestation and pollution to name a few, which results in climatic changes and consequences measured in terms of human suffering which are likely to be acute.

The common view of disaster is due for a radical change. Though triggered of by natural events such as floods and earthquakes, disasters are increasingly man made. Some disasters (floods, droughts, famines) are caused more by environmental and resource mismanagement than by too much or too little rainfall. The impact of other disasters which are triggered by acts of nature (earthquake, volcano, tsumani, hurricane) are magnified by unwise human actions. Disasters are social and political events which can be and often are prevented. In the developing countries, where the poor are forced to overuse their land and live on dangerous grounds, disasters are taking a rising toll. By emphasizing mitigation instead of development, current disaster relief is often inadequate to the task it sets itself.

We can only tackle the root causes if disaster prevention and response are designed so as to incorporate both developmental and environmental strategies. We must get at the root causes and reverse the trends of increasing poverty and environmental degradation before it is too late. A sustainable eco-system must be our aim, as one in which the global family can live in balanced harmony with the whole of nature. The rural poor, who are the principal victims of the three elements which between them make up the major part of the developing countries disasters—deforestations, soil erosion and desertification should be central to the work of all disaster agencies. All the trends emphasize that ignorance and grinding poverty accelerate the onslaught of disasters and exacerbate the cruel impact they have, particularly on vulnerable groups of people. The poor, the handicapped, the infant and the aged are the first to lose their basic right to food, shelter and health. They need and deserve our help. The social development of people and their communities in disaster prone areas has been grossly ignored by governments and agencies alike. Such appalling human conditions can best be fought through the weapons of self-reliance, literacy, preventive health care and equitable pricing structures for rural food producers, that is, helping people to respond to their own basic needs, within their environment.

The common view of natural disaster is due for a radical change. A new term may even be needed, such as 'nature disaster" to distinguish calamities associated with the forces of nature from such tribulations as war and factory explosions. Today humans are playing too large a role in natural disasters for us to go on calling them natural.

So a distinction must be made between the "trigger events" too little rain, too much rain, earthshocks, hurricanes—which may be natural and the associated disasters which may be largely man made. Scientists, politicians, decision makers and the general public have been very slow to make the basic distinction between the trigger and the disaster.

Most of the scientific effort and money devoted to natural disaster has been spent on studying climatological and geological triggers—over which humans have very little control—rather than on studying the wide range of human actions—over which humans do have some control—which bring more disasters upon people every year.

Contemporary natural disasters research has become the single greatest impediment to improvement in both the understanding of natural calamities and the strategies to alleviate them.

Researchers have concentrated on the physical aspects of disasters rather than the social and political aspects, governments have been lured into putting their trust in grand physical prevention and mitigation measures.

Despite the death, destruction and after affects of major natural disasters, they have received surprisingly little scientific attention. Science has not even had mu :h success defining what it means by the term 'disaster'. Dictionaries use words such as 'misfortune' or 'calamity' implying, that for them to be a disaster, people must suffer. Thus, a cyclone or an earthquake is not a disaster unless it kills people or damages their property. This seems obvious but it is not since 1966 the UN Educational, Scientific and Cultural Organisation (UNESCO) has listed each year's natural disasters earthquakes, sunami (large ocean waves) storm surges and volcanic eruptions.

This definition had the effect of separating the disaster event—destruction, death and injuries from the trigger mechanisms— high winds, earth shocks, lack of rain, excess of water, lava and high waves. It also served to emphasize that most of research on disaster by climatologists and geologists is really on the trigger mechanisms. Other definition of disaster include:

> "An event (or series of events) which seriously disrupts normal activities" Cisin and Clark (1962). "An accident on a new large scale" Walker (1973).

Tribals are unable to draw immediate attention of the policy makers, concerned government activists, anthropologists, etc. The ethnographic studies and the applied anthropology fail to cater to the needs of the tribals. Therefore, the anthropology of disaster management becomes a necessary dimension of Anthropology of 21st century: The century of Anthropology.

Anthropology of 21st century: The century of Anthropology has to widen its horizon according to need of the Man of 21st Century. The science celebrating its century has to be careful in selecting priorities of research and other academic pursuits.

The Indian anthropology will have to grow and shape its branches under the influence of world anthropology.

When one compares the number of people killed per disaster against the income of the country involved, one finds a steep rise in mortality with decreasing income. Gunnar Hagman of the Swedish Red Cross finds evidence that most disaster's are found in middle income countries and most property damage is caused in the rich nations. It is presumed that the middle income nations may have the most disaster events because of an aggressive economic development policy which includes over cultivation, deforestation and other forms of environmental degradation. Both Tokyo, Japan and Managua, Nicaragua are prone to earthquakes. But the people of Tokyo are far less vulnerable to injury by earthquake because Tokyo has strictly enforced building codes, zoning regulations and earthquake training and communications system. In Managua, there are still many people living in top heavy, mud brick houses on hillsides. They are vulnerable to such disasters. The idea of anthropology of disaster management raises questions for the various groups interested in disasters.

- For governments: Can government be more effective in protecting its people from disasters by working to change patterns.
- For relief, aid and volunteer agencies active in disasters: Might it make more sense to invest some effort and funds in development before a disaster occurs, rather than putting all efforts after the event.
- For journalists: Is it enough to merely count the dead and describe the damage? or is it a journalists' job to look behind the scenes of destruction to expose ways in which people, politics and social systems have been responsible for any given disaster.
- For those responsible for development: Are they putting too much emphasis on "growth at any price", a policy which may have more and more people on the margins of society dangerously exposed to disasters?

Many people of the world, specially of Third World are more or less permanently affected by disaster processes and hundreds of millions are vulnerable to flood and droughts and to shortages of food, water and fuel wood. As natural disasters and many resource shortages are on the increase, it is obvious that the current development efforts are having little effect in these areas. This may be partly because rural development is rarely the priority it ought to be.

Prevention is urgent as the increasing frequency and severity of disasters are scaling the point of being unmanageable. In large parts of Asia, Africa and Latin America, the ecological base for human existence is being so damaged that it can no longer support the growing population of these regions.

Most disaster problems in the Third World are unsolved development problems. Disaster prevention and mitigation is thus primarily an aspect of development. Disasters can actually become "vehicles for change and involve both development and relief agencies in long-term programmes aimed both at development and at disaster prevention and mitigation.

Disasters are not unforeseen events and the technology now exists to identify the hazards that threaten a community and to estimate the areas and the settlements that will be affected. In most places and segments of society where calamities are occurring, the natural events are about as certain as anything within a person's lifetime. The very essence of disaster mitigation is long-term planning, while the very essence of Third World poverty is the struggle of day to day existence. The local people are more concerned with their children's education or lack of it, their health and the scarcity of medicine in the dispensaries and the difficulties of selling their crops at a decent price, which relates to the problems of access to markets in the accessible terrain. So vulnerability to natural hazards has to be recognised within the cultural and economic context of poverty and deprivation. And as with our own society, long-term logical action is frequently overwhelmed by short-term expediency.

Effective disaster mitigation and prevention depends on long-term planning for development towards a more sustainable and less vulnerable society. Some relief agencies are embarking on new types of community based disaster prevention programmes. Improved self-reliance in respect of food and fuel, access to land, employment, better health and nutrition, family planning and education are important components of disaster prevention. Disaster prevention and the elimination of poverty are closely linked as are poverty and environmental degradation. Many relief agencies are beginning to complement their emergency aid with their development programmes and are now working towards gaining knowledge, experience, training personnel and public backing to initiate new ideas into practice, in order to understand and minimize the problems of disasters.

Current Status of Displacement and Development

Development is an ongoing process which leads to commissioning of various kinds of development projects such as: Construction of new irrigation dams, establishing new factories, mines, road construction, railways and many other projects related to infrastructural growth leading to regional/ national economic development. This often necessitates the government to acquire land which leads to 'involuntary displacement' of people from the original home land.

Development leading to displacement of people from their own land is inevitable. All activities mentioned above, force the otherwise stable, sedentary population to move away from their original places of home and work. It uproots people from their original land and creates psycho-sociological stress leading to many dysfunctional consequences. More often, both social and economic benefits of such developmental projects are not shared equally by displaced population.

The problem of displacement is normally related to economic aspects but truly speaking, it has more of psycho-sociological implications. Though the meagre economic compensation provides temporary relief to evacuees, but it leads to many psycho-sociological and cultural problem of serious nature. The displacement demands change in the lifestyle of people and forces them to adjust in a totally alien social milieu. This causes a situation of psychological stress. Compulsory and involuntary displacement together with, "rarely fair' payment of compensation are its two main reasons as a problem (Menezes, 1991). According to him, the current system fails to acknowledge that an 'oustee' is deprived of a historical right of access to a large number of resources, entire way of life and is not given any opportunity to demand an adequate price for this loss. Apart from his private land and cultural historical heritage, an oustee holds several other livelihood generating assets which are not legally acknowledged. Evidences suggest that these psycho-sociological problems are not well considered neither by the planners nor by those who are the key participants in the implementation of such projects. Therefore, the understanding and management of these problems are more important for effective implementation of these projects.

Displaced Population

The report of the Commissioner for Scheduled Castes and Scheduled Tribes (1990), points out that when the land is acquired and under the present law, only its property form is considered vital, questions concerning the very survival of the displaced persons are settled on this basis. Even those, who are identified, are very inadequately compensated. Lack of accurate data on such crucial issues, such as this, is itself an indication of both the Central and State governments degree of concern for the rehabilitation of oustees (Viegas,

1987). This current status of displacement is leading to an alarming situation. How to sustain the historical right which the oustee has been deprived of, is an important issue today.

Rehabilitation and Development

Rehabilitation is more often understood as economic rather than psycho-sociological phenomenon resulting from displacement. It is normally perceived as a 'planned change effort'. In a strict senses, it implies that, while there is a change the overall effects of the change is to restore the situation to its original condition. In other words, change or no change (Franks, 1991). Though rehabilitation is sought for development but its nature is quite different from other developmental processes. All developmental efforts imply planned change to improve existing conditions, whereas rehabilitation is designed to restore the status quo. This makes it imperative to understand the term rehabilitation in a much wider perspective, and its components which make it different from other developmental processes.

Components of Rehabilitation

Rehabilitation can be described as having the following components:

(i) Antecedent conditions: Displacement and rehabilitation of people are required when certain 'antecedent conditions' exist in the situation. For example, National long-term interest for socio-economic development of the country leading to commissioning of various developmental projects; National calamities, such as, war and political turmoil; Natural disasters, such as, floods, earthquakes, drought and also man made disasters.

(ii) Cognitive state of the individuals involved, i.e., their perception and awareness of the situation, such as:

- Fears and apprehensions about the possible problems to be faced by the affected people.

- Fears and apprehensions about their acceptability by the host population.
- Fears and apprehensions about fulfilment of government promises with respect to providing facilities.
- Attitudes about various 'developmental projects' and about 'government'.

(iii) Affective state of the individuals involved in the situation: Perception of a situation may affect the people in a variety of ways such as, developing anxieties, psychological tension, stress and hostility.

(iv) Manifest behaviour: Psychological effects manifest themselves in variety of behavioural patterns. These range from passive resistance to active resistance, overt aggression and finally agreeing for displacement under stress lending to many other dysfunctional behaviour patterns resulting in poor mental health.

(v) Rehabilitation: Displacement leading to rehabilitation of people through various rehabilitation programmes such as: Allotment of land: houses, monetary compensation, occupation and many other facilities required for resettlement.

(vi) Further demands by people from government: Any rehabilitation results in an aftermath which manifests itself in further demands by people from government.

Rehabilitation Process

Drawing upon the ways in which components of rehabilitation are described, it is apparent that, displacement leading to rehabilitation can be described as a dynamic process having definite sequential stages coming one after the other. Each stage has its own characteristics which influences the process in its own way. Displacement leads to deterioration of the situation in the initial stages and subsequently to restoration of the situation, quite close to status quo.

Rehabilitation process comprises the following six stages:

(i) Latent Stage: It refers to the "Antecedent condition", for example, commissioning of developmental project leading to displacement and rehabilitation of population. The nature of antecedent condition will determine the ways of handling the situation in terms of "preparedness measures" and "coping strategies" by the government, other agencies, affected people and also by society. These will influence the characteristic pattern of behaviour of individuals at the next stage, which will also accordingly affect the "Preparedness measures and Coping strategies" for the subsequent stages leading to rehabilitation thereby characterized by certain stable aspects of condition, perceptions, affects and behaviour discussed later.

(ii) Cognitive Stage: Fears and apprehensions such as:

- Loss of home
- Loss of primary sources of gratification of needs
- Fear of change of basic style of living
- Loss or change in occupation (source of Livelihood)
- Fear of adjustment in new jobs
- Loss of social relationships
- Fear of acceptability by the host population
- Lack of confidence in 'Government initiatives' and 'Programmes'.

All the above listed fears and apprehensions are the natural outcomes of displacement and are unavoidable. These must be acknowledged by all concerned. Correct diagnosis of the situation, appropriate 'preparedness measures' and 'coping strategies' to minimize them, can greatly reduce the severity of onset of next stage of the rehabilitation process.

(iii) Affective Stage: Perceived fears and threats may or may not affect the people equally under normal circumstances. These come on the surface and show up in various forms, such as, anxiety, tension, stress and may also lead to hostility. Effective handling of 'affective stages' would accordingly affect the state of next stage of the rehabilitation process.

(iv) Manifest Stage: Degree of psychological tension/stress will greatly influence the behavioural patterns at the manifest stage. People's passive and active resistance to 'evacuating the home land', and demand for better compensation may lead to aggressive behaviour and mass agitation. Quite often they finally agree for displacement under great stress leading to further deterioration of mental health.

(v) Rehabilitation Stage: This stage finally leads to rehabilitating displaced people through various 'Rehabilitation Programmes'.

(vi) Rehabilitation Aftermath: Howsoever effectively the various stages of rehabilitation process are handled, it will still lead to an 'aftermath' in terms of further demands by the people leading to increased dependency on the government.

Psycho-sociological Consequences of Displacement

It is universally acknowledged that displacement is stressful and sometimes leads to traumatic conditions. In spite of this, the psycho-sociological issues have been neglected in the displacement of people under various projects. Rehabilitation programmes often lack specific components of the aspects of mental health of people. There is no evidence of discussion of the mental health problems and its implications for assessing cost and benefit of development projects.

A broadly defined psycho-sociological perspective can have important implications for designing rehabilitation policies. It allows us to anticipate inevitable problems that result from displacement of population to assess the consequence of particular policies.

A systematic analysis of what happens to individuals who are subjected to displacement from their homeland and require rehabilitation, will help us to provide the ways and means to minimize the adverse impact of involuntary displacement on mental health of people. Fears and apprehensions discussed earlier are usually perceived as potential threats by the affected population. These are natural and constitute the major components of displacement process resulting in dysfunctional behaviour patterns. These must be considered by all concerned involved in the management of the process. It is imperative to have indepth understanding of the consequences and subsequent careful handling, to minimize their adverse impact on mental health of people. This can be studied at two levels: Individual level and Group level.

Impact at Individual Level

Loss or Change in Primary Sources of Satisfaction of Needs: The major fear associated with displacement is, loss or change in the primary sources of satisfaction of needs. All behaviours are instigated by needs and are directed towards goals that can satisfy these needs. Personality has a system of organized needs such as

(1) Physiological needs, e.g., thirst, hunger, sex etc.,
(2) Safety needs, e.g., security and order,
(3) Social needs, e.g., need to belong, identification and love,
(4) Esteem needs, e.g., need to achieve, need to control, self-respect and
(5) Self-actualisation, e.g., need for identity and self-fulfilment (Maslow, 1954).

Physiological needs are largely determined by the innate factors but others are greatly influenced by the nature of the social environment. Human beings are constantly seeking for pleasures, reflected through satisfaction of above mentioned needs in their unique manner through their established sources of livelihood, social relations, social status, kinship ties, etc. Any change or blockage, though temporarily, in the manner of satisfying these needs, will result in varying degrees of tension and stress in different people. Therefore, social environment together with the satisfaction of needs in an acceptable manner, become extremely important. For example, the satisfaction of the security need which constitutes an important need among the hierarchy of needs in Indian culture is greatly affected by the process of displacement. The compulsive change in the basic style of satisfaction of these needs is usually not welcomed by the people and hence often resisted. People may start perceiving themselves as having low self-worth, 'self-respect' and develop 'negative attitude' towards themselves. In an extreme situation, they may also develop identity crisis. All these result in lack of adjustment, leading to psychological stress or shock or trauma. The major factor associated with this is loss or change in the sources of occupation/livelihood leading to varying degrees of occupational redundancy and loss of social relationships.

(a) Occupational Disruption

Fear of change of source of livelihood leads to 'Occupational disruption'. This may lead to low to high degree of Occupational redundancy'. This loss, even if substituted by the new ways of managing earning of livelihood, often leads to a state of mental stress. Loss of agricultural land by the landowners, though made up by 'Economic compensation' and also new occupational opportunities under various "Rehabilitation programmes' by the government, could not fulfil the psychological loss such as, social status enjoyed through Feudalistic culture', and the village leadership leading to psychological satisfaction. All these sources of satisfaction of needs usually get blocked by the relocation process in the new .environment.

Loss of land and property is a blow to the oustees, who

are unable to secure an alternative source of livelihood because of lack of education and skill. Evidence suggests that many development projects created new occupational opportunities but the people were unable to get the share in the benefits of the project. The displaced persons, by and large, were forced into daily wage labour, for example, the persons displaced by the Pong Dam, who returned to Himachal Pradesh or decided to migrate to other states, in the hope of comparatively more comfortable life, were forced to become landless migrant labourers. Another example is that of 16,080 tribal families from 170 villages displaced by Ukai-Kakarpur Project on river Tapi in Gujarat. Surveys reported that 42 per cent of all the families, landed or landless were forced to migrate for work for varying periods of time, most of them in the sugar-cane factories (Mankodi and Gangopadhyay, 1983). All these occupational disruptions, especially loss of job/sources of livelihood, lead people to experience feelings of insecurity, defunctness, powerlessness and loss of self-confidence, leading to stress and in extreme cases, to psychological shock. The change in the job is also associated with variety of problems, such as, lack of skill and interest in the new job. Though people are provided training for the new jobs under various Occupational Rehabilitation Programmes, yet they are unable to use their potentials which demotivates them in the new jobs. They also develop feelings of low Self-efficacy (Grist, 1987), Self-esteem (Brockner, 1988), Self-management (Manz & Sims, 1980), Self-montoring (Snyder, 1987), and Alienation, leading to a great stressful situation.

(b) Loss of Social Relationships

Displacement also forces individuals to change the pattern of social relationships, individuals have to undergo an entire process of resocialization and adjustment in a new social milieu. This leads to loss of existing social relationships. Kinship ties which are important sources of individual's gratification of social needs are in no way less important for an individual's survival. Evidence also suggests that the oustees are sometimes rejected by the parent group. The hostile behaviour of host population further makes the resocialization difficult, for the oustees. Having faced rejection by the parent group and unacceptance by the host population, the oustees go through a tremendous psychological trauma and face an identity crisis; This sometimes leads people to go for second displacement, as in the case of Pong dam oustees (MARG, 1987).

Compensation Package

Inadequate or in appropriate compensation package also results in psychological tension/stress among the oustees. It has been reported that adequate or inappropriate compensation packages to the oustees have also resulted in lot of psychological stress for the people. The illiterates found it difficult to utilize the compensation amount appropriately. This has led to social evils like alcoholism, gambling and prostitution (Advani, 1990).

Impact at Group Level

Displacement also results in disintegration of family, other social groups and occupational groups. Evidence from Augucha Mines of Hindustan Zinc Ltd., at Bhilwara, Rajasthan suggests that providing occupation to one representative of each evacuee's family by HZL, helped families, but created family tension resulting in breaking of joint family system and difficulties in getting match in their own community for their children (Advani, 1990).

All these psycho-sociological factors discussed above, result in psychological tensions, stress, hostility, sometimes leading to trauma. These get manifested in variety of dysfunctional behaviours leading to mental ill health and sometimes to mental sickness.

Management of Displacement and Rehabilitation Process

In order to achieve the efficacy of various objectives of

resettlement and rehabilitation projects, minimizing the adverse effects of displacement must form the primary focus, The success of these projects depends upon, how effectively the displacement is managed and the various rehabilitation programmes are perceived, as appropriate and adequate sources of gratification of needs by the affected population. This makes it imperative to plan, design and implement strategies as 'preparedness measures' and 'rehabilitation programmes', to cope with negative aspects of displacement, at the appropriate stages of the rehabilitation process.

Need for a 'National Policy'

Recognizing the adverse impact on human beings, the sufferings and hardships caused by involuntary settlement, the World Bank Policy states as its first requirement, that "whenever feasible, the involuntary resettlement must be avoided or minimized and alternative developmental solutions must be explored" (Cemea, 1988). Notwithstanding this policy, there have been cases, when projects have been designed and approved without examining such possible alternatives. Lack of provision of psycho-sociological consideration in the Land Acquisition Law 1994 and also 'Land Acquisition Amendment Act 1984, further weakens the implementation of the Bank Policy. Though rehabilitation has normally been envisaged as a planned change effort, evidences suggest that implementation of each project, called for an ad hoc policy of its own. The Bank Policy can be made effective only, if a well-defined National Policy is designed. Introducing of psycho-sociological perspective in the Land Acquisition Law will also greatly enhance the efficacy of bank policy. Therefore, the need for a well-defined national policy is a first pre-requisite for effective implementation of resettlement and rehabilitation projects.

(c) Manifest Stage

Careful and timely handling of cognitive and affective stage through appropriate preparedness measures would greatly reduce the psychological tension and stress generating dysfunctional behaviour at the manifest stage. In many cases the government has taken an unduly long time in deciding the compensation package, forcibly evacuated the people and acquired the land. Evidences suggest that people have shown their actual resistance and resorted to mass agitation under certain development projects. Such a situation can be effectively handled through negotiations between government and affected population. All infrastructural facilities such as land, houses, schools, hospitals, etc., should be provided to people before displacement. This would help in minimizing resistance.

(d) Rehabilitation Stage

Rehabilitation programmes necessarily need to he designed according to the felt needs of the affected population. Data about population, procured earlier as preparedness measures, must be appropriately used for designing the programmes.

Rehabilitation programmes should make use of available skills and talents and also focus upon providing new skills and competencies to the affected population, to equip them to face the outer world. Efforts should be made to develop settler's commitment to self-support and sustenance, to avoid onset of settlers dependency syndrome psycho-therapeutic/ health programmes in the form of family counselling, stress reducing exercises, community programmes and other socio-occupational programmes should form an essential complement of the rehabilitation package along with adequate compensation package. The perception of compensation package, as adequate and good, is greatly influenced by, how effectively the psychological tension, stress and traumatic situation is handled through these programmes.

(e) Rehabilitation Aftermath

Effective management of earlier stages will greatly reduce the further demands by the people from the government.

Summing Up

The population which is more often displaced by the developmental projects usually belong to lower strata of society, such as Scheduled Castes and Scheduled Tribes who are more affected as compared to other displaced population. Therefore, as a part of socio-economic development, it must concern with safeguarding the interests of minority, the affected population, and minimizing the negative impacts of relocations.

In spite of intentions of the government to provide a comfortable rehabilitation to the affected population, no attention has been paid to the psycho-sociological consequences associated with the process. Though rehabilitation projects are often viewed as a planned change effort with developmental objectives, they are rarely implemented in a manner to achieve those objectives. People have been made to evacuate from their land forcefully and have been made to experience psychological shocks, undergo trauma, more often resulting in mental illness. In fact, if these psychological consequences are not effectively handled, perhaps, new resettlement colonies created under the so-called development projects, having objectives of overall development of people, for better quality of life, leading to national development, will turn into mental asylums. It is, therefore, the right time to reflect on this problem and seriously evaluate the extent to which the policies, planning and strategies together, with their implementation by the government, have been inadequate and draw lessons for further action.

All managers, who are responsible for managing rehabilitation of people and concerned community, must appreciate and understand the complex psycho-sociological nature of displacement. Rehabilitation must be addressed as a planned changed effort, having sequential stages requiring detailed advance planning for each stage. Steps are needed to arrest the psychological consequences resulting at each stage. This requires correct diagnosis, designing and implementing appropriate interventions as preparedness measures and coping strategies.

REFERENCES

Brockner, J. (1988), *Self Esteem at Work*, Lexington: MA, Lexington Books, Chapts. 1-4.

Cemea, Michael, M. (1988), *Involuntary Resettlement in Development Projects*, World Bank Technical Paper Number 80, Washington: World Bank, 4..

Cisin and Clark (1962), *Man and Society in Disaster.*

Commissioner for Scheduled Castes and Scheduled Tribes. *Twenty-Ninth Report of the Commissioner for SC and ST*, New Delhi: The Manager of Publications, Government of India, 245, 1987-89.

Franks, Tom (1991), Institutional Change and Project Rehabilitation, Hardware, Software and Liveware, in Project Rehabilitation in Development Countries, ed. by Colin, Kirkpatrick, London: Routledge 213.

Galbraith, John Kenneth (1983), The Anatomy of Power, Boston: Houghton Hifflin.

Gist, M.E. (1987), "Self Efficacy: Implementation for Organization Behaviour and Human Resource Management," Academy of Management Review, July, 472-85.

Government of Orissa (1968), *Report on the Benefits of Hirakud Irrigation: A Socio-economic Study*, Cuttack: Bureau of Statistics and Economics, Government of Orissa, 13.

6

Mega Cities and Natural Disasters

Because mega-cities are a relatively recent phenomenon, the literature on mega-city disasters is sparse. Much more is known about the relationship between natural disasters and urbanization in general.

Despite some tendencies toward uniformity and homogenization, there is a great deal of variety among mega-cities and considerable uncertainty about their eventual dimensions. Different types of mega-city are likely to have quite different disaster-susceptibilities and different capabilities for response. Mega-cities may grow, becoming both more complex and more alike. Or there may be perhaps two or three basic variants. For example, if the organization of the global economic, and political system continues to be dominated by a relatively few countries, it may well be that the natural hazard profiles of mega-cities in the dominant (rich) countries will continue to diverge from those of the (poor) rest, thereby rendering problematic the exchange of hazard experience and hazard-reduction technologies between both. On the other hand, there is evidence that some of the characteristics of third world cities are beginning to show up in places such as Los Angeles and Miami, thus raising the possibility of eventual reconvergence.

Both in rich and poor countries, the growth of such giant urban agglomerations poses major metropolitan planning problems which must be solved in a broad regional context. Food, fuel, electric power, and drinking water must be brought in from considerable distances, and massive quantities of waste materials must be disposed of. The giant metropolis needs very sophisticated transportation systems if it is to function effectively, and city dwellers may have to travel considerable distances to recreational facilities and surviving farm and wilderness areas. *Most major cities also have some special problems resulting from the peculiarities of their sites, for example subsidence, earthquakes, and air and groundwater pollution buildups in Mexico City, and flooding and typhoon damage in Dacca.* (Bromley et al., 1989, p. 372; emphasis added).

Large cities of antiquity certainly experienced heavy losses as a result of natural disasters, but the data are highly incomplete. Chandler and Fox (1974) show that at least a score of cities each recorded tens of thousands of deaths in the wake of earthquakes, floods, volcanic eruptions, and other events. But few of these places had populations that exceeded 200,000 and most were considerably smaller.

The Tokyo-Yokohama metropolitan area was probably the first mega-city to be devastated by a natural disaster. The Great Kanto earthquake (1923) killed approximately 100,000 people in Tokyo and destroyed more than 700,000 houses in a city of over 2 million (Seidensticker, 1983, p. 259). In the half-century between 1945 and 1995, around 100 natural disasters affected large cities. The most physically destructive single events during this period took place in: Nagoya (typhoon, 1959), Tangshan (earthquake, 1976), Bucharest (earthquake, 1977), Mexico City (earthquake, 1985), Miami/ Dade County (hurricane, 1992), and Kobe (earthquake, 1995). Latest to add is Mumbai (rainflood, 2005). However, a focus on great catastrophes may be misplaced, because the aggregate impacts of lesser events can be much larger. This is particularly so in third world mega-cities, where small storms, floods, and seismic shocks, events that would be considered inconsequential elsewhere, often wreak disproportionately heavy losses. In such places, natural hazard is a more or less chronic everyday problem. Earthquakes, severe storms, and wildfires appear to be the most frequent catastrophic urban events.

It is worthwhile noting that urban areas are the sites of many different types of disaster: natural, technological, biological, and social. Thus far, most of these have been simple events of one type, but compound events that involve two or more of these components are beginning to appear (e.g. floods that disperse toxic materials, earthquakes that rupture oil pipelines and storage tanks, droughts that uncover flooded waste disposal sites). The potential for further "surprises" is obvious.

Of late it has ben noticed that rapid large-scale urbanization - is a major contributor to the rising global toll of disaster losses (National Research Council, 1987; Science Council of Japan, 1989, pp. 13-14; US Office of Science and Technology Policy, 1992, p. 10). The world's big cities are rapidly becoming more exposed and more vulnerable to natural hazards and disasters (Havlick, 1986). Unfortunately, the special problems of urban disasters have not received much attention from scholars and professionals (Somma, 1991). "Too much of our efforts to assist... for too long have been focused on rural populations which are of ever diminishing relative magnitude and importance" (Jones and Kandel, 1992, p. 70). Much of the most useful information on urban disasters is part of a "grey literature" that is not readily available to potential users.

During the 1990s a number of researchers addressed the intersecting problems of cities and disasters. One of these was the disaster relief expert Frederick Cuny, whose strong convictions about the pivotal role of cities in international disaster operations began to appear in print just before his disappearance and probable murder in Chechnya (Cuny, 1994). Other notable contributions during this period include Sylves and Waugh's (1990) case-studies of emergency operations in American cities; Zelinsky and Kosinski's (1991) valuable compilation of data on urban evacuations; Berke and Beatley's (1992) analysis of earthquake planning in mid-sized US cities (Salt Lake City, Palo Alto, Charleston); a path-breaking edited collection of papers by geographers on housing and hazards in cities in less developed countries (Cairo, Bhopal, Mexico City, Agadir, Caracas, Hong Kong) (Main and Williams, 1994); a special issue of a European geography journal that focuses on geological hazards in mountain cities (*Revue de Geographic Alpine*, 1994); and the proceedings of a workshop on urban hunger in developing countries organized by the International Geographical Union's Commission on Vulnerable Food Systems (Bohle, 1994). The headquarters staff of the UN-sponsored International Decade for Natural Disaster Reduction (1990-2000) has also published a slim volume that reviews projects designed to improve urban disaster mitigation in 11 different countries and supplies information about organizations that are active in this field (IDNDR, 1996). Though all of these publications deal with hazards and disasters in exclusively urban settings, none focuses specifically or exclusively on large cities. Recent works with a more explicit focus on mega-city hazards include collections of papers prepared by contributors to a World Bank-sponsored conference (Kreimer and Munasinghe, 1992) and by members of the International Geographical Union's Study Group on the Disaster Vulnerability of Megacities (Parker and Mitchell, 1995). In addition, the UK Institution of Civil Engineers has published a report on mega-city vulnerability (Institution of Civil Engineers, 1995). A number of noteworthy individual papers have also appeared (e.g. Aguilar et al, 1995; Boone, 1996; Dando, 1994; Degg, 1993; Driever and Vaughn, 1988; Ezcurra and Mazari-Hiriart, 1996; Firman and Dharmapatni, 1994; Guterbock, 1990; Jairo-Cardenas, 1990; Kirn, 1990; McGranahan and Songsore, 1994; Masure, 1994; Mitchell, 1993a; Reed, Tromp, and Lam, 1992; Setchell, 1995; Steedman, 1995; UNEP/WHO, 1994).

Due to the likely impact of natural disasters on mega-cities is so great and so little understood, "the vulnerability of mega-cities" was identified as a high-priority topic for research and action during the International Decade for Natural Disaster Reduction (IDNDR). A major effort in support of that theme was mounted by the global scientific and technology community under the auspices of the International Council of Scientific Unions (ICSU). At ICSU's invitation, the International Association of Engineering Geologists and the World Federation of Engineering Organizations were encouraged to bring together a variety of academic and professional groups with the objective of formulating a collaborative agenda for mega-cities and disasters. This included projects by the UK Institution of Civil Engineers and the International Geographical Union as well as the World Bank and Habitat, among others. Independent but related programmes were also organized by the global community of landscape architects and other professional bodies. Most of these activities involve organizations of scientists, engineers and urban managers.

The intellectual principle on which the IDNDR rests is a well-founded recognition that society already possesses a great deal of valuable information about the reduction of natural disasters but has largely failed to put that information to appropriate use. For most of the scientific and engineering community the main task is to apply existing knowledge about disaster reduction to a series of specific contexts - in this case, mega-cities. It is assumed that, like Archimedes, managers can stand on the stable base of accumulated technical knowledge and engage the lever of science to "move" the world of urban disasters. Undoubtedly, if resolutely followed, this strategy will produce important benefits, especially when it results in genuine partnerships between the producers and users of scientific information (Mitchell, 1988).

For a student of natural hazards, the city is but one

among many physical settings of extreme events, albeit a setting that usually makes few concessions to the natural systems that are the agents of disaster. Conversely, from the perspective of urban managers, natural disasters are just one among many problems that must be confronted within city boundaries - and an infrequent one, at that Hazard management has a place in the spectrum of urban issues but that place must be negotiated among competing demands for attention to other problems (e.g. new urban in-migrants, decaying infrastructure, poor housing, hazardous facilities, deindustrialization, pollution, homelessness, lack of mass transit, street crime, inadequate social services, ethnic and racial tensions).

Nor is it simply that natural disasters must compete with other urban issues for public attention; they are intimately bound up with those issues. For example, the flood and landslide disasters of Rio de Janeiro, Caracas, and Tijuana are closely connected to problems of obtaining affordable housing faced by poor migrants from rural areas. Prospects for earthquake hazard reduction in Tokyo are affected by the high cost of urban land, which encourages crowded neighbourhoods, restricts open space, and pushes new developments onto hazard-susceptible low-lying filled land in Tokyo Bay. The protection of Kolkata or Lagos against flooding is also tied up with inadequate means for disposing of solid wastes, antiquated or non-existent sewage systems, and budgetary conflicts between city and national governments. The fragmentation ("de-urbanization") of metropolitan populations and governments has a significant bearing on the design and operation of hazard-management systems in mega-cities of the United States (e.g. Los Angeles, Miami) and other developed countries. The implications are clear. If natural disasters are to be reduced in a big-city setting, the Archimedean metaphor of science-driven solutions is not an appropriate guide. Urban disasters are not merely a kind of inert problem that will yield to the direct application of scientific knowledge -they push back In other words, not only do disasters affect cities but urbanization affects the creation of vulnerability, the scope for mitigating action, and a wide range of related topics. Thus, no doubt urbanization provides an interactive context for disaster.

There is one further twist to the relationship between disasters and mega-cities — perhaps the most important factor of all. Both elements of the problem - cities and disasters - are now changing in complex ways. The nature of disasters is changing: new kinds are emerging - some of them unprecedented. The management of disasters is changing: in many countries, existing institutions and policies are coming under increased criticism and there are calls for new ones. The ways we think about disasters are changing: for example, a post-modernist dialogue is beginning to appear in the professional literature. Equally, the nature of cities is changing: not only are they more numerous, bigger, and non-Western, but their economic and cultural functions are in flux, casting previous models of urban development into doubt. The management of cities is changing: pressed from below by burgeoning demands from their rapidly growing and diversifying populations, governments of mega-cities are also shifting to adjust to other pressures such as the changing role of national governments in the face of global economic integration and the reluctance of those governments to honour existing commitments to assist the cities. Urban mass movements and emergent neighbourhood organizations are also exerting pressure for the "reinvention" of mega-city governments. As big cities become increasingly important actors on the world stage, their populations are drawing on the experience of peer cities beyond national boundaries. As a response to such changes, it is no surprise that the intellectual basis of urban analysis is also in flux.

Under such circumstances, the Archimedean metaphor requires further modification. Not only are the problem spheres of disasters and urbanization interactive (i.e. urban disasters "push back"), but given the speed and scope of changes that are now afoot in both spheres there may no longer be a truly stable base from which the leverage of scientific knowledge can be pivoted. This means that taken-for-granted assumptions about scientific information and disaster reduction need to be critically examined in light of the highly changeable contexts that bracket both disasters and mega-cities. Until these contexts are better known, the transfer of knowledge and technology among countries and cities should proceed with caution. Mega-city disaster-reduction initiatives will have to be carefully tailored to local conditions and specific settings.

In coming to grips with the complexities of a dynamic set of relationships between mega-cities and natural disasters it may be helpful to think in terms of a contextual model. Such a model is intended to show how a more or less discrete process relates to the broader environment of which it is a part. The central process is one of hazard and the larger context is that of urbanization. Both components of the model can be considered separately and in conjunction. The hazard component includes four main elements: physical processes, human populations, adjustments to hazard, and net losses. As people seek to adjust to hazardous natural environments, these four elements modify each other through seven endogenous feedback relationships. A change in one or more elements may set in motion a cascade of reflexive changes in the others. The stimulus for change may be some or all of the following: an extreme natural event such as an earthquake or a storm; community encroachment into an area of known hazard; urban technologies that inadvertently alter existing physical risks; the development of vulnerable groups, institutions, or technologies; the adoption of specific new hazard-management measures and the decay of old ones; and a broad-based commitment to raise general thresholds of public protection against hazards of various kinds.

Change can also come from outside the hazard system. That context includes exogenous factors or processes that interact with components of hazard, but are largely independent of them. These include variables such as the stages of city development (including the growth of mega-cities), the internal structure and functioning of urban areas under different sociocultural, political, and economic systems, and the urban implications of a wide range of contemporary changes in science, technology, environment, economics, politics, and culture. Among the latter are: the flow of new scientific information and the diffusion of new technologies; the growing recognition that humanity now has the capability to affect environmental change on a global scale; worldwide economic restructuring and integration; the collapse of an existing international geopolitical order and the development of replacement arrangements (e.g. continental trading blocs, ethnically fragmented states, "reinvented" governments, non-governmental organizations, urban mass movements); and the adoption of "post-modern" modes of thought and action both within the intellectual community and beyond.

In the same way that a viewer can construct different interpretations of an illusion by focusing on either the figure or the ground, it is possible to arrive at an explanation of urban disasters that depends on disaster agents and proximate human responses or to fashion an explanation around the distal structuring characteristics of urban systems and urban lifeways. The latter approach may redefine the meaning of disaster in an urban setting and predispose cities to "disasters" that are different from those natural scientists customarily think of. But urban disasters are not just amalgams of disaster and urbanization; they are the products of a set of changeable relations between both components. This feature makes it difficult to fashion effective programmes of urban disaster reduction by employing only the perspectives on hazards management or urban management. The permutations of natural hazard and urbanization produce different outcomes in different settings at different times. Moreover, the set of possible permutations is significantly larger than the set of outcomes to date; an understanding of this fact opens up a vast untapped potential for intervention to make cities safer places.

Evidence of increasing disaster-susceptibility in megacities bespeaks a change in the balance of hazard and opportunity in urban life. Of course changes in the mix of urban hazards and shifts in the hazard-opportunity balance have gone on throughout history. For several centuries the balance has tilted steadily towards higher levels of safety and opportunity for most city residents, while hydrological, meteorological, and geological hazards have declined relative to other types of threat. Urban concentrations of wealth, knowledge, talent, and power have justified - and made possible - extraordinary efforts to protect people and property against the more obvious extremes of Nature. The avoidance, prevention, and mitigation of natural hazards were a primary responsibility of those who ruled the ancient cities of Egypt, China, and Central America (Tuan, 1979; Wu Qingzhou, 1989). Dyking, drainage, and irrigation schemes were among the earliest urban public works in these places. The suppression of fire was a high priority in the crowded cities of medieval Europe and elsewhere at other periods (Rosen, 1986). A widely shared commitment to protect urban lives and property against natural extremes continues today. Contemporary Japanese cities are showplaces of hazard engineering, the metropolitan areas of Rotterdam and London are flanked by some of the world's most modern and technologically advanced flood defences, Mexico City has invested in the world's only public earthquake alarm system (*New York Times*, 19 December 1993), and the vast drainage network of greater Los Angeles has been so extensively modified by humans that it is now an almost totally artificial construct (Cooke, 1984; McPhee, 1989).

Heightened urban sensitivity to hazards and the benefits

of hazard reduction do not mean that big cities have been - or are - entirely safe from extreme natural events. Nor do they mean that cities have been free of other types of hazard. (The historical record of urban epidemics, riots, fires, industrial accidents, and similar social ills is salutary.) But, over the long run, it is clear that a quite remarkable record of success has attended efforts to provide many urban dwellers with improved security against geological, meteorological, and hydrological hazards.

Now there is growing concern that cities are becoming so numerous, so large, so complex, and so volatile that the balance between risk and reward will tilt back towards conditions of increased natural hazard in the absence of determined efforts to reverse that trend. A world of mega-cities may well be more risky, more exposed, and more vulnerable than the world we currently inhabit. The scale of potential mega-city losses imposed by floods, storms, earthquakes, and other phenomena compels attention to the problem. So too does the timing, for we are fast becoming a predominantly urban world, a world where half the urban population will be citizens of mega-cities.

An Agent of Disaster

Before examining the links between mega-cities and disasters it is necessary to identify the general hazard-intensifying and disaster-forcing aspects of urbanization. Urban development increases disaster-susceptibility in a number of ways. First is the frequent association of cities with naturally risky locations such as seacoasts and floodplains because such places also confer important benefits. Initial settlements may take advantage of available safe sites but subsequent growth typically spills over into adjacent high-risk areas. Coastal metropolises of the eastern United States (Boston, New York, Miami, Houston) and the seaward-expanding cities of Japan are good examples.

Again the physical process of building cities often creates

or exacerbates existing environmental risks. For instance, paving over watersheds reduces infiltration, speeds runoff, and increases flood volumes; constructing coastal defences may reduce supplies of beach sand and facilitate erosion during storms. As the leading edge of urban development marches across the landscape, the incidence of natural disasters tends to keep pace (Cooke, 1984). The human role in creating conditions for disaster is clearly visible. Bangkok *klongs* (canals) that used to accommodate overflow from the Chao Phraya River have been filled in to create streets that are now chronically flood prone, while the city continues to subside owing to pumping of water from underlying aquifers.

The cities increase disaster potential by concentrating people and investments. A disproportionate amount of material wealth is bound up with cities in the form of buildings (ceremonial, commercial, industrial, and residential) and infrastructure (i.e. the complex and expensive networks of lifelines that sustain urban populations and make it possible for them to interact with each other and the outside world). When an extreme event occurs, urban losses are often very heavy. In a matter of hours, hurricane Andrew inflicted over US$20 billion of property damage on the Miami metropolitan area, whereas it took about six weeks of heavy flooding in mostly rural sections of nine Midwestern states to produce approximately half as much material loss (Myers and White, 1993).

The built environment is continuously wearing out but the rate of urban replacement rarely matches the rate of urban obsolescence. As a consequence, most cities contain large concentrations of old buildings that fail to meet present standards for hazard-resistant construction. Differential ageing and uneven replacement of the physical stock typically produce a complex patchwork of disaster-susceptibilities.

Many urban areas contain populations that are particularly vulnerable to disaster. For example, metropolitan areas often attract large numbers of in-migrants, most of them poor and all of them separated both from the familiar landscapes of home, whose risks were known, and from traditional support networks or customary behaviours that provided a modicum of security in the event of disaster.

Only few governments of rapidly growing cities have been able to allocate significant resources to hazard reduction when they are already stretched to breaking point by the task of providing basic support services for their expanding populations. In short, cities often contain all of the ingredients for disaster: heightened risks, concentrated exposure, and increased vulnerability.

Changing Patterns of Urbanization

In 1990 urban dwellers accounted for 47 per cent of the world's population but that number is expected to rise to around 63 per cent by 2020. Some 6,000 years separated the earliest urban centres from the first cities of more than 1 million people. Now there are about 300 such places and their numbers are growing rapidly. At the beginning of the twentieth century approximately 2 per cent of all humans lived in just 14 mega-cities. Today the proportion is close to 20 per cent and it will probably rise to around 30 per cent by the year 2020 (Fellman et al., 1992, p. 371).

Moreover, the size of mega-cities is increasing rapidly. In 1900 there were no cities of more than 10 million and only three that exceeded 3 million (London, Paris, and New York). Now there are about 60 cities with populations greater than 3 million and 14 super-mega-cities of more than 10 million. What is, by some counts, the world's largest city (Mexico City) currently contains at least 15 million people. The entire contiguous area of Mexico City (i.e. the central city plus adjacent smaller cities, towns, and suburbs) may hold more than 20 million. It is projected that there will be two or three urbanized areas of 20 million by the year 2000 (Mexico City,

Sao Paulo, and perhaps Tokyo-Yokohama) and another 20 of between 10 and 20 million (Jones and Kandel, 1992, p. 75).

Urban analysts recognize a number of different cultural variants of city form and structure, each with their own characteristic patterns of land use and population distribution. For example, Latin American cities tend to be made up of concentric zones, with old but well-maintained housing near a single central business district and poor shanty towns on the periphery. Industrial areas and the elite residential zone cut across these rings in the form of wedge-shaped blocks of territory. In contrast, the typical North American city more or less reverses this pattern, with a ring of decayed housing surrounding the central business district and affluent suburbs on the periphery. Also the central business district may be in decline, its functions challenged by many secondary shopping and industrial nodes scattered throughout the metropolis. West European cities often have well-marked historic cores with many preserved public buildings, surrounded by old houses - newly upgraded by middle-class gentrifiers - side by side with the cramped homes of working-class residents. Segregated urban ethnic neighbourhoods are less marked than in the United States. Suburbs may be either rich or poor and are often flanked by green belts with dormitory villages in the countryside beyond. African and south Asian cities tend to contain substantial tracts of market gardens within the built-up area. Middle Eastern cities often preserve distinct religious "quarters." The former socialist cities of Russia and Eastern Europe have a high percentage of their land given over to industrial districts and relatively few socio-economic contrasts among neighbourhoods. For much of the post-Second World War period, new investment was denied to Shanghai and other coastal cities of China, as national leaders sought both to hold down the growth of all large cities and to spread economic development more widely into the interior. The contrast between outmoded facilities and today's resurgent economic boom in the coastal mega-cities of China is striking (Gaile, 1983; Sit, 1988; *New York Times*, 22 December 1993).

These examples do not exhaust the catalogue of cultural and regional variations of urbanization but suffice to make the point that cities are functionally organized in different ways that have distinctive areal expressions. These patterns are then draped over a varied physical landscape and adjusted to it, a process that helps to disguise the underlying organizing principles. When a natural disaster strikes, it disrupts - and may destroy - not just the lives of citizens and the city's physical fabric but also the functional organization of the metropolis. However, the same organizing principles typically reassert themselves during post-disaster reconstruction.

Different types of organization have different loss potentials, different vulnerabilities, and different prospects for recovery. Likewise, different types of city require different types of preparedness-planning and different hazard-mitigation strategies. For example, a single central business district plays an irreplaceable role in Lima (Peru), a city that contains 30 per cent of the country's population and 70 per cent of its industry; the several business districts of a typical multi-nucleated North American city share economic functions and rarely serve the entire nation. Likewise, the Lima periphery would hardly be a suitable location for the replication of suburban watershed management schemes borrowed from an American mega-city. In similar vein, the in-city agricultural lands of African and South-East Asian cities provide amounts of open space for hazard refuges and post-disaster relief staging areas that could only be dreamed about in the typical large Japanese city.

The preceding variants notwithstanding, there are also significant similarities among mega-cities. For example, the great majority are ports -very often the most important ports in the respective countries. Therefore protection against waterborne hazards and disasters is likely to be a shared concern, and safeguarding marine facilities, ship channels, and water-dependent land uses may receive high priority.

Polycentre and Periphery Perspectives

Much of the concern about natural disasters in mega-cities of developed countries stems from the fact that such places contain a large proportion of the world's material investments and economic wealth. A disaster that takes many human lives is clearly possible in cities such as London, Los Angeles, or Tokyo, but such places are much more likely to suffer heavy economic and material losses in the wake of extreme natural events. As hurricane Andrew demonstrated for Greater Miami and the Hanshin earthquake for Kobe, a single metropolitan disaster in a rich country can produce economic losses that rock the global reinsurance industry.

But, the issue of mega-city disasters in rich countries is not simply one of losses that are inflicted on the affected communities themselves; it is increasingly connected with the roles that such places play in the global economy and the capacity of disasters to disrupt global economic functioning (Sassen, 1991). Several years ago the world's business community was jarred by reports that a major earthquake in Tokyo might precipitate a collapse of the global economic system (M. Lewis, 1989). This revelation followed on the heels of a record 1987 windstorm in southern England that had shut down the London Stock Exchange and may have helped to trigger the worst international stock market crisis since the Great Depression (Mitchell, Devine, and Jagger, 1989). Since then a series of other events has further underlined the disaster-vulnerability of mega-cities that anchor the global finance and trading network. They include: an underground flood that immobilized much of Chicago's financial district; riots and the possibility of a great earthquake in Los Angeles; an earthquake that disrupted the San Françisco Bay Area; and the bombing of the World Trade Center in New York. Between them these six mega-cities house the headquarters of more than 60 per cent of the world's leading private corporations (Berry, 1990).

Now there is evidence that the urban-based new information technologies on which the global economy increasingly depends are highly vulnerable to disruption by storms, floods, earthquakes, and other unexpected events. Nineteen mega-cities together make up a global "poly-centre" that directs and controls the international entrepreneurial system (Berry, 1990). Fifteen of these places account for 70 per cent of all electronic data flows in the contemporary world (J. Lewis, 1990). Not only are mega-cities of the polycentre full of expensive buildings and infrastructure and strategic economic functions, their sophisticated but demanding technologies that make for economic (and perhaps geopolitical) dominance may be susceptible to new kinds of vulnerability. In these cities, as well as the familiar consequences of natural disasters, there is considerable potential for disaster "surprises" in the future (Mitchell, 1996).

What do we know about the ability of mega-cities in developed countries to respond to severe natural events? The Loma Prieta earthquake and other recent mega-city disasters provided evidence that some of the measures that have proven to be effective in reducing losses in smaller cities may not work quite so well in emerging Western mega-cities (Mitchell, 1993a). Prediction, warning, and evacuation systems that depend on sophisticated technology and highly effective public bureaucracies are particularly open to question. In addition, big-city disasters possess features that have not been common in smaller communities and that may raise entirely new problems of disaster management. For example, disaster impacts in mega-cities that dominate mass media markets are likely to be extensively, continuously, and obsessively reported whereas impacts on other communities that have less access to these channels are likely to be overlooked. The consequences for skewing post-disaster relief are considerable. Secondly, the complex societal mixes of mega-cities pose new problems for the delivery of emergency response services and disaster relief; linguistic, ethnic, and other differences are often marked in such places. Thirdly, the sheer size and complexity of mega-city infrastructure networks make them particularly liable to disruption. Finally, recovery is apt to occur more slowly than in smaller places. In short, past lessons of disaster management may no longer be applicable in the mega-cities of the polycentre.

In places such as Manila, Dhaka, Ankara, or Lima there is the potential for heavy loss of life during disasters as well as catastrophic material destruction. The situation in Lima is typical. This is a city that has suffered severe earthquakes at least five times in the past 300 years. At the end of the Second World War, just over half a million people lived in the metropolitan area. Today, there are more than 5 million. Vast numbers of poor rural peasants have flooded into Lima. Not all groups are equally exposed to hazard. Indeed, the pattern of hazard-susceptibility is a complex one that has evolved in response to changes in demography, economics, land ownership, building practices, and other factors. Middle- and upper-income groups live in well-constructed houses that often comply with antiseismic codes and are sited in neighbourhoods with wide streets and ample open spaces. If affected by an earthquake there are enough resources to ensure quick recovery. The peripheral shanty towns *(pueblos jovenes)* are also low-density settlements, this time composed of light bamboo structures that do not collapse when the ground moves. People are poor, but levels of social organization are high. In contrast, seismic vulnerability is high in the inner-city slum areas. Here many poor families are crowded into old adobe brick structures, adjoining streets are narrow, and open spaces are non-existent. There are few neighbourhood organizations or other local institutions that might be called on in the event of a disaster. Here earthquake protection measures are minimal or, more often, non-existent.

As summarized by one observer, the situation is full of bleak prospects:

> The inhabitants of critical areas would not choose to live there if they had any alternative, nor do they neglect the maintenance of their overcrowded and deteriorated tenements. For them it is the best-of-the-worst of a number of disaster-prone scenarios such as having nowhere to live, having no way of earning a living and having nothing to eat. Given that these other risks have to be confronted on a daily basis, it is hardly surprising that people give little priority to the risk of destruction by earthquake. (Maskrey, 1989, p. 12).

To sum up, there is a high degree of uncertainty about the future of mega-cities. Their growth seems assured, but at what density? New ones may spring up in unexpected places under the influence of changing geo-economic forces. Increasingly similar in outward form, mega-cities in different cultures and continents may still retain distinctively different internal structures. The divisions between rich mega-cities and poor ones may become wider and their disaster-susceptibilities may also diverge. But, at the same time, the differences between all mega-cities and their rural hinterlands may become sharper. It would be foolhardy to assume that the disaster-susceptibility of any one mega-city will be quite like that of any other.

The US Federal Emergency Management Agency (FEMA) has been a particular target. It has been accused of providing insufficient and inappropriate relief to disaster victims. It has also been criticized for encouraging the occupation of hazardous lands by offering low-cost insurance to rich investors; and it has drawn fire for devoting too much effort to cleaning up after past disasters and too little effort to reducing the probability of future disasters. FEMA's mishandling of relief in the wake of hurricane Andrew (Florida, 1992) triggered a major investigation by the US Congress. Critics called for the nation's armed forces to replace FEMA, and large numbers of military personnel have, in fact, been deployed after recent disasters. The military is commonly in charge of disaster management in third world nations because it is often the only institution capable of providing aid during disasters and one of the few organizations that can be counted on to enforce government policies at other times. But in the United States and other Western nations proposals for a larger military role in civilian affairs are often controversial. Advocates of civil authority and legal due process are concerned that increased military involvement in disasters may signal an erosion of citizen rights and responsibilities, while others point to the reduction in international tensions and the need for more cost-effective national institutions as grounds for making creative use of military expertise in new roles.

Without going into detail, it is worthwhile to note that there is a widespread loss of faith in the ability of national public agencies to combat natural and technological hazards in many other countries. The failures of Soviet agencies in connection with the Armenian earthquake (1988) and the Chernobyl nuclear power station fire (1986) have been well documented and they are believed to have contributed to the collapse of the Soviet government. British civil defence agencies have also been roundly criticized for inadequate preparedness and lack of attention to hazard mitigation (Mitchell, 1989; Parker and Handmer, 1992).

Partly because government agencies have come under attack, there has been a determined effort to shift the burden of disaster management onto private individuals and institutions. In countries such as the United States, Germany, and the United Kingdom, this began with a conservative revolution in politics led by people such as Margaret Thatcher, Ronald Reagan, and Helmut Kohl. In the context of hazard management, policy reforms commonly took the form of insurance schemes (flood insurance, earthquake insurance, crop insurance, etc.), limitations on central government spending for disaster relief and recovery, an end to public subsidies for building in hazardous areas, and penalties for people who wilfully build - or rebuild - in such places.

Now there is a growing body of evidence that such policies may not work as intended. For example, insurance is not the panacea it was once proclaimed to be. Many potential victims are uninsured or underinsured and those who have -adequate insurance often experience serious problems securing reimbursements. Not all perils are covered by insurance, and major problems arise when hazards involve several perils (e.g. hurricanes bring floods, erosion, wind damage, landslides, and other events). Cut-backs in government funding of social services have become common throughout the developed world in recent years, and spending on disasters is no exception. As a result, policies that emphasize private responsibilities for hazard management may help to widen the gap between richer and better-educated victims - that is, those who can afford to make provisions for their own security - and the poor or disadvantaged groups that lack such a capacity. In short, a hazard-protection system that relies primarily on market mechanisms may well be detrimental to broader public interests.

British experience with the great storm of 15 October 1987 illustrates several of these problems (Mitchell, Devine, and Jagger, 1989). Before the storm, local governments and private individuals in England had been encouraged to be self-reliant and not to expect the national government to provide recovery funds in the event of a disaster. But the storm - which recorded the highest wind speeds in 250 years - blew down some 15 million trees and inflicted economic losses greater than any natural disaster in Britain since the end of the Second World War. In the process it exposed the limitations of local resources for coping with disasters and it compelled a major reversal of national policies that would have left local governments to take care of natural disasters.

If there is concern about the general effectiveness of disaster management by the private sector, there is deep consternation about the future of hazard insurance systems. Lack of insurance coverage and inadequate reimbursements are continuing problems, but the central issue is that very large disasters may bankrupt the entire international insurance system. Insurance and reinsurance companies in Germany, Japan, and the United States are all deeply troubled by this prospect. These include Lloyd's of London, which ran up losses of US$4.2 billion in 1993 as a consequence of heavy pay-outs to victims of earthquakes, hurricanes, and pollution emergencies (*New York Times*, 30 April 1993). In 1989, the Loma Prieta earthquake (northern California) and hurricane Hugo (Puerto Rico, Virgin Islands, South Carolina) inflicted severe losses on the American insurance industry and the global reinsurance market. But these losses were nothing compared with the losses sustained in 1992 as a result of three "superstorms" that occurred within a few weeks: typhoon Omar (Guam), hurricane Andrew (Florida), and hurricane Iniki (Hawaii). The total bill for insured storm losses was at least US$20 billion. Yet worse is possible - indeed likely. It is estimated that a single large hurricane could cause US$30-40 billion in insured losses and that a major earthquake in Tokyo or southern California might wreak even worse damage. These are the kinds of event that could disrupt investment markets throughout the world and trigger a collapse of the global financial system. Such circumstances underline the increasing interdependence of global society and its vulnerability to strategic loss.

Failure to make use of available hazard-reduction information and measures of known effectiveness constitutes another general policy issue. It is one that helps to stimulate the ongoing UN-sponsored International Decade for Natural Disaster Reduction (Mitchell, 1988). In many places it would be possible to mitigate losses simply by putting what is known into effect. For example, the value of warning and evacuation systems has been proven repeatedly; yet such systems are often underused. Likewise, hazard-mitigation schemes offer reliable paths toward reducing the long-term costs of disasters but they are often resisted in favour of immediate post-disaster relief, insurance, and compensation programmes. Why do individuals and governments fail to make optimal use of available knowledge? There is no single answer to this question. A large number of factors are involved.

- lack of agreement about definition and identification of problem;
- lack of awareness of hazards;
- misperception or misjudgement of risks;
- lack of awareness of appropriate responses;
- lack of expertise to make use of responses;
- lack of money or resources to pay for responses;
- lack of coordination among institutions;
- lack of attention to relationship between "disasters" and "development";
- failure to treat hazards as contextual problems whose components require simultaneous attention (i.e. reciprocity);
- lack of access by affected populations to decision-making;
- lack of public confidence in scientific knowledge;
- conflicting goals among populations at risk;
- fluctuating salience of hazards (competing priorities);
- public opposition by negatively affected individuals and groups.

Underlying all of these specific reasons is a larger problem. It is this: society fails to treat natural hazards as complex systems with many components that often require simultaneous attention. We tinker with one or another aspect of these systems when what is required are system-wide strategies. Perhaps even more important, we fail to address the direct linkage between natural hazard systems and economic investment decisions that drive the process of "development" and affect the potential for disasters. That such links exist has been known for a very long time:

> If a man owes a debt, and the storm inundates his field and carries away the produce, or if the grain has not grown in the field, in that year he shall not make any return to the creditor, he shall alter his contract and he shall not pay interest for that year. (*The Code of Hammurabi,* King of Bablyon, *c.* 2250 B.C.)

But most of the decisions that are taken to build new facilities or redevelop old ones, or to adopt new production and distribution processes, or to develop new land, or to effectuate a myriad of other development goals are not currently very sensitive to considerations of natural hazards. They should become so. And that is a task that will require a great deal of effort by natural hazard scientists to go beyond the laboratory and the research office or the field study site to acquire an understanding of how best to apply their expertise in public settings. It will also require the users of scientific information about hazards (architects, engineers planners, banks and mortgage companies, international development agencies, and investment financiers) to nurture a mutually interactive relationship with the scientists who are producers of that information. "Development" is only one of the major public issues that overlaps with natural hazards reduction. Others include: environmental management; public health; security (personal, social, and national); and urbanization. All of them are major problem sets in their own right, each patterned by philosophical and managerial disputes and unresolved issues. Efforts to work out mutually supportive policies and programmes raise entirely new sets of contextual issues for hazards experts. How shall the different kinds of policies for these broad problem sets be articulated? Can they be organized around a single concept such as sustainable development, or will it be necessary to make trade-offs among each of them separately on an ad hoc basis? Some of the experience gained from attempts to work out sustainable development programmes in the World Bank and elsewhere might prove useful here (Cohen and Leitmann, 1994; Goode, 1996; Jones and Ward, 1994; Stren et al., 1992; White, 1994; and Wikan, 1995). So might the experience of "harmonizing" laws and regulations among countries that join together in new continental-sized free trade blocs (e.g. the European Union or the North American Free Trade Agreement).

The difficulties of merging hazards reduction in the overlapping context of sustainable development are instructive and require further comment. The rising incidence of disasters throughout the world is one of the most commonly cited indicators of non-sustainable development. (The other major villains are loss of biodiversity, impairment of natural systems, and global economic crises.) As Odd Grann, Secretary General of the Norwegian Red Cross, has said:

> All major disaster problems in the Third World are essentially unresolved development problems. Disaster prevention is thus primarily an aspect of development, and this must be a development that takes place within the sustainable limits.

The evidence that disasters and development are connected is simply too overwhelming to be ignored. In the case of problems such as drought and famine in the African Sahel or the deaths of poor slum dwellers in landslides that affect the unstable slopes of Latin American cities, the connections between disasters and development are clear. But it is another matter entirely to believe that most or all natural disasters will disappear if only we adopt sustainable development policies and programmes. "Sustainable" development does not necessarily equal "safe" development.

It will probably always be necessary to support and nourish institutions that have the capability of responding to unexpected natural disasters. Much of what our existing hazard-management organizations do could be described as preparing for and coping with "routine disasters," that is, problems that were bound to occur sooner rather than later and for which we have developed reliable management responses. These are the sorts of things that it is hoped will diminish if sustainable development is properly implemented.

Clearly, the roster of hazard-management issues is packed with still unresolved old issues and emerging new ones. Among the topics that require attention are the following:

- the changing contributions of people, natural systems, and technology to the creation of hazard;
- measures to encourage improved use of available information about hazards (including scientific knowledge and folk wisdom);
- global interdependence and the vulnerability of large institutions (e.g. economies, cities) to major disruptive events;
- the relative human impacts of cumulative small-scale hazards and single large disasters;
- innovative procedures for coping with unprecedented hazards (i.e. surprises);
- attitudes toward risk and hazard;
- equity in the distribution *of* hazard costs and benefits;
- the illumination of polarizing debates about appropriate hazard-management strategies (e.g. "top-down" versus "bottom-up," centralization versus decentralization, rights versus responsibilities, anticipation versus reaction);
- alternative means for sustaining stakeholder involvement in decision-making beyond periods of acute crisis; and

- coalition-building between hazards interest groups and others that address overlapping problems (e.g. sustainable development).

Changes in the Theory of Hazards and Disasters

The theory of research on natural hazards and disasters has been extensively reviewed elsewhere (Emel and Feet, 1989; Hewitt, 1983; Kates, 1978; Mitchell, 1984, 1987, 1989, 1990, 1991, 1993b; O'Riordan, 1986; White, 1973; Whyte, 1986; Whyte and Burton, 1980). We will focus only on recent (i.e. circa post-1988) changes. Two major research paradigms were in existence by the late 1980s: an older, human ecology one, which focused on decision-making by individuals and groups in the face of extreme events, and a newer, political economy paradigm, which emphasized underlying political, economic, and social structures that create conditions of hazard and prevent populations at risk from taking appropriate safety measures. Since 1988, debates between proponents of each paradigm have continued (Emel and Peet, 1989; Hewitt, 1992; K. Smith, 1992; Blaikie et al., 1994), but the two groups have tended to focus on different topics. Human ecologists have carried their ideas forward in a specialized literature on the social amplification of risk and risk communication, particularly in the context of major technological hazards (Greenberg et al., 1989; Wynne, 1989). Political economists have preferred to examine issues of vulnerability and equity, although others have also addressed those themes (Anderson and Woodrow, 1991; Dow, 1992; Kates and Weinberg, 1986; J. Lewis, 1990; Liverman, 1990; Taylor, 1990).

There have been some attempts at intellectual synthesis, including the creation of a new subfield - political ecology (Blaikie and Brookfield, 1987; Dalby, 1992; Little and Horowitz, 1987). Such syntheses incorporate elements of both paradigms and sometimes also include other perspectives (Alexander, 1993; Bryant, 1991; Palm, 1990). At the same time, a number of scholars have sought to forge links between hazards research and overlapping fields, in the hope of providing explanations for a wider range of problems. For example, medical researchers have called for attention to biological and disease hazards that were formerly neglected, and students of geopolitics have underscored the growing importance of environmental disasters as threats to national and global security (Dalby, 1992; Lewis and Mayer, 1988; Mintzer, 1992).

Overall there has been a recognition that broader interpretive frameworks are necessary - frameworks that incorporate both society and nature and a variety of contextual variables (Mitchell, Devine, and Jagger, 1989). However, whereas some have approached the task of extending hazards theory by means of synthesis among existing approaches, others have subjected long-accepted foundational concepts to critical analysis. For example, students of industrial disasters have questioned assumptions about a return to "normal" that underlie cyclical equilibrium models of disaster (Couch, 1996; Edelstein, 1988). They suggest that some disasters are essentially open-ended processes that may persist indefinitely. Other have criticized a widespread assumption among hazards researchers that public leaders want scientists to help them reach good decisions by eliminating uncertainty. Waterstone counters that the manipulation of uncertainty is a core political device that few leaders willingly surrender (Waterstone, 1993, p. 150). Wynne (1992) has also expressed doubts about the applicability of "uncertainty" as a basic concept in hazards studies. Drawing on a variety of evidence about recent surprises, he argues that many types of hazards may be better understood as indeterminate phenomena. Such risks as stratospheric ozone depletion, the build-up of greenhouse gases in the atmosphere, and the hazards of new industrial technologies are unprecedented in human experience; they represent a break with past knowledge. By invoking the concept "indeterminacy," Wynne and others imply that hazards research is pressing against the limits of scientific methods and scientific philosophies (Wynne, 1992;

P.J. Smith, 1990). Funtowicz and Ravetz (1990) have come to similar conclusions by examining the quality of scientific knowledge about global environmental hazards. When assessing emergent types of hazard they judge that we may need to think of several orders of scientific knowledge, each characterized by different degrees of certainty and reliability. O'Riordan and Rayner (1991) carry this analysis further and call for the creation of risk-management institutions that explicitly seek to combine science and politics. O'Riordan (1986) has also gone on record in support of creative use of knowledge from the arts and humanities to inform hazards research and education.

Thoughts like these lie at the interface between science and other forms of knowing. They are part of a general questioning of established knowledge that constitutes "postmodern discourse" in the social sciences and, especially, the humanities. In a surprising turn of events, hazards research - an interdisciplinary social science with ties to the natural sciences - is now beginning to be fertilized by ideas from the humanities. It is not easy to characterize either postmodernism or the special attributes of postmodernist theory (see Harvey, 1989; Hayles, 1991; Rosenau, 1992). Postmodernism is both a cultural condition and an "intellectual construct. As a cultural condition, it is identified with certain architectural and artistic styles that involve the unexpected juxtaposition of forms and characters, transitory states, fluidity, and eclecticism. As an intellectual construct, postmodernism can be viewed as one outcome of a long-running border war between science and the humanities, wherein the allegiance of social scientists has been divided. The basic ideas of postmodernism have been fashioned by literary theorists and other humanists who have been concerned about the excesses and limitations of rational analysis and the neglect of alternative forms of knowing. Their thesis is as follows. The dominant global society is a product of the European Enlightenment. This "modern" society has endured for several hundred years, founded on beliefs about rationality in the organization and functioning of both the natural and social worlds and on the capacity of people to discover these truths and to act in light of them for their own benefit (i.e. to achieve "progress"). It is now argued that modernity has run its course and is being replaced by a fundamentally different "postmodern" era.

For social scientists, the salient characteristics of postmodern thought are: its rejection of grand theory and so-called metanarrative; its adherence to pluralist interpretations; its characterization of change as discontinuity; its celebration of difference, contingency, and the primacy of local experience; its use of paradox and metaphor as investigative tools; and its non-pejorative assessment of alternative (i.e. non-scientific) forms of knowing. In the words of one commentator:

> Post-modernists rearrange the whole social science enterprise. Those of a modern conviction seek to isolate elements, specify relationships, and formulate a synthesis; post-modernists do the opposite. They offer indeterminacy rather than determinism, diversity rather than unity, difference rather than synthesis, complexity rather than simplification. They look to the unique rather than the general, to intertextual relations rather than causality, and to the unrepeatable rather than the re-occurring, the habitual, or the routine. Within a post-modern perspective social science becomes a more subjective and humbling enterprise as truth gives way to tentativeness. Confidence in emotion replaces efforts at impartial observation. Relativism is preferred to objectivity, fragmentation to totalization. Attempts to apply the model of natural science inquiry in the social sciences are rejected because post-modernists consider such methods to be part of the larger techno-scientific corrupting cultural imperative, originating in the West but spreading out to encompass the planet. (Rosenau, 1992, pp. 8-9).

Few hazards researchers have self-consciously placed

their work in a postmodern context, but there are clear echoes of postmodern sensibility in many recent critiques of the field (Cooke, 1992; Curry, 1988; Taylor and Buttel, 1992). The following statement by Hewitt is a good example.

[The] elements of today's dominant view of hazards ... are fully symptomatic [of] the abstracted, gender-blind, class-blind, secular and amoral, mechanistic and technocratic style of work that prevails in international "Big Science" and the preoccupations of agencies and publics in the wealthier and more powerful centers.... They not only display the Enlightenment desire to generalize and command "rational" interpretation by reducing everything to a common language and set of concepts. They are repeatedly beguiled by the most "advanced" or fashionable concepts, the worries of "fast-breaking" technologies in their own places of origin, and a belief these define and alone can solve "problems" elsewhere (Hewitt, 1992, p. 58).

Hewitt's statement is an indictment of current theory as well as current practice in the management of hazards. He is not alone in holding such views. This is not to say that contemporary hazards research is riven by postmodern critiques. The challenges that I have reported here are not yet a dominant presence in the field. But they are beginning to tap into a distinct undercurrent of disquiet among many who are conscious of the limitations of existing theory and practice (Frowning and Shetler, 1992).

Whether postmodernist critiques will fundamentally alter the nature of hazards research is an open question. At first glance there are grounds for scepticism. The existence of close links between research and praxis suggests that there will be strong counterpressures to resist any theory that calls for thoroughgoing institutional and social change - and evinces deep suspicion of the very organizations that are most involved with the making and execution of policy. Of course, current debates about hazards need not lead to postmodern theories of hazard that blend the contributions of scientists and humanists. Other purely scientific ("modern") approaches are possible, including those based on theories of evolution, chaos, and complexity (Argyros, 1991; Waldrup, 1992). (For example, some Russian colleagues are developing ideas about processes that limit the disturbance of large systems that are based on the application or extension of the well-known Le Chatelier Principle in chemistry.) But hazards researchers have been slow to link up with this more formal work, most of which is firmly in the tradition of Enlightenment thought. It is too soon to assess the advantages that a "science of chaos and complexity" might offer to hazards scholars.

Mega-Cities and Natural Disasters Reconsidered

This is a process with which Japanese society has had considerable experience from the late nineteenth century onwards. And the Japanese experience offers instructive parallels, both in a general sense and in a more restricted one that applies specifically to issues of hazard and disaster. After the Meiji restoration, contacts between Japan and the rest of the world were managed in such a way as to permit Japan to benefit while at the same time preventing Japanese society from being inundated by foreign cultural influences. A successful transition to a new social order was obtained. As part of that transition, Western science came to Japan and with it an interest in the scientific and technical analysis of natural hazards and disasters. Out of this arose leading institutions of disaster research and a distinctive style of hazards management that attracts visitors from all over the world. Whether one learns about the means by which Kagoshima beneficially coexists with its hyperactive backyard volcano, or the gated rivers of the Japanese coast, or Nagoya's three-tiered elevated highway, ground-level park, and underground flood reservoir scheme, or Tokyo's firewall high-rise complex, there can be no mistaking the fact that a very distinctive blend of scientific knowledge, technological innovation, and societal cooperation has been achieved in a variety of big-city contexts.

In coming to grip with the burgeoning disaster potential of the world's mega-cities, the hazards community and the urban community are embarking on a somewhat similar exercise in cultural contact, this time among professional and academic cultures as well as national ones. We cannot know how the contact will turn out, but we can make sure that the best thinking from each community is incorporated into the process.

REFERENCES

Abu Sin, M.E. (1991), "Migration from Eastern Gezira into Greater Khartoum - A case study in rural-urban migration and population integration processes." *GeoJournal* 25(1): 73-80.

Agmad, Adil Mustafa (1993), "The neighborhoods of Khartoum: Reflections on their functions, forms and future." *Habitat* 16(4): 27-45.

Aguilar, Adrian Guillermo, Exequiel Ezcurra, Teresa Garcia, Marisa Mazari-Hiriat, and Irene Pisanty (1995), "The basin of Mexico." In Jeanne X. Kasperson, Roger E. Kasperson, and B. L. Turner II (eds.), *Regions at Risk.* Tokyo: United Nations University Press, pp. 304-366.

Alexander, David (1993), *Natural disasters.* New York: Chapman & Hall.

Anderson, Mary B. and Peter J. Woodrow (1991), "Reducing vulnerability to drought and famine: Developmental approaches to relief." *Disasters* 15(1): 43- 54.

Argyros, Alexander J. (1991), *A blessed rage for order: Deconstruction, evolution, and chaos.* Ann Arbor: University of Michigan Press.

Bakhit, Abdel Hamid (1994), "Availability, affordibility and accessibility of food in Khartoum." *GeoJournal* 34(3): 253-255.

Berke, Philip R. and Timothy Beatley (1992), *Planning for earthquakes: Risk, politics, and policy.*

Baltimore, MD: Johns Hopkins University Press.

Berry, Brian J.L. (1990), "Urbanization." In B. L. Turner II, William C. Clark, Robert W. Kates, John F. Richards, Jessica T. Mathews, and William B. Meyer (eds.), *The earth as transformed by human action: Global and regional changes in the biosphere over the past 300 years.* Cambridge: Cambridge University Press, pp. 103-119.

Blaikie, P. and H. Brookfield (1987), *Land degradation and society*. London: Methuen.

Blaikie, Piers, Terry Cannon, Ian Davis, and Ben Wisner (1994), *At risk: Natural hazards, people's vulnerability and disasters*. London: Routledge.

Bohle, Hans-Georg (1994), "Cities of hunger: Urban food systems in developing countries." *GeoJournal* 34(3): 243-244 (see also additional papers, pp. 245-304).

Boone, Christopher G. (1996), "Language politics and flood control in nineteenth-century Montreal." *Environmental History* 1(3): 70-85.

Bromley, Ray, Peter Hall, Ashok Dutt, Debnath Mookherjee and John E. Benhart (1989), "Regional development and planning." In Gary L. Gaile and Cort J. Willmott (eds.), *Geography in America*. Columbus, OH: Merrill Publishing Company, pp. 351-386.

Browning, Larry D. and Judy C. Shetler (1992), "Communication in crisis, communication in recovery: A postmodern commentary on the Exxon Valdez disaster." *International Journal of Mass Emergencies and Disasters* 10(2).

Brunn, Stanley D. and Jack F. Williams (1993), *Cities of the world: World regional development*, 2nd edn. New York: HarperCollins.

Bryant, E.A. (1991), *Natural hazards*. Cambridge: Cambridge University Press.

Chandler, Tertius and Gerald Fox (1974), 3000 *years of urban growth*. New York: Academic Press,

Chudacoff, Howard P. and Judith E. Smith (1994), *The evolution of American urban society*. Englewood Cliffs, NJ: Prentice-Hall.

Cohen, Michael A. and Josef L. Leitmann (1994), "Will the World Bank's real 'New Urban Policy' please stand up?" *Habitat International* 18(4): 117-126.

Cooke, Ronald U. (1984), *Geomorphological hazards in Los Angeles*. London: Alien & Unwin.

Couch, S. R. (1996), "Environmental contamination, community transformation, and the Centralia mine fire." In James K. Mitchell (ed.), *The long road to recovery: Community responses to industrial disaster*. Tokyo: United Nations University Press, pp. 60-85.

Cronon, William (1991), *Nature's metropolis: Chicago and the Great West*. New York and London: W. W. Norton.

Cuny, Frederick C. (1994), "Cities under seige: Problems, priorities and programs." *Disasters* 18(2): 152-159.

Curry, Michael (1988), "Commentary on 'Geographers and nuclear war: Why we lack influence on public policy'." *Annals of the Association of American Geographers* 78(4): 720-724.

Dalby, Simon (1992), "Ecopolitical discourse: 'Environmental security' and political geography." *Progress in Human Geography* 16(4): 503-522.

Dando, W.A. (1994), *Urban famines in a future world of mega-cities: A commentary*. Professional Paper No. 20. Indiana State University, Terre Haute, Department of Geography and Geology, pp. 81-87.

Davis, Mike (1992), *City of quartz: Excavating the future in Los Angeles*. New York: Vintage Books.

Degg, Martin (1993), "The 1992 'Cairo Earthquake': Causes, effect and response." *Disasters* 17(3): 226-238.

Dow, Kirstin (1992), "Exploring differences in our common future(s): The meaning of vulnerability to global environmental change." *Geoforum* 23(3): 417-436.

Driever, Steven L. and Danny M. Vaughn (1988), "Flood hazard in Kansas City since 1880." *Geographical Review* 78(1): 1-19.

Earthquake Engineering Research Institute (1985), *Proceedings - U.S.-Japan Workshop on Urban Earthquake Hazards Reduction*. Publication No. 85-03. Berkeley: EERI.

Edelstein, M. R. (1988), *Contaminated communities: The social and psychological impacts of residéntial toxic exposure*. Boulder, CO: Westview Press. El-Bushra,

El-Sayed and Naila B. Hijazi (1995), "Two million squatters in Khartoum urban complex: The dilemma of Sudan's national capital." *GeoJournal* 35(4): 505-514.

Emel, J. and J. R. Peet (1989), "Resource management and natural hazards." In J.R. Peet and N. Thrift (eds.), *New models in geography: The political-economy perspective*. London: Unwin Hyman.

Ezcurra, Exequiel and Marisa Mazari-Hiriart (1996), "Are megacities viable? A cautionary tale from Mexico City." *Environment* 38(1): 15, 26-35.

Fellmann, Jerome, Arthur Getis, and Judy Getis (1992), *Human geography: Landscapes of human activities*. Dubuque: Wm. C. Brown.

Firman, Tommy and Indira Dharmapatni (1994), "The challenges to sustainable development in Jakarta Metropolitan Region." *Habitat International* 18(3): 74-94.

Fishman, Robert (1987), *Bourgeois Utopias: The rise and fall of suburbia*. New York: Basic Books.

Frater, Alexander (1991), *Chasing the monsoon.* New York: Alfred A. Knopf.

Gaile, Gary L. (1983), "Reanalyses of Chinese spatial inequality." *Professional geographer* 35: 281-283.

Gilbert, Alan and Josef Gugler (1992), *Cities, poverty and development: Urbanization in the third world.* Oxford: Oxford University Press.

Goode, Judith (1996), "On sustainable development in the mega-city." *Current Anthropology* 36(1): 131-133.

Guterbock, Thomas M. (1990), "The effect of snow on urban density patterns in the United States." *Environment and Behavior* 22(3): 358-386.

Hall, Peter (1988), *Cities of tomorrow: An intellectual history of urban planning and design in the twentieth century.* Oxford: Basil Blackwell.

Hansel, G. (1991), "Rural-urban migration and the problem of town planning - The case of Um Badda, Omdurman." *GeoJournal* 25(1): 27-30.

Harvey, D. (1989), *The condition of postmodernity: An enquiry into the origins of cultural change.* Oxford: Blackwell.

Havlick, Spencer W. (1986), "Third world cities at risk: Building for calamity." *Environment* 28(9): 6-11, 41-45.

Hayles, Katherine, ed. (1991), *Chaos and order: Complex dynamics in literature and science.* Chicago: University of Chicago Press.

Hewitt, Kenneth (1983), *Interpretations of calamity.* Boston: Alien & Unwin. ——— 1992. "Mountain hazards." *GeoJournal* 27(1): 47-60.

Ibrahim, F.N. (1991), "The southern Sudanese migration to Khartoum and the resultant conflicts." *Geo Journal* 25(1): 13-18.

——— (1994), "Hunger-vulnerable groups within the metropolitan food system of Khartoum." *GeoJournal* 34(3): 257-261.

——— (1995), "Cultural change and the chances of reintegration after reimmigration to home areas - The case of the Southern Sudanese dislocated population in Greater Khartoum." *GeoJournal* 36(1): 103-107.

IDNDR (International Decade for Natural Disaster Reduction) (1990), *International Conference 1990 Japan: Toward a less hazardous world in the 21st century: Proceedings.* September 27-October 3,1990, Yokohama and Kagoshima.

——— 1(996), *Cities at risk: Making cities safer ... before disaster strikes.* Supplement to No. 28, *Stop Disasters.* Geneva: IDNDR.

Institution of Civil Engineers (1995), *Megacities: Reducing vulnerability to natural disaster.* London: Thomas Telford.

Jairo-Cardenas, J. (1990), "Natural disasters and urban struggle for housing." *Architecture et Comportement/'Architecture and Behaviour* 6(2): 177-191.

Jones, Emrys (1990), *Metropolis.* New York: Oxford University Press.

Jones, Gareth A. and Peter M. Ward (1994), "The World Bank's 'new' Urban Management Programme: Paradigm shift or policy continuity?" *Habitat International* 18(3): 33-51.

Kates, Robert W. (1978), *Risk assessment of environmental hazard.* SCOPE (Scientific Committee on Problems of the Environment) Report No. 8. New York: Wiley.

Kates, Robert W. and Alvin M. Weinberg, eds. (1986), *Hazards: Technology and fairness.* Washington, D.C.: National Academy Press.

Kim, Kwi-Gon (1990), "Risk assessment in urban planning and management: A metropolitan example." *Habitat* 14(1): 177-190.

Kreimer, Alcira and Mohan Munasinghe, eds. (1992), *Environmental management and urban vulnerability.* World Bank Discussion Paper 168. Washington, D.C.: World Bank.

Lewis, James (1990), "The vulnerability of small island states: The need for holistic strategies." *Disasters* 14(3): 241-249.

Lewis, Michael (1989), "How a Tokyo earthquake could devastate Wall Street and the world economy." *Manhattan, inc.*, June: 69-79.

Little, Peter D. and Michael M. Horowitz, eds. (1987), *Lands at risk in the Third World: Local level perspectives.* Boulder, CO: Westview Press.

McHarg, Ian (1969), *Design with nature.* New York: Natural History Press (especially "The City: Health and pathology," pp. 187-195).

McPhee, John (1989), *The control of nature.* New York: Farrar, Straus & Giroux.

Main, Hamish and Stephen Wyn Williams, eds. (1994), *Environment and housing in Third World cities.* Chichester: Wiley.

Maskrey, Andrew (1989), *Disaster mitigation: A community based approach.* Development Guidelines No. 3. Oxford: Oxfam.

Masure, P. (1994), "Risk management and preventive planning in mega-cities: A scientific approach for action." *Regional Development Dialogue* 15(2): 183-188.

Miller, Ross (1990), *American apocalypse: The great fire and the myth of Chicago.* Chicago: University of Chicago Press.

Mintzer, Irving M. (1992), *Confronting climate change: Risks, implications and responses.* Cambridge: Cambridge University Press.

Mitchell, James K. and Neil Ericksen (1992), "Effects of climate changes on weather-related disasters." In Irving Mintzer (ed.), *Confronting climate change: Risks, implications and responses.* Cambridge: Cambridge University Press, pp. 141-152.

Mitchell, James K., Neal Devine, and Kathleen Jagger (1989), "A contextual model of natural hazard." *Geographical Review* 89(4): 391-409.

Myers, Mary Fran and Gilbert F. White (1993), "The challenge of the Mississippi flood." *Environment* 35(10): 6-9, 25-35.

O'Riordan, Timothy (1986), "Coping with environmental hazards." In Robert W. Kates and Ian Burton (eds.), *Themes from the work of Gilbert F. White*, vol. 2 of *Geography, resources, and environment.* Chicago: University of Chicago Press, pp. 272-309.

Palm, Risa (1990), *Natural hazards: An integrative framework for research and planning.* Baltimore, MD: Johns Hopkins University Press.

Parker, D. J. and J.W. Handmer, eds. (1992), *Hazard management and emergency planning: Perspectives on Britain.* London: James & James.

Parker, Dennis J. and James K. Mitchell (1995), "Disaster vulnerability of mega-cities: An expanding problem that requires rethinking and innovative responses." *GeoJournal* 37(3): 295-301 (see also additional papers, pp. 303-388).

Perlman, Janice E. (1987), "Megacities and innovative technologies." *Cities*, May: 128-136.

Reed, Stuart, Fred Tromp, and Alain Lam (1992), "Major hazards - Thinking the unthinkable." *Environmental Management* 16(6): 715-722.

Revue de Geographic Alpine (1994), "Croissance urbaine et risques naturels dans les montagnes des pays en developpement," No. 4.

Rosen, Christine Meisner (1986), *The limits of power: Great fires and the process of city growth in America.* New York: Cambridge University Press.

Rosenau, P.M. (1992), *Post-modernism and the social sciences: Insights, inroads, and intrusions.* Princeton, NJ: Princeton University Press.

Ruppert, Helmut (1991), "The responses of different ethnic groups in the Sudan to rural-urban migration." *GeoJournal* 25(1): 7-12.

Sachs, Ignacy (1988), "Vulnerability of giant cities and the life lottery." In Mattei Dogan and John D. Kasarda (eds.), *A world of giant cities*, vol. 1 in *The metropolis era.* Newbury Park, CA: Sage Publications, pp. 337-350.

7

Tsunamis

The most disastrous face of Tsunami was witnessed only recently when entire south and south east Asia was hit. Millions of people lost their life and an unestimable loss of property and resources.

"Tsunami" is a Japanese word meaning "harbor wave." It is a water wave or a series of waves generated by an impulsive vertical displacement of the surface of the ocean or other body of water. Other terms for "tsunami" found in the literature include: seismic sea wave, Flutwellen, vloedgolven, raz de mare, vagues sismique, maremoto, and, incorrectly, tidal wave. The term "tidal wave" is frequently used in the older literature and in popular accounts, but is now considered incorrect. Tides are produced by the gravitational attraction of the sun and moon and occur predictably with twelve hour periods. The effects of a tsunami may be increased or decreased depending on the level of the tide, but otherwise the two phenomena are independent.

Although there are warning systems for tsunamis occurring around the Pacific, including local and regional warning systems in Hawaii and Alaska, the risks from future tsunamis are still not fully known. Some events, such as that in Prince William Sound, Alaska, in March 1964, can be devastating over large distances. Even over short distances along a coast, the heights of a tsunami wave will vary considerably. An important part of the risk assessment is to gain a clearer understanding of the effects of past tsunamis.

Introduction to Tsunamis

A tsunami, which is sometimes incorrectly referred to as a tidal wave, is a series of large waves created when either nearshore or undersea earthquakes occur causing sudden movement of the seafloor. The seafloor's movement generates a sudden impulse that causes the water column to displace vertically. The result is a large train of waves. As the wave approaches shallow water, it slows down, but the energy of the wave remains constant. This action causes the wave to increase in height, as high as 30.5 meters (100 feet), in some instances.

There is a very short time span for people to evacuate following an earthquake or tsunami warning. Tsunami events affecting the U.S. and its territories have been responsible for almost 470 fatalities and hundreds of millions of dollars in property, infrastructure, transportation, and lifeline damage. The U.S. has not experienced a major tsunami since the Great Alaskan Earthquake at Prince William Sound on March 28, 1964. That event killed 10 people and caused more than $7 million in property damage in Crescent City, California. It caused 106 fatalities and more than $84 million in damage in Alaska.

The Pacific Northwest is vulnerable to tsunamis generated by local and distant earthquakes throughout the Pacific Ocean basin. The greatest tsunami threat for the Pacific Northwest results from earthquakes generated along the Cascadia Subduction Zone (CSZ).

The last major tsunami event in the Cascadia region was the 1964 Alaskan earthquake mentioned above, which produced waves of more than 4 meters (13 feet) at several locations along the west coast. Since that time, several earthquakes in the Pacific Basin have resulted in tsunami warnings and/or measurable events along the west coast, including the April 1992 Cape Mendocino earthquake.

While none of these events have resulted in major damage, the great increase in coastal development in recent decades warrants attention and mitigation for tsunami hazards.

Even since the disaster have been talked about it was taken up always lightly because such events never took place as been dictated by weather department or else were being talked by a person believed to have exploited. After Tsunami episode people started realising the talks given by, Brahma Kumaris under Shiva baba for total disaster, any moment, taking place in this world destroying every one except few, who would be called, Gods of Ist period of age, Sat Yuga again would reappear. Whether it would be sea which occupies three fourth of the Clobe and other rivers mingling with that, would form a sizeable height not reachable by steps or any building. The damns are believed to be sustaining an earthquake of maximum intensity of 7.3 on richter scale. Imagine the consequences of a land slide shown on television when a number of villages were washed away in Uttaranchal. The earthquakes mystery is different as electric poles, boundary walls, structures tumble down as debris lies on the ground.

It is of course not possible to predict the time and intensity of the disaster as anything can happen. The rails could collide headway with another rail or Aeroplanes blast away, the tornadoes push up all those upside down in the air for more than a kilometre. Only efforts could be made to deal the disaster after it covers as within seconds the picture becomes different.

WORLDWIDE OCCURRENCE OF TSUNAMIS

Tsunamis have been reported since ancient times. They have been documented extensively, especially in Japan and the Mediterranean areas. The first recorded tsunami occurred off the coast of Syria in 2000 B.C. Since 1900 (the beginning of instrumentally located earthquakes), most tsunamis have been generated in Japan, Peru, Chile, New Guinea and the Solomon

Islands. However, the only regions that have generated remote-source tsunamis affecting the entire Pacific Basin are the Kamchatka Peninsula, the Aleutian Islands, the Gulf of Alaska, and the coast of South America. Hawaii, because of its location in the center of the Pacific Basin, has experienced tsunamis generated in all parts of the Pacific.

The Mediterranean and Caribbean Seas both have small subduction zones, and have histories of locally destructive tsunamis. Only a few tsunamis have been generated in the Atlantic and Indian Oceans. In the Atlantic Ocean, there are no subduction zones at the edges of plate boundaries to spawn such waves except small subduction zones under the Caribbean and Scotia arcs. In the Indian Ocean, however, the Indo-Australian plate is being subducted beneath the Eurasian plate at its east margin. Therefore, most tsunamis generated in this area are propagated toward the southwest shores of Java and Sumatra, rather than into the Indian Ocean.

The Most Dangerous Tsunami Experience

Huge tidal waves, triggered by a massive underseaearthquake off Sumatra in Indonesia, killed over 1,50,000 people—fishermen, people living in the coastal regions, tourists, holiday-makers, people going for a morning walk and even children playing cricket on the beach—on December 26, 2004, just a day after Christmas. For millions of survivors of what is called tsunami—earthquake-driven killer waves—the future has become a hideous nightmare in India, Sri Lanka, Indonesia, Thailand, Malaysia, Myanmar, Maldives—in all twelve countries.

The earthquake, which had its epicentre 257 km south and south-west of Banda Aceh, Sumatra, measured 8.9 on the Richter scale making it the most powerful since 1900 and the strongest since a 9.2 tremor slammed Alaska in 1964. The marauding killer waves spared none and nothing—buldings, cars, trucks and even a running train in Sri Lanka and thousands of innocent lives. Man and everything he built seemed vulnerable before the waves that rose as high as six meters throughout the Indian Ocean and the Andaman Sea. The worst affected States in India were Tamil Nadu, Pondicherry, Andhra Pradesh and Kerala. The island Andaman and Nicobar were badly muded by the demon waves.

The word tsunami is of Japanese origin which means "harbour wave.'Tsu' means harbour and 'nami' stands for wave. Tsunamis are large waves that are generated when the sea floor is deformed by scismic activity, vertically displacing the overlying water in the ocean.

The United States Geological Survey recorded the magnitude of the earthquake of Sumatra at 8.9 with the epicentre lying 10 km below the seabed. Aftershocks struck in the magnitude 7 range. The quake occurred at a place where several massive geological plates push aganist each other with massive force.

CHARACTERISTICS OF TSUNAMI

Most tsunamis are caused by a rapid vertical movement along a break in the Earth's crust (i.e., their origin is tectonic). A tsunami is generated when a large mass of earth on the bottom of the ocean drops or rises, thereby displacing the column of water directly above it. This type of displacement commonly occurs in large subduction zones, where the collision of two tectonic plates causes the oceanic plate to dip beneath the continental plate to form deep ocean trenches. Most

Subduction occurs along most of the island arcs and coastal areas of the Pacific, the notable exception being the west coast of the United States and Canada. Movement along the faults there is largely strike-slip, having little vertical displacement, and the movement produces few local tsunamis.

Volcanoes have generated significant tsunamis with death tolls as large as 30,000 people from a single event. Roughly one fourth of the deaths occurring during volcanic eruptions where tsunamis were generated, were the result of the tsunami rather than the volcano. A tsunami is an effective transmitter of energy to areas outside the reach of the volcanic eruption itself. The most efficient methods of tsunami generation by volcanoes include disruption of a body of water by the collapse of all or part of the volcanic edifice, subsidence, an accompanying or preceding the eruption. Roughly one-half of all volcanic tsunamis are generated at calderas or at cones within calderas. Submarine eruptions may also cause minor tsunamis.

Locally destructive tsunamis may be generated by subaerial and submarine landslides into bays or lakes. Lituya Bay, Alaska, has been the site of several landslide-generated tsunamis, including one in 1958 that produced a splash wave that removed trees to a height of 525 m. It also caused a tsunami of at least 50 m in the bay. The 1964 Prince William Sound earthquake triggered at least four submarine landslides, which accounted for 71 to 82 of the 106 fatalities in Alaska for the 1964 event. However, it is tectonic earthquake-generated tsunamis (those produced by a major deformation of Earth's crust) that may affect the entire Pacific Basin.

Other possible but less efficient methods of tsunami generation include: strong oscillations of the bottom of the ocean, or transmission of energy to a column of water from a seismic impulse (e.g., a deep-focus earthquake that has no surface rupture); transmission of energy from a horizontal seismic impulse to the water column through a vertical or inclined wall such as a bathymetric ridge; strong turbidity currents; underwater and above-water explosions. Several mechanisms commonly are involved in the generation of a tsunami (e.g., vertical movement of the crust by a seismic impulse or an earthquake, and a submarine landslide).

Our knowledge of tsunami generation is incomplete, because the generation phenomena has not been observed nor measured directly. However, studies of tsunami data suggest that the size of a tsunami is directly related to: the shape of the rupture zone, the rate of displacement and sense of motion of the ocean-floor in the source (epicentral) area, the amount of displacement of the rupture zone, and the depth of the water in the source area.

It is also observed that long-period tsunamis are generated by large-magnitude earthquakes associated with seafloor deformation of the continental shelf; while, shorter period tsunamis are generated by smaller magnitude earthquakes associated with seafloor deformation in deeper water beyond the continental shelf.

Once the energy from an undersea disturbance has been transmitted to the column of water, the wave can propagate outward from the source at a speed of more than 1,000 km per hour depending on the depth of the water. Because the height of the long-period waves in the open ocean is commonly 1 m or less and their wavelength is hundreds of kilometers, they pass unnoticed by observers in ships or planes in the velocity of its waves is reduced, and the height of each wave increases. The waves pile up on shore especially in the region of the earthquake source, producing a "local tsunami." Some dramatic examples of such local tsunamis include those generated by landslides or by volcanic eruptions, which have caused "runup" heights of 30 to 50 m in some coastal areas.

"Runup" is the maximum height of the water observed above a reference sea level. Two other terms may be determined from the runup value: (1) tsunami magnitude, which is defined (Iida and others, 1967) as

$$m = \log_2 H$$

and (2) tsunami intensity, which is defined (Soloviev and Go, 1974) as

$$I = \log_2(2^{1/2} * H),$$

where H in both equations is the maximum runup height of the wave.

If the energy produced by the generating disturbance is sufficiently large, such as that released by a major deformation of the crust in a trench area, the resulting tsunami wave may cross the open ocean and emerge as a destructive wave many thousands of kilometers from its source. The severity of a tsunami of this type—called a "remote-observed and perhaps cause damage throughout the Pacific Ocean Basin (e.g., the Chile tsunami of May 1960).

Radiation of a remote-source tsunami from the focus of an earthquake is directional, depending on the geometry of the seafloor in the source region. The source region for major tectonic earthquakes is usually elliptical, and the major axis is as much as 600 km long and corresponds to the activated part of the fault. The major part of the tsunami energy is transmitted at right angles to the direction of the major axis, both toward the near shore and along a great circle path toward the shore on the opposite side of the ocean. Thus, tsunamis in Chile have severe impact on Japan; and those in the Gulf of Alaska on the west coast of North America. Hawaii, which lies in the central Pacific Basin, is vulnerable to remote-source tsunamis generated both in the North Pacific and along the coast of South America.

The velocity (V) of a tsunami in the open ocean is expressed as the product of the square root of the depth of the water (d) and the acceleration of the force of gravity (g).

$$V = (dg)^{1/2}$$

Because the speed of the tsunami depends on the depth of the ocean basin, the waves decrease in speed as they reach shallower water. The wavelength is shortened, the energy within each wave is crowded into progressively less water, increasing the height of the wave. The tsunami may increase in height from 1 m in the open ocean to more than 20 m during runup. Also, if underwater ridges are present, they may act as collecting lenses and further intensify the tsunami.

If the tsunami encounters a coastal scarp, the height of its waves increases. Because the long-period wave can bend around obstacles, the tsunami can enter bays and gulfs having the most intricate shapes. Experience has shown that wave heights increase in bays that narrow from the entrance to the head, but decrease in bays that have narrow entrances. Shores of islands protected by coral reefs commonly receive less energy than unprotected coastlines lying in the direct path of an approaching tsunami. Islands in a group may "shadow" one another reducing the tsunami effect. Small islands may experience reduced runup as the tsunami waves may refract around them.

A tsunami wave may break on the beach, appear as flooding, or form a "bore"(violent rush of water with an abrupt front) as it moves up a river or stream. When the trough of the wave arrives first, the water level drops rapidly. Where this occurs the harbor or offshore area may be drained of its water, exposing sea life and ocean bottom. This phenomenon may be the only warning to residents that a large tsunami is approaching. Fatalities have occurred where people have tried to take advantage of this situation to gather fish or explore the strange landscape. The wave returns to cover the exposed coastline faster than the people can run. Although there may be an interval of minutes—or perhaps an hour—between the arrival of waves, the second, third, or later waves can be more destructive than the first. Residents returning too soon to the waterfront, assuming that the worst has past, represent another kind of preventable fatalities.

8

The International Decade for Natural Disaster Reduction

We have seen, above, the types of responses which can *be* made to geohazards and of how these responses apply in the context of health and safety and planning legislation and policy in the United Kingdom. However, it is not yet clear that any lessons learnt from experience in Britain and elsewhere are being applied in the areas where such hazards are both more common and more hazardous. To do so we need to examine briefly the international response to geohazards.

Considering that natural disasters have claimed about 3 million lives in the past two decades, adversely affected 800 million more people and resulted in immediate damages in excess of US$23 billion, and recognising the potential positive effects of scientific and technical advances in the field of natural disasters, the United Nations General Assembly decided in resolution 42/169 of 11 December 1987:

> "to designate the 1990s as a decade in which the international community, under the auspices of the United Nations, will pay special attention to fostering international cooperation in the field of natural disaster reduction."

As modified by resolution 43/202 (United Nations, 1988) and 44/236 (United Nations, 1989), the objective of this International Decade for Natural Disaster Reduction is:

> "to reduce through concerted international actions, especially in developing countries, loss of life, property damage and social and economic disruption caused by natural disasters

such as earthquakes, wind-storms (cyclones, hurricanes, tornadoes, typhoons), tsunamis, floods, landslides, volcanic eruptions, wildfires, grasshopper and locust infestations drought and desertification and other calamities of natural origin."

The General Assembly also established five goals for the Decade:

(a) "to improve the capacity of each country to mitigate the effects of natural disasters expeditiously and effectively, paying special attention to assisting developing countries in the assessment of disaster damage potential and in the establishment of early warning systems and disaster-resistant structures when and where needed;

(b) "to devise appropriate guidelines and strategies for applying existing scientific and technical knowledge, taking into account the cultural and economic diversity among nations;

(c) "to foster scientific and engineering endeavours aimed at closing critical gaps in knowledge in order to reduce loss of life and property;

(d) "to disseminate existing and new technical information related to measures for the assessment, prediction and mitigation of natural disasters; and

(e) "to develop measures for the assessment, prediction, prevention and mitigation of natural disasters through programmes of technical assistance and technology transfer, demonstration projects, and education and training tailored to specific disasters and locations and to evaluate the effectiveness of those programmes."

Day-to-day activities of the Decade are to be coordinated by a small secretariat in association with the UN Disaster Relief Organisation (UNDRO) in Geneva. Preparations for the Decade began with the establishment in 1988 of:

(a) a UN Steering Committee, composed of all the relevant entities of the United Nations system; and

(b) a Scientific and Technical Committee on the International Decade for Natural Disaster Reduction of 20-25 scientific and technical experts to develop overall programmes to be taken into account in bilateral and multilateral cooperation for the Decade, paying attention to priorities and gaps in technical knowledge identified at the national level, to assess and evaluate the activities carried out in the course of the Decade and to make recommendations on the overall programmes in an annual report to the Secretary-General.

In addition to these organisational arrangements, Resolution 44/236 also established the policy measures to be taken at national level. These include:

(a) formulation of natural disaster mitigation programmes and economic, land-use and insurance policies for disaster prevention, all fully integrated into national development programmes;

(b) participation in concerted international action for the reduction of natural disasters, with the establishment, where appropriate, of national committees in co-operation with the relevant scientific and technological communities;

(c) encouragement of support from both the public and private sectors in contributing towards achieving the aims of the Decade;

(d) keeping the Secretary-General informed so that the United Nations may become an international centre for the exchange of information and coordination of international efforts;

(e) taking the necessary measures to increase public awareness of damage risk probabilities and of the significance of preparedness, prevention, relief and short-term recovery activities with respect to natural disasters;

(f) paying due attention to the impact of natural disasters on health care and to activities to mitigate the vulnerability of critical social and economic infrastructure;

(g) improving the early international availability of emergency supplies through the identification and storage of such supplies in disaster-prone areas.

Through the activities of the International Decade for Natural Disaster Reduction, it is expected that significant strides can be made in the application of some of the lessons already learnt in different countries to be applied on a much wider scale in order to reduce the impact of geohazards. Whilst it is not expected in the majority of cases that the events which lead to hazards can be avoided, it is expected that the hazard involved can be reduced. It is perhaps of interest in this context to examine briefly the reaction in Britain to the International Decade and how that could assist the achievement of its objective and goals.

It has clearly not been possible to review the whole field of policies in response to geohazards. All that has been attempted is an explanation of the types of response which are operated, with some examples from the developed world of the legislation which has been enacted to implement those responses. In particular, brief examples have been quoted from Britain of the development of health and safety legislation with respect to underground mining and of the planning and related legislation and policy statements in amplification of that legislation.

During the 1990s, there is considerable potential for advances to be made on a world scale through the activities of the International Decade for Natural Disaster Reduction.

Whilst there may be lessons to be learnt from those countries in the developed world which have a well developed legislative and policy framework for dealing with natural disasters, whether due to geohazards or not, it will be important not to try to impose solutions on countries which do not yet have this framework. To attempt to do so will undoubtedly, and justifiably, meet with political resistance and will be unlikely to be commendable to the population of the country affected.

It is important, however, that the lessons that can be learnt are applied as wisely as possible, particularly in the light of the growing world population and its increasing concenration in both urban areas and in areas which are prone to geohazards.

In South America, for example, the population has increased by a factor of three in the last our decades. Hermelin (1989) illustrated these factors in Colombia, where, between 1960 and 1983, population increased from 15.5 million to 27.5 million whilst experiencing an enormous increase of urban population. At the end of the 1950s, rural population in Colombia was 73%; it is now 34%, and the country has now more that 30 cities with more than 100,000 inhabitants. Medellin, the second largest city, has grown from 500,000 in 1951 to 2.3 million in 1988. Needless to say, much of this urban increase has occurred through the occupation of areas which are not necessarily suitable for such uses. e.g. because they are too steep, unstable, subject to flooding, etc.

It is also evident that some of these lessons are being learnt and Hermelin (1989) gave a useful resume of the development of environmental management in Colombia in the last 20 years or so from the adoption of the National Code on Natural Resources and Environment in 1974 to the adoption of the Urban Reform Law in 1989, under which cities and villages must prepare a Development Plan which necessarily has to include a set of regulators on urban land uses and the identification of natural risks. However, he also stated that, at the time of writing only one province in Colombia had taken action to enforce the Urban Reform Law.

Thus, although some significant steps have been taken, there remain problems in the implementation and enforcement of the necessary policies and legislation which will bring about a much-needed reduction in the exposure of human society to the environmental risks arising from geohazards. These problems arise both from the technical nature of the hazards and from the social and economic structure of the societies affected.

For example, the trigger level for any evacuation procedures for an impending disaster will be difficult to establish, and it will be difficult to persuade people whose immediate concern is merely staying alive that they should not develop (often illegally) shanty towns in the most hazardous areas, which is where they tend to be located. The Superbarrio (Superman) figure who appeared in Mexico City after the 1985 earthquake may be an effective means of protest after the event to ensure that the needs of the people are given more consideration in reconstruction, but to a large extent that is too late.

Much more effort needs to be concentrated on disaster prevention and preparedness, and this has been rightly stressed by the United Nations with respect to the International Decade.

In many countries, as in the UK, the targeting of new development away from hazardous zones may be relatively straightforward, provided that such zones have been identified and the procedures are in place to consider them in the planning of new development. However, it is certain that, in many places where development already exists, there are geohazards which have either only been recognised subsequent to the development or were not considered to be hazardous at the time of the development. In such situations there may be serious difficulties in avoiding serious personal disruption in developing a hazard management programme. It is likely that, in many such cases, crisis management and planning for losses may be the only viable option.

Two particular elements of policy are seen as essential in dealing with geohazards and these have been recognised in relation to the International Decade. They are:

1. Enhancement of scientific advances to improve hazard management procedures; and
2. Dissemination of both scientific knowledge and policy mechanisms.

It is equally clear that public awareness is all important. If the general public are aware and accept what is needed in particular hazard management situations, then it is more likely that the politicians and decision-makers will also be aware, and a response will be forthcoming. It is perhaps important, therefore, that the level of publicity and education in respect of the various scientific and policy aspects of geohazards will need to be not at the level of the scientific or technical journal or conference (though these are obviously of value), but at the level of the popular press.

At the beginning of the International Decade for Natural Disaster Reduction, it is important that we look forward with optimism to the time when the press will be reporting geo-events as *hazards which have been overcome* or *avoided* rather than as the natural disasters which are reflected in the references at the end of this paper. We have a much greater understanding today of the causes of such hazards than ever we had in the past and we are much nearer to developing the necessary policy responses to deal with them. The opportunity is there for all to share in this understanding and to learn from both the successes of others and the mistakes that have been made.

9

Declaration of Guayaquil El Nino

GUAYAQUIL, ECUADOR, 13 NOVEMBER 1998

The Government of Ecuador, representatives from public and governmental authorities from countries affected by El Niño, representatives from concerned agencies and organizations from the United Nations system, the Permanent Commission of the South Pacific, and experts from the international scientific community as well as participants from other concerned sectors of society, assembled on the occasion of the First Intergovernmental Meeting of Experts on El Niño, called for by the United Nations General Assembly in its resolution 52/200:

Reaffirm their commitment to continue in their efforts to reduce the negative impacts of the El Niño phenomenon, in line with resolution A/C.2/53/L.30 of the fifty-third United Nations General Assembly which calls, inter-alia, for the full and continued implementation of General Assembly resolution 52/200.

Conclude that the global pattern of climate extremes associated with the 1997-1998 El Niño event caused loss of life, the destruction of shelter and food reserves, the disruption of food production and transport systems, and sudden exposure to extreme health risks; they imposed continuing poverty on peoples and set back development in many parts of the globe.

Underline that natural disaster reduction forms an integral

part of sustainable development strategies, at all levels, and must take into full consideration the interrelationship between climate variabilities such as the El Niño and the La Niña phenomena, the consequences of global climate change and the vulnerability of communities at risk from natural disasters that may be induced by extreme climatic conditions.

Emphasize the need for synergies between science and technology, public and private sector decision makers and planners, as well as the public at large, in order to ensure the effective planning and implementation of measures that would prevent the negative impacts of the El Niño phenomenon and similar climate variabilities.

Call at the same time for integrated approaches to identify positive effects of such phenomena, in order to determine how to draw maximum benefits, where possible.

Recognize the opportunities for interdisciplinary and multisectoral research, applied science and technology, and preventive action which are provided by the United Nations Inter Agency Task Force on El Niño, within the framework of the International Decade for Natural Disaster Reduction.

Agree that natural disasters are of global concern, and have their most severe impacts on vulnerable communities, as well as economic and social infrastructures in the developing world, and can therefore contribute to increased poverty if no concrete action is taken towards integrated preventive strategies.

Express their strong conviction that it is necessary to strengthen scientific research on the El Niño and related processes in order to improve the forecasts and apply the results of the scientific research for mitigation of damages and the realisation of potential beneficial effects particularly in support of vulnerable communities.

Express their concern for the loss of human life and the

destruction of economic resources, in particular in the South East Pacific region, which have occurred as a result of the 1997-1998 El Niño event, as well as in other countries which have suffered recently from the devastating impacts of climatic extremes.

Reiterate their wish to intensify international cooperation, including multilateral projects for scientific cooperation and technology transfer designed to enhance the resilience of urban infrastructures and agricultural zones in order to lessen the negative impacts of El Niño.

Conclude that urgent actions are required to strengthen many existing intergovernmental programmes to achieve the objectives of United Nations General Assembly Resolution 52/200:

" Improved monitoring of the climate system, especially through the development of regional networks and the implementation of operational systems that have demonstrated proven value from research. Commitment of new funding for multi-purpose space based systems and in-situ observing networks of the Global Climate Observing System is necessary to achieve this objective.

" Expanded ongoing research directed towards improved prediction of climate variability on seasonal to interannual time-scales. The World Climate Research Programme has demonstrated its effectiveness as a research framework, and commitment of new funds to the Climate Variability and Predictability Programme (CLIVAR) will give an important impetus to this established activity.

" Development and implementation of new climate early warning systems at the regional levels where required, and the strengthening of existing systems. The technological infrastructure, including specialized observing networks and regional communications and computing capabilities for data collection, analysis and prediction are costly and beyond the financial reach of most developing countries. Commitment of new funds will be necessary to establish a network of national and regional centres and is essential for supporting national climate services in countries of the developing world.

" Ensuring that the information needs of national sectors vulnerable to climate extremes are met through regional and sector specific studies to develop knowledge of vulnerability and sensitivity that is essential to underpin sound planning for protection, prevention and mitigation of negative impacts of El Nino and related events. Commitment of new funds for the purpose of impact assessments and the development of appropriate response strategies is required to reduce climate risk and establish safe community habitats.

" Capacity building at the regional and national levels in the areas of observational techniques, data management and processing and in the use and interpretation of climate information and predictions for the early warning and prevention of natural disasters

Emphasize the importance of developing regional models for the South East Pacific and other affected areas to match the scientific aspects with the social and economic factors.

Emphasize that the South East Pacific region represents one natural, strategic and continuous case study platform for ongoing research on the prediction and monitoring of the El Niñ o phenomenon, on the forecasting of its effects, on projecting its impacts and providing early warning, and for developing and applying preventive measures.

Also emphasize that it is of utmost importance to join efforts of all countries affected by El Niño for the permanent study and monitoring of the phenomenon globally, in real time, which would enable the timely formulation of prevention and mitigation measures, through the creation of an international specialized center in the South East Pacific region.

Recommend immediate action to assess the feasibility of establishing an International Center for the Research of the El Niño Phenomenon, in Guayaquil, as proposed by the Government of Ecuador, and suggest that such action be undertaken within the context of the United Nations Inter Agency Task Force on El Niño, and the results to be reflected in the report on the implementation of the United Nations General Assembly Resolution A/C.2/53/L.30 to the next United Nations General Assembly through the 1999 substantive session of the Economic and Social Council.

Take note, with appreciation, of the results of the ninth Session of the Joint IOC/WMO/CPPS Technical Group carried out in Guayaquil on November 5-7, 1998.

Entrust the Government of Ecuador, the agencies and organizations of the United Nations involved and the Permanent Commission of the South Pacific, to present the conclusions and the recommendations of the International Seminar on the 1997-1998 El Niño Event: Evaluation and Projections, in appropriate international forums related to the impacts of El Niño and related climate events.

Entrust the Government of Ecuador to present the results of this First Intergovernmental Meeting of experts on El Niño and this Declaration to the current fifty-third session of the United Nations General Assembly.

10

Environment and Policy Retrospective (1972-2002): Global Overview

Disasters can occur as a consequence of the impact of a natural or a human-caused hazard. Natural hazards comprise phenomena such as earthquakes, volcanic activity, landslides, tsunamis, tropical cyclones and other severe storms, tornadoes and high winds, river and coastal flooding, wildfires and associated haze, drought, sand and dust storms, and infestations. Human-caused hazards may be intentional, such as the illegal discharge of oil, or accidental such as toxic spills or nuclear meltdown. All of these can expose people, ecosystems, flora and fauna to threats. The poor are the most vulnerable to disasters because they have fewer resources and capacity to prevent or cope with the impacts.

Natural Disasters

People and the environment are increasingly suffering from the effects of natural disasters. There are a number of reasons for this such as high population growth and density, migration and unplanned urbanization, environmental degradation and possibly global climate change. The sheer scope of the socio-economic impacts of natural disasters has brought about a shift in the political approach to dealing with the concept of risk in modern societies.

Comparing the past two decades, the number of people killed in natural and non-natural disasters was higher in the 1980s (86328 annually) than in the 1990s (75252 annually).

However, more people were affected by disasters in the 1990s — up from an average of 147 million a year in the 1980s to 211 million people a year in the 1990s. While the number of geophysical disasters has remained fairly steady, the number of hydrometeorological disasters (those caused by water and weather) has increased (see figure on page 271). In the 1990s, more than 90 per cent of those killed in natural disasters lost their lives in hydrometeorological events such as droughts, windstorms and floods. While floods accounted for more than two-thirds of people affected by natural disasters, they are less deadly than many other types of disaster, accounting for only 15 per cent of deaths (IFRC 2001).

The social and economic costs of disasters vary widely and are difficult to estimate on a global basis. Insurance claims tend to be misleading as an estimate of the economic impact of disasters. Considering insured damage claims for the 1999 floods in Austria, Germany and Switzerland, at least 42.5 per cent of damage was covered by disaster insurance. But in Venezuela the same year, only 4 per cent of flood damage was covered (CRED-OFDA 2002). There is a need for reliable and systematic data on disasters to help assess their socio-economic and environmental impacts in both the short and the long term. But although communities in developing countries suffer from numerous local-scale disasters such as wildfires, small floods, droughts and pest infestations, these are often not reflected in disaster statistics.

The most expensive disasters in purely financial and economic terms are floods, earthquakes and windstorms but events such as drought and famine can be more devastating in human terms. While earthquakes accounted for 30 per cent of estimated damage, they caused just 9 per cent of all fatalities due to natural disasters. In contrast, famine killed 42 per cent, but accounted for just 4 per cent of damage over the past decade (IFRC 2001). In 1999, global financial losses from natural catastrophic events were estimated to exceed US$100 billion — the second highest figure on record. A total of 707 large events were recorded compared to 530 to 600 events in previous years. It is even more striking that the number of major catastrophic events over the past decade has increased threefold in comparison with the 1960s, while the rate of economic losses has increased by a factor of almost nine over the same period (Munich Re 2001).

Between 1995 and 1997, the impacts of natural hazards cost the United States at least US$50 billion a year, or the equivalent of about US$1 billion a week (IDNDR 1999a). The economic losses of the United States because of the 1997-98 El Nino event were estimated at US$1.96 billion or 0.03 per cent of GDP. Ecuador suffered equivalent financial losses but this represented 11.4 per cent of its GDP. The floods in China in 1991, 1994-95 and 1998 caused losses ranging from US$20 to 35 billion (CNC-IDNDR 1999).

The annual loss from natural disasters over the period from 1989 to 1996 is estimated to range from 3 to 6 per cent of China's GDP, averaging 3.9 per cent. In December 1999, the Anatol, Lothar and Martin storms generated losses in northern Europe amounting to US$5-6 billion (Munich Re 2001). Less developed countries with limited economic diversity and poor infrastructure must not only rely mostly on external relief if a disaster happens but their economies need more time to recover. In developed economies, governments, communities and individuals have greater capacities to cope with disasters, the economic losses are to some extent absorbed by a diversified economy, and most assets are insured.

Among the least developed countries, 24 of the 49 face high levels of disaster risk; at least six of them have been affected by between two and eight major disasters per year in the past 15 years, with long-term consequences for human development (UNDP 2001). Since 1991, more than half of all the disasters reported occurred in countries with medium levels of human development (see 'Socio-economic background'). However, two-thirds of those killed came from countries with low levels of human development, while just 2 per cent came from highly developed countries. The effect of development on disasters is dramatic: on average, 22.5 people die per reported disaster in highly developed countries, 145 die per disaster in countries with medium human development, and 1052 people die per disaster in countries with low levels of development (IFRC 2001).

A number of experts link the current trend in extreme weather events with an increase of the global mean temperature. Many parts of the world have suffered major heat waves, floods, droughts and other extreme weather events. While individual events, such as El Nino-related phenomena (see box), cannot be directly linked to human-induced climate change, the frequency and magnitude of these types of events are predicted to increase in a warmer world. The changes in the global mean temperature are 'very likely' to affect parameters such as precipitation patterns, wind velocities, soil moisture and vegetation cover which appear to influence the occurrence of storms, hurricanes, floods, drought and landslides (IPCC 2001). For example, the extent of damage from storm surges can be directly linked to sea level variations.

Climate change and variability alone do not explain the increase in the impacts related to disasters. 'Natural' can be a misleading description for disasters such as the droughts, floods and cyclones which afflict much of the developing world. Identifying human-induced root causes, and advocating structural and political changes to combat them, is long overdue (IFRC 2001). For example, destruction of the natural environment because of logging or inappropriate land uses for short-term economic gain is one of the major factors promoting floods or mudslides such as those that hit Venezuela in December 1999. Similarly, the migration of population to urban and coastal areas increases human vulnerability as population densities increase, infrastructure becomes overloaded, living areas move closer to potentially dangerous industries, and more settlements are built in fragile areas such as floodplains or areas prone to landslides. As a result, natural catastrophes affect more people and economic losses are increased. For example, despite the fact that seismic activity has remained constant over recent years, the effects of earthquakes on the urban population appear to be increasing.

Socio-economic Effects of 1997-98 El Nino

The 1997-98 El Nino event affected virtually every region: Eastern Africa suffered drought and unusually high rainfall; Southeast Asia and North America, abnormally warm periods; South Asia, drought; Latin America and the Caribbean, unusually high rainfall and drought; and the Pacific Islands unusually high rainfall. The global socio-economic impacts were varied:

- More than 24 000 people died because of high winds, floods or storm tides that occurred during intense storms.
- More than 110 million people were affected and more than 6 million people were displaced as community infrastructures, including housing, food storage, transport and communications, were lost during storms.
- Direct economic losses exceeded US$34 billion.
- Waterlogging of fields reduced agricultural production in many regions; in others, the absence of storms and rain led to prolonged dry spells, loss of crops and reduction in water supplies.
- Wildfires were more frequent and widespread during extended dry periods.
- Increased incidence of disease followed the prolonged

disruption to weather and rainfall patterns that resulted in contamination of water supplies or a more favourable environment for disease-carrying insect vectors.

(Sources: *WMO 1999, UNU 2001*)

Human-induced Disasters

A number of major accidents involving chemicals and radioactive materials have drawn attention worldwide to the dangers of mismanagement, particularly in the transport, chemical and nuclear power sectors. These events often have impacts that transcend national boundaries; they also emphasize the fact that issues of technological safety concern more than just the developed countries.

Some disasters have resulted in the introduction of voluntary or mandatory regulations designed to prevent similar occurrences. Public concern following the explosion in 1976 at a pesticide plant in Seveso, Italy, with the release of 2,3,7,8-tetrachlorodibenzo-p-dioxin (TCDD), led to the introduction in 1982 of a European Directive on the major-accident hazards of certain industrial activities. Similarly, other major accidents, such as the methyl isocyanate leak at Bhopal, India, in 1984 and the Switzerland-Sandoz warehouse fire in Basel in 1989, stimulated legislation in many countries to prevent and control chemical incidents. Influenced by the Bhopal accident, in particular, the International Labour Office developed in 1993 the Convention Concerning the Prevention of Major Industrial Accidents No. 174 and the Prevention of Major Industrial Accidents Recommendation No. 181. These documents call for an international exchange of relevant information, development of policies aimed at addressing the major accident risks, hazards and their consequences, and recognition that a major accident could have serious impacts on human life and the environment.

Major nuclear accidents such as those at Three Mile Island in the United States in 1979 and at Chernobyl in 1986 have not only catalysed action to strengthen nuclear safety and emergency preparedness but also forced many countries to abandon or severely restrict development of the nuclear power sector. Following the Chernobyl accident, two major international treaties were adopted — the Convention on Assistance in the Case of Nuclear Accident or Radiological Emergency and the Convention on the Early Notification of a Nuclear Accident. Most recently, the 1994 Convention on Nuclear Safety, committing parties to a higher level of nuclear safety, and the 1997 joint Convention on the Safety of Spent Fuel Management and on the Safety of Radioactive Waste Management were adopted.

The 1989 *Exxon Valdez* oil spill in Alaska resulted in enormous environmental and economic damages and catalysed the development of the 'Valdez Principles' — a voluntary code of conduct for corporate behaviour towards the environment — by the Coalition for Environmentally Responsible Economics (CERES). The 'Valdez Principles' guide corporations in the establishment of environmentally sound policies and require the raising of corporate environmental safety standards and the taking of responsibility for environmental harm that may be caused by them (Adams 1994).

International Policy Responses

Until the 1970s, the international community considered disasters as exceptional circumstances, when local coping capacities were exhausted and external emergency relief was required. The term disaster management was generally equivalent to disaster response and tended to be within the exclusive competence of organizations such as the Red Cross and Red Crescent Societies or national civil defence institutions.

In 1971, the United Nations Disaster Relief Office, now the United Nations Office for the Coordination of Humanitarian Affairs (UNOCHA), was established to mobilize and coordinate relief activities from all sources in times of disaster. The concept of disaster preparedness was developed during the 1970s and 1980s, and included training and some cross-sectoral activities to increase capacity for rescue, relief and rehabilitation during and after a disaster. But even the most pessimistic forecasts could not have foreseen the upward spiral in negative socio-economic consequences of natural disasters in the closing decades of the 20th century.

China Committed to Risk Reduction

The Chinese government is shifting the focus of its disaster policies from improving response capabilities to reducing hazards and risks. During the past ten years, national coordination has been vested in the Chinese National Committee (CNC) for the IDNDR, an inter-ministerial organization composed of representatives from 28 ministries, departments and commissions. Since 1989, CNC has been working on the National Natural Disaster Reduction Plan of the People's Republic of China (1998-2010). It has also helped to develop and coordinate policies and plans for national and local disaster reduction activities.

Motivated by the seriousness of the 1991 floods in China, the Chinese authorities recognized the need 'to integrate disaster reduction into the comprehensive plan for national economy and social development'. The Chinese National Centre for Natural Disaster Reduction has now been established within the Chinese Academy of Sciences. The centre compiles and analyses data on disasters, and passes the results to the State Council for decision-making responsibilities.

China experienced its worst floods in more than 100 years in 1999, which affected more than 300 million people. The floods galvanized more political commitment for the integration of risk and disaster prevention programmes into national social and economic planning. However, China believes that there were fewer losses during the 1999 floods in the Yangtze River Valley, despite higher water levels, because of the US$7.6 billion invested in water conservancy measures since the costly 1998 floods. (Source: *CNC-IDNDR 1999)*

The 1990s was declared the International Decade for Natural Disaster Reduction (IDNDR), one of the principal goals of which was to inculcate a culture of disaster prevention through the wider application of known scientific and technological mechanisms by a better-informed population. In the words of United Nations Secretary-General Kofi Annan, 'We must, above all, shift from a culture of reaction to a culture of prevention. The humanitarian community does a remarkable job in responding to disasters. But the most important task in the medium and long-term is to strengthen and broaden programmes which reduce the number and cost of disasters in the first place. Prevention is not only more humane than cure, it is also much cheaper' (IDNDR 1999b). The IDNDR successfully placed risk reduction higher on the political agenda, as well as setting out a number of priorities to be undertaken by countries and regions in the 21st century.

An increasing number of governments and international organizations are promoting risk reduction as the only sustainable solution for reducing the social, economic and environmental impacts of disasters. Risk reduction strategies include:

- vulnerability mapping;
- identification of areas that are safe for settlement and development;
- adoption of building codes based on disaster resilient engineering and on local hazard risk assessments; and
- enforcing these plans and codes by economic and other incentives.

At the global level, the UN has established an International Strategy for Disaster Reduction (ISDR), a global platform aimed at helping all communities to become resilient to the effects of natural disasters and to proceed from protection against hazards to the management of risk through the integration of risk prevention into sustainable development. The strategy—based on the IDNDR experience and developments such as the 1994 Yokohama Strategy and Plan of Action for a Safer World and the 1999 Strategy 'A Safer World in the 21st Century: Disaster and Risk Reduction' — reflects a cross-sectoral and interdisciplinary approach to disaster reduction.

Implementation of the strategy, which is based on the establishment of partnerships between governments, non-governmental organizations, UN agencies, the scientific community and other stakeholders in the disaster reduction community, is an integral part of efforts aimed at promoting the overall goal of sustainable development. It is also an indispensable element in the search for solutions designed to counter the increasing threat posed by natural hazards (ISDR 1999).

Prevention and Preparedness to Reduce the Costs of Disasters

The fundamental goal of the UNEP disaster management programme is to reinforce the centrality of environmental concerns in disaster management. The other cornerstone is the adoption of preventive strategies and practical measures to reduce the potential loss of human lives and property, as well as destruction of the environment.

The success of this approach depends on increasing public awareness of the risks that natural, technological and environmental hazards pose to societies, and on educating people about the value of existing approaches for prevention and preparedness. UNEP contributes to this process through its programmes on environmental law, early warning and assessment, and Awareness and Preparedness for Emergencies at Local Level (APELL).

UNEP's APELL programme, developed in conjunction with governments and industry, recognizes that the incidence and effects of environmental disasters can be reduced by prevention and preparedness initiatives at the local level. The APELL concept has been successfully introduced to more than 30 countries and in more than 80 industrial communities worldwide. The UNEP strategy includes the promotion of cleaner production processes and technologies, and helping countries establish cleaner production centres.

A major objective of the UNEP early warning and assessment programme is to evaluate the increasing vulnerability of human society due to widespread environmental and climatic change in order to emphasize the need for sound integrated environmental management, and to provide early warning of emerging threats for preparedness and response.

Appendices

APPENDIX—I

A COMPREHENSIVE APPROACH ROAD MAP FOR A PLAN PREPARATION PROCESS (PPP)

1. HPC was set up in August 1999 to prepare a Disaster Management Plan for the country for natural disasters, to comprise of national, state and district level plans. At the very outset a need was felt that, from the point of view of consequence management, the distinction of natural and non-natural was academic and the committee should address all types of disasters. The terms of reference of HPC were accordingly modified in February 2000.
2. The approach of HPC is holistic, in line with the Yokohama Strategy evolved during the International Decade of Natural Disaster Reduction (IDNDR) i.e. planning for prevention, mitigation, and preparedness and thereafter response planning, will go a long way to reduce the loss of life and property due to disasters. Effort of HPC is, not to develop a plan de novo, but to build on what obtains at different levels and streamline such bottlenecks as may be existing.
3. 30 odd types of disasters have been identified and the same have been grouped into five categories.
   - (i) Water and Climate related disasters,
   - (ii) Geologically related disasters,
   - (iii) Biologically related disasters,

(iv) Chemical, industrial and Nuclear related disasters, and

(v) Accident related disasters.

The grouping of disasters is at Annexure III. For facility of plan preparation, five sub-groups comprising of concerned depts, have been formed and convenor depts have been indicated to coordinate the preparation of the plan of each sub-group.

4. District Plan

HPC gave top priority to this. A source book has been evolved in consultation with the state Relief Commissioners, Experts and the LBSNAA, Mussoorie in which a format for model District Disaster Management Plan has been suggested. It is proposed that the district plan could be-

(i) For each group of disasters.

(a) one volume of essential details with historical perspective ana current data,

(b) second set of volumes for each type of disaster falling in that group, laying out a prevention plan, a mitigation plan, a preparedness plan, a preparedness plan, and a response plan.

(ii) Districts would start this exercise of plan preparation with the most immediate and frequent disasters, which all the district. The district plan will include plans for the local bodies like municipalities, town areas etc. The mega corporations would be having separate plans on similar lines, for which the state urban development departments would need to take the desired initiative.

(iii) Disasters like drought take a long time to

develop, and the very first signs need to be attended to. Can states adopt schemes like the Employment Guarantees Scheme (EGS) of Maharashtra, where on the first signal of distress the district collector is able to intervene? This is not the same as GOI having schemes in the ministry of rural development to provide for rural employment, GOI funds reach the states only after they have utilised the previously released funds, and, in view of the resource crunch, district collectors are unable to provide relief on the first signal of distress. A state level EGS could take care of such situations, well in time.

5. The State Plan

The state plan would be prepared by the 5 sub-groups similar to the G.O.I. exercise.

(i) Each sub-group would have its own plan-

(a) One volume of essential details with historical perspective and current data.

(b) Second set of volumes for each type of disasters falling in that group, laying out a state-wide or region wise Prevention Plan, and Prevention Strategy; a state-wide, or region-wise Mitigation Plan and Mitigation Strategy; a state-wide, or region-wise Prepareness Plan; a state wide, or region-wise Response Plan.

(ii) The states need to set up the five sub-groups for the five categories of disasters in order to take in hand the process of preparation of the state plan.

6. The National Plan

The National Plan will primarily be a Response Plan of the five sub-groups with

(i) Prevention Plan of inter-state and sub-continental features,
(ii) Prevention Strategy of inter-state and international issues,
(iii) Mitigation Plan of inter-state and sub-continental features,
(iv) Mitigation Strategy of inter-state and international issues,
(v) Preparedness Plan at the national level, and
(vi) SAARC and international initiative in this regard.

7. Updating the Plan and its Rehearsal

A plan is only as good as it is updated and rehearsed. It is suggested that every year "last week of April" be observed as "updating the plan' week and every year "first week of May" be observed as "rehearsing the plan' week throughout the country at district, state and national level to ensure that the plan is implementable. The quality of rehearsal would need to be assessed objectively, one mark for a prescribed act done, zero mark for a prescribed act not done.

8. (i) There is need to integrate the school, college and university systems with disaster preparedness and response mechanism as they are a major systemic casualty of a super disaster, and have a major stake in preventing them, and also in mitigating their impact. Involvement of students and youth would prepare them for discharging their responsibility towards the vulnerable sections of society.

(ii) Development plans at national, state and district level need to apportion funds for prevention and mitigation of disasters, as cost-effectiveness of prevention and mitigation is estimated to reduce relief costs to up to one tenth. Role of NIRD and SIRD's in this regard needs to be emphasised. NIRD may be requested to organise a workshop of SIRD's to evolve norms for apportioning development funds (plan funds) for prevention and mitigation of disasters at national, state and district level.

(iii) This will call for involving and motivating the people's representatives. NGO's etc. A national level consultation with NGOs is being planned at four locations. This should trigger off statewide and district level NGO consultations in association with the people's representatives, and Panchayati Raj bodies.

(iv) There is need for collaboration between Dept. of Space (DOS), Dept of Science and Technology (DST) and Dept of Mines (DOM) at GOI level, and NRSA along with State Remote Sensing Application Centers (SRSAC), Survey of India, Geological Survey of India to prepare geomorphological maps in the scale 1: 50,000 to enable preparation of block-level landuse plans, and block-level drainage plans which would be useful to identify risk-prone areas in the blocks for preparation of micro-watershed plans with the help of village level maps of the State Land Records Department.

9. Trigger Mechanism

The proposed trigger mechanism is a device to minimise response time when disaster strikes.

(i) Civil Defence warden system is a good response mechanism; can it be extended to the whole country? Panchayat members could be wardens in the rural areas.

(ii) Communication links: VHF at each Tahsil/ Taluka; V-sat at each District headquarters; HAM (Help All Mankind) radio promotion programme to be taken up.

(iii) District Control Room/ Shadow Control Room;

State Control Room/ Shadow Control Room; Central Control Room, control room in the convenor/ nodal dept. of each sub-group, control room in each dept. constituting the sub-groups set up by the HPC.

(iv) L1, L2, L3 levels of each type of disaster to be predetermined, to lay out procedures to trigger off the Basic Initial Response Management Steps (BIRMS) without formal orders form anywhere. Sub-groups at national and state levels to address this exercise at the earliest. Normally L2 level of the district will be the L1 level at the state hqs; and L3 level of the district will be the L2 level of the state hqs; L3 level of the state hqs; would normally be the L1 level at the centre.

(v) Police wireless network and Police Control Rooms to be alternate communication system.

(vi) Sub-groups to lay out 'dos' and 'don'ts' for each type of disaster for people and the relief volunteers and personnel, to facilitate relief and rescue activities when disasters strike. These ought to be passed on to the State Resource Centres of the National Literacy Mission for communication the same to the Zilla Saksharta Samitis.

10. Making available consultants at the state and district level; NCDM (IIPA) to oversee this role of state ATIs, along with preparing a panel of consultants at the national level.

(i) State ATIs to play a role in preparing, firstly

(a) The district plans by training officials and non-officials for prevention, mitigation, preparedness and response to disaster; and later, the state plans,

(b) Monitoring the preparation process of district and state plans.

(ii) IIPA/ NCDM to orient central ministries, departments and PSUs, as well as state ATIs, in the trigger mechanism; state ATIs to do a similar exercise with state departments and PSUs.

(iii) State ATIs to play a role in drafting a state act for disaster prevention, mitigation, preparedness and response. Techno-legal regime Vs Techno-socio-movement to be weighed and planned for each state.

11. Networking of knowledge and the learning exercise:

(i) Data from every disaster occurring should be meticulously recorded to serve as a guide for future- this learning exercise should be formalised. A national level consultation is taking place in this regard at Bhopal on 14th and 15th July.

(ii) Similar state and district level exercises need to be organised.

12. So, while the national plan would be ready soon, the state and district plans ought to evolve as suggested in tune with, the best wisdom available in each state and its districts; NCDM would be expected to assist and oversee the entire process till completion of this effort. Thereafter, the process of improving on the plans would continue in line with fresh experience from time to time.

One of the important activities which ought to be taken up on the widest possible scale during normal times, is PLANTING TREES AND SHRUBS of appropriate species of prevent disasters and also to mitigate their impact.

APPENDIX—II

THE COASTAL REGULATION ZONE NOTIFICATION

(As Amended by Notification Dated 16.8.1994, 31.1.1997, 9.7.1997 and Supreme Court Judgment Dated 18.4.1996)

MINISTRY OF ENVIRONMENT AND FORESTS
(Department of Environment, Forests & Wildlife)

NOTIFICATION

New Delhi, the 19th February, 1991
Gazetted on 20.2.1991

Notification under section 3(1) and section 3(2)(v) of the Environment (Protection) Act, 1986 and Rule 5(3)(d) of Environment (Protection) Rules, 1986, Declaring Coastal Stretches as Coastal Regulation Zone (CRZ) and Regulation Activities in the CRZ.

S.O. 114(E).- Whereas a Notification under Section 3 (1) and Section 3(2)(v) of the Environment (Protection) Act, 1986, inviting objections against the declaration of Coastal Stretches as Coastal Regulation Zone (CRZ) and imposing restrictions on industries operations and processes in the CRZ was published vide S.O. No 941 (E) dated 15th December, 1990.

And whereas all objections received have been duly considered by the Central Government:

Now, therefore in exercise of the powers conferred by Clause (d) of sub-rule (3) of Rule 5 of the Environment (Protection) Rules, 1986, and all other powers vesting in its behalf, the Central Government hereby declares the coastal stretches of seas, bays, estuaries, creeks, rivers and backwaters which are influenced by tidal action (in the landward side) upto 500 metres from the High Tide Line (HTL)* and the land between the Low Tide Line (LTL) and the HTL as Coastal Regulation Zone and imposes with effect from the date of this Notification, the following restrictions on the setting up and expansion of industries operations or processes etc., in the said Coastal Regulation Zone (CRZ).

Note: The distance from the High Tide Line shall apply to both sides, in the case of rivers creeks and backwaters may be modified on a case by case basis for reactions to be recorded while preparing the Coastal Zone Management Plans. However, this distance shall not be less than [2][100] metre or the width of the creek, river or backwater whichever is less. The distance upto which development along rivers, creeks and backwaters is to be regulated shall be governed by the distance upto which the tidal effect of sea is experienced in rivers, creeks or back-waters, as the case may be, and should be clearly identified in the Coastal Zone Management Plans.]

Prohibited Activities

The following activities are declared as prohibited within the Coastal Regulation Zone, namely:

(i) setting up of new industries and expansion of existing industries, except those directly related to water front or directly needing foreshore facilities;

(ii) manufacture or handling or storage or disposal of hazardous substances as specified in the Notifications of the Government of India in the Ministry of Environmental & Forest. No. S.O. 594(E) dated 28th July, 1989, S.O. 966(E) dated 27th November, 1989 and GSR 1037(E) dated 5th December, 1989; except transfer of hazardous substances from ships to ports,

---

* For purposes of this Notification, the High Tide Line means the line on the land upto which the highest water line reaches during the spring tide and shall be demarcated uniformly in all parts of the country by the demarcating authority so authorised by the Central Government in consultation with the Surveyor General of India.

terminals and refineries and vice versa in the port areas:

[3][Provided that Government of India in the Ministry of Surface Transport, on a case to case basis, may permit storage of the petroleum products as specified in Annexure-III appended to this notification within the existing port limits of existing ports and harbours and in those areas of ports that have not been classified as CRZ-I subject to implementation of safety regulations including guidelines issued by Oil Safety Directorate in the Government of India, Ministry of Petroleum and Natural Gas after ensuring proper location of site and availability of necessary equipment to meet the safety norms and the exigencies arising due to any accident or spillage].

(iii) Setting up and expansion of fish processing units including warehousing (excluding, hatchery and natural fish drying in permitted areas);

[3]Provided that existing fish processing units for modernisation purposes may utilise twenty five per cent additional plinth area required for additional equipment and pollution control measures only subject existing Floor Space Index, Floor Area Ratio norms and subject to the condition that the additional plinth area shall not be towards seaward side of existing unit and also subject to the approval of State Pollution Control Board or Pollution Control Committee].

(iv) setting up and expansion of units/mechanisms for disposal of waste and effluents, except facilities required for discharging, treated effluents into the water course with approval under the Water (Prevention and Control of Pollution) Act, 1974; and except for storm water drains:

(v) discharge of untreated wastes and effluents from industries cities or towns and other human settlements. Schemes shall be implemented by the concerned authorities for phasing out the existing practices, if any, within a reasonable time period not exceeding three years from the date of this notification;

(vi) dumping of city or town waste for the purposes of land filling or otherwise the existing practice, if any, shall be phased out within a reasonable time not exceeding three years from the date of this Notification;

(vii) dumping of ash or any wastes from thermal power stations;

(viii) [4][land reclamation, bunding or disturbing the natural course of sea water, except those required for construction of port, harbours, jetties, wharves, quays, slipways, bridges and sea-links and for other facilities that are essential for activities permissible under the notification or for control of coastal erosion and maintenance or clearing of waterways, channels and ports and for prevention of sandbars and also except for tidal regulators, storm water drains and structures for prevention of salinity increase and for sweet water recharge;

(ix) mining of lands, rocks and other substrata materials except those rare mineral not available outside the CRZ areas;

[5][Provided that in the Union Territory of the Andman and Nicobar Islands, mining of sands may be permitted by the Committee which shall be constituted by the Lieutenant Goovernor of the Andaman and Nicobar Islands consisting of Chief Secretary; Secretary, Department of Environment; Secretary, Department of Water Resources; and Secretary, Public Works Department Committee may permit mining of sand form non-degraded areas for construction purposes from selected sites, in a regulated manner on a case to case basis, for a period upto the 31st day of March, 1998. The quantity of sand mined shall not exceed the essential requirements for completion of

construction works including dwelling units, shops in respect of current year and 1997-98 annual plans. The permission for mining of sand may be given on the basis of a mining plan from such sites and in such quantity whcih shall not have adverse impacts on the environment.]

(x) harvesting or drawal of ground water and construction of mechanisms therefore within 200 m of HTL: in the 200 m to 500 m zone it shall be permitted only when done manually through ordinary wells for drinking, horticulture agriculture and fisheries;

[6][Provided that drawal of ground water is permitted, where no other source of water is available and when done manually through ordinary wells or hand pumps, for drinking and domestic purposes, zone between 50 to 200 m from High Tide Line in case of seas, bays and estuaries and within 200 m or the CRZ, whichever is less, from High Line in case of rivers, creeks and backwaters subject to such restrictions as may be deemed necessary, in areas affected by sea water intrusion, that may be imposed by a authority designated by State Government/Union Territory Administration].

(xi) construction activities in ecologically sensitive areas as specified in Annexure-I of this Notification;

(xii) any construction activity between the Low Tide Line and High Tide Line except facilities for carrying treated effluents and waste water discharges into the sea facilities for carrying sea water for cooling purposes. Oils gas and similar pipelines and facilities essential for activities permitted under this Notification; and

(xiii) dressing or altering of sand dunes hills, natural features including landscape changes for beautification, recreational and other such purpose, except as permissible under this Notification.

Regulation of Permissible Activities

All other activities, except those prohibited in para 2 above, will be regulated as under:

(1) Clearance shall be given for any activity within the Coastal Regulation Zone only if it requires water front and foreshore facilities.

(2) The following activities will require environmental clearance from the Ministry of Environment & Forests, Government of India, namely:

(i) Construction activities related to Defence requirements for which foreshore facilities are essential (e.g. slipways, jetties etc.); except for classified operational component of defence projects for which a separate procedure shall be followed. (Residential buildings, office buildings, hospital complexes, workshops shall not come within the definition of operational requirements except in very special cases and hence shall not normally be permitted in the CRZ);

(ii) Operational constructions for ports and harbours and light houses and constructions for activities such as jetties wharves, quayst slipways;

[7][provided that for expansion or modernisation of existing ports and harbours including fishing harbours operational constructions for ports and harbours and construction of jetties, wharves, quays, slipways, Single Point Mooring and Single Buoy Mooring and for reclamation of facilities essential for operational requirements of ports and harbours in areas within the existing port limits, except the areas classified as category CRZ-I(i), shall require environmental clearance from Government of

India in the Ministry of Surface Transport, which shall take decision on these activities on the basis of Environmental Impact Assessment Report.

Provided further that reclamation for commercial purposes such as shopping and housing complexes, hotels and entertainment activities shall not be permissible].

(iii) Thermal power plants (only foreshore facilities for transport of raw materials facilities for intake of cooling water and outfall for discharge of treated waste water cooling water); and

(iv) [8][All other activities with investment exceeding rupees five crores except those activities which are to be regulated by the concerned authorities at the State/Union Territory level in accordance with the provisions of paragraph 6, sub-paragraph (2) of Annexure 1 of the notification].

(3) (i) The coastal States and Union Territory Administrations shall prepare, within a period of one year from the date of this Notification. Coastal Zone Management Plans identifying and classifying the CRZ areas within their respective territories in accordance with the guidelines given in Annexures-I and II of the Notification and obtain approval (with or without modifications) of the Central Government in the Ministry of Environment & Forests;

(ii) Within the framework of such approved plans, all development and activities within the CRZ other than those covered in para 2 and para 3 (2) above shall be regulated by the State Government, Union Territory Administration or the local authority as the case may be in accordance with the guidelines given in Annexures-I and II of the Notification; and

(iii) In the interim period till the Coastal Zone Management Plans mentioned in para 3(3)(i) above are prepared and approved, all developments and activities-within the CRZ shall not violate the provisions of this Notifications. State Governments and Union Territory Administrations shall ensure adherence to these regulations and violations, if any, shall be subject to the provisions of the Environment (Protection) Act, 1986.

Procedure for Monitoring and Enforcement

The Ministry of Environment & Forests and the Government of State or Union Territory and such other authorities at the State or Union Territory levels, as may be designated for this purpose, shall be responsible for monitoring and enforcement of the provisions of this notification with in their respective Jurisdictions.

APPENDIX—III

COASTAL AREA CLASSIFICATION AND DEVELOPMENT REGULATIONS

Classification of Coastal Regulation Zone

6(1) For regulating development activities, the coastal stretches within 500 metres of High Tide Line of the landward side are classified into four categories, namely:

Category I (CRZ-I):

(i) Areas that are ecologically sensitive and important, such as national parks/marine parks, sanctuaries, reserve forests, wildlife habitats, mangroves, corals/coral reefs, areas close to breeding and spawning grounds of fish and other marine life, areas of outstanding natural beauty/historical/heritage areas, areas rich in genetic-diversity, areas likely to be inundated due to rise in sea level consequent upon global warming and such other areas as may be declared by the Central Government or the concerned authorities at the State/Union Territory level from time to time.

(ii) Area between the Low Tide Line and the High Tide Line.

Category-II (CRZ-II):

The areas that have already been developed upto or close to the shoreline. For this purpose, "developed area" is referred to as that area within the municipal limits or in other legally designated urban areas which is already substantially built up and which has been provided with drainage and approach roads and other infrastructural facilities, such as water supply and sewerage mains:

Category III (CRZ-III):

Areas that are relatively undisturbed and those which do not belong to either category-I or II. These will include coastal zone in the rural areas (developed and undeveloped) and also areas within Municipal limits or in other legally designated urban areas which are not substantially built up.

Category-IV (CRZ-IV):

Coastal stretches in the Andaman & Nicobar, Lakshadweep and small islands except those designated as CRZ-I, CRZ-II or CRZ-III.

Norms for Regulation of Activities

6(2) The development or construction activities in different categories of CRZ areas shall be regulated by the concerned authorities at the State/Union Territory level, in accordance with the following norms:

CRZ-I

No new construction shall be permitted within 500 metres of the High Tide Line. No construction activity, except as listed under 2(xii), will be permitted between the Low Tide Line and the High Tide Line;

[9][provided that construction of dispensaries, schools, public rain shelters, community toilets, bridges, roads, jetties, water supply, drainage, sewerage which are required for traditional inhabitants of the Sunderbans Biosphere reserve area, West Bengal, may be permitted, on a case to case basis, by an authority designated by the State Government].

CRZ-II

[10](i) Buildings shall be permitted neither on the seaward side of the existing road (or roads proposed in the approved Coastal Zone Management Plan of the area) nor on seaward side of existing authorised structures. Buildings permitted on the landward side of the

existing and proposed roads/existing authorised structures shall be subject to the existing local Town and Country Planning Regulations including the existing norms of FSI/FAR:

provided that no permission for construction of buildings shall be given on landward side of any new roads (except roads proposed in the approved Coastal Zone Management Plan) which are constructed on the seaward side of an existing road.

(ii) Reconstruction of the authorised buildings to be permitted subject with the existing FSI/FAR norms and without change in the existing use.

(iii) The design and construction of buildings shall be consistent with the surrounding landscape and local architectural style.

CRZ-III

(i) The area upto 200 metres from the High Tide Line is to be earmarked as 'No Development Zone'. [11][No construction shall be permitted within this zone except for repairs of existing authorised structures not exceeding existing FSI existing plinth area and existing density, and for permissible activities under the notification including facilities essential for such activities. An authority designated by the State Government/Union Territory Administration may permit construction of facilities for water supply, drainage and sewerage for requirements of local inhabitants.] However, the following uses may be permissible in this zone - agriculture, horticulture, gardens, pastures, parks, play fields, forestry and salt manufacture from sea water.

(ii) Development of vacant plots between 200 and 500 metres of High Tide Line in designated areas of CRZ-III with prior approval of MEF permitted for construction of hotels/beach resorts for temporary occupation of tourists/visitors subject to the conditions as stipulated in the guidelines at Annexure-II.

(iii) [12][Construction/reconstruction of dwelling units between 200 and 500 metres of the High Tide Line permitted so long it is with in the ambit of traditional rights and customary uses such as existing fishing villages and goathans. Building permission for such construction/reconstruction will be subject to the conditions that the total number of dwelling units shall not be more than twice the number of existing units; total covered area on all floors shall not exceed 33 per cent of the plot size; the overall height of construction shall not exceed 9 metres and construction shall not be more than 2 floors (ground floor plus One floor).

Construction is allowed for permissible activities under the notification including facilities essential for such activities. An authority designated by State Government/Union Territory Administration may permit construction of public rain shelters, community toilets, water supply, drainage, sewage, roads and bridges. The said authority may also permit construction of schools and dispensaries, for local inhabitants of the area, for those panchayats the major part of which falls within CRZ if no other area isavailable for construction of such facilities].

(iv) Reconstruction/alterations of an existing authorised building permitted subject to (i) to (iii) above.

CRZ-IV

Andaman & Nicobar Islands

(i) No new construction of buildings shall be permitted within 200 metres of the HTL;

(ii) The buildings between 200 and 500 metres from the High Tide Line shall not have more than 2 floors (ground floor and 1st floor), the total covered area on all floors shall not be more than 50 per cent of the plot size and the total height of constructions shall not exceed 9 metres;

(iii) The design and construction of buildings shall be consistent with the surrounding landscape and local architectural style.

(iv) [13][(a) Corals and sand from the beaches and coastal waters shall not be used for construction and other purposes:

(b) Sand may be used from the beaches and coastal waters, only for construction purpose unto the 31st day of March, 1990 and thereafter it shall not be used for construction and other purposes].

(v) Dredging and underwater blasting in and around coral formations shall not be permitted; and

(vi) However, in some of the islands, coastal stretches may also be classified into categories CRZ-I or II or III with the prior approval of Ministry of Environment and Forests and in such designated stretches, the appropriate regulations given for respective Categories shall apply.

Lakshadweep and Small Islands

(i) For permitting construction of buildings, the distance from the High Tide Line shall be decided depending on the size of the islands. This shall be laid down for each island in consultation with the experts and with approval of the Ministry of Environment & Forests, keeping in view the land use requirements for specific purposes vis-a-vis local conditions including hydrological aspects erosion and ecological sensitivity;

(ii) The buildings within 500 metres from the HTL shall not have more than 2 floors (ground floor and 1st floor), the total covered area on all floors shall not be more than 50 per cent of the plot size and the total height of construction shall not exceed 9 metres;

(iii) The design and construction of buildings shall be consistent with the surrounding landscape and local architectural style;

(iv) Corals and sand from the beaches and coastal waters shall not be used for construction and other purposes;

(v) Dredging and underwater blasting in and around coral formations shall not be permitted; and

(vi) However, in some of the Islands, coastal stretches may also be classified into categories CRZ-I or II or III, with the prior approval of Ministry of Environment & Forests and in such designated stretches, the appropriate regulations given for respective Categories shall apply.

APPENDIX—IV

GUIDELINES FOR DEVELOPMENT OF BACH RESORTS/HOTELS IN THE DESIGNATED AREAS OF CRZ-III FOR TEMPORARY OCCUPATION OF TOURIST/ VISITORS, WITH PRIOR APPROVAL OF THE MINISTRY OF ENVIRONMENT AND FORESTS

7(1) Construction of beach resorts/hotels with prior approval of MEF in the designated areas of CRZ-III for temporary occupation of tourists/visitors shall be subject to the following conditions:

(i) The project proponents shall not undertake any construction (including temporary constructions and fencing or such other barriers) within 200 metres (in the landward side) from the High Tide Line and within the area between the Low Tide and High Tide Line;

[(ia) live fencing and barbed wire fencing with vegetative cover may be allowed around private properties subject to the condition that such fencing shall in no way hamper public access to the beach];

(ib) no flattening of sand dunes shall be carried out;

(ic) no permanent structures for sports facilities shall be permitted except construction of goal posts, net posts and lamp posts.

(id) construction of basements may be allowed subject to the condition that no objection certificate is obtained from the State Ground Water Authority to the effect that such construction will not adversely affect free flow of ground water in that area. The State Ground water in that area. The State Ground Water Authority shall take into consideration the guidelines issued by the Central Government before granting such no objection certificate.

Explanation

Though no construction is allowed in the no development zone for the purposes of calculation of FSI, the area of entire plot including [15][50% of] the portion which falls within the no development zone shall be taken into account.

(ii) The total plot size shall not be less than 0.4 hectares and the total covered area on all floors shall not exceed 33 per cent of the plot size i.e. the FSI shall not exceed 0.33. The open area shall be suitably landscaped with appropriate vegetal cover;

(iii) The construction shall be consistent with the surrounding landscape and local architectural style;

(iv) The overall height of construction upto the highest ridge of the roof, shall not exceed 9 metres and the construction shall not be more than 2 floors (ground floor plus one upper floor);

(v) Ground water shall not be tapped within 200 m of the HTL; within the 200 metre - 500 metre zone it can be tapped only with the concurrence of the Central/State Ground Water Board;

(vi) Extraction of sand, levelling or digging of sandy stretches except for structural foundation of building, swimming pool shall not be permitted within 500 metres of the High Tide Line;

(vii) The quality of treated effluents, solid wastes, emissions and noise levels etc. from the project area must conform to the standards laid down by the competent authorities including the Central/State Pollution Control Board and under the Environment (Protection) Act, 1986;

(viii) Necessary arrangements for the treatment of the effluents and solid wastes must be made. It must be ensured that the untreated effluents and solid wastes are not discharged into the water or on the beach; and no effluent/solid waste shall be discharged on the beach:

(ix) To allow public access to the beach, atleast a gap of 20 metres width shall be provided between any two hotels/beach resorts; and in no case shall gaps be less than 500 metres apart; and

(x) If the project involves diversion of forest land for non-forest purposes, clearance as required under the Forest (Conservation), Act, 1980 shall be obtained. The requirements of other Central and State Laws as applicable to the project shall be met with.

(xi) Approval of the State/Union Territory Tourism Department shall be obtained.

7(2) In ecologically sensitive areas (such as marine parks, mangroves, coral reefs, breeding and spawning grounds of fish, wildlife habitats and such other areas as may be notified by the Central/State Government/Union Territories) construction of beach resorts/hotels shall not be permitted.

APPENDIX—V

LIST OF PETROLEUM PRODUCTS PERMITTED FOR STORAGE IN PORT AREAS

[See Paragraph 2, Sub-paragraph (ii)]

(i) Crude Oil;
(ii) Liquefied Petroleum Gas;
(iii) Motor Spirit;
(iv) Kerosene;
(v) Aviation Fuel;
(vi) High Speed Diesel;
(vii) Lubricating Oil;
(viii) Butane;
(ix) Propane;
(x) Compressed Natural Gas;
(xi) Napatha;
(xii) Furance Oil;
(xiii) Low Sulphur Heave Stock]

MINISTRY OF ENVIRONMENT AND FORESTS GOVT. OF INDIA

ORDER

New Delhi, the 26th November, 1998

S.O. 991 (E).—In exercise of the powers conferred by sub-sections (1) and (3) of section 3 of the Environment (Protection) Act, 1986 (29 of 1986) (hereinafter referred to as said Act) and in supersession of the Order of the Government of India in the Ministry of Environment and Forests number J-17011/18/96-IA-III dated 13th August, 1998, except as respects things done or omitted to be done before such supersession, the Central Government hereby constitutes an authority to be known as the National Coastal Zone Management Authority (hereinafter referred to as the Authority) consisting of the following persons, for a period of two years, with effect from the date of publication of this Order in the Official Gazette, namely:

1.	Additional Secretary (Impact Assessment), Ministry of Environment and Forests, New Delhi.	Chairman.
2.	Chief Town Planner, Ministry of Urban Affairs and Employment, New Delhi.	Member.
3.	Director General (Tourism), Minister of Tourism, New Delhi.	Member.
4.	Fisheries Development Commissioner, Ministry of Agriculture, New Delhi.	Member.
5.	Joint Secretary (Ports), Ministry of Surface Transport, New Delhi.	Member
6.	Director, National Institute of Oceanography, Panjim, Goa.	Member
7.	Director, Central Marine Fisheries Research Institute, Cochin.	Member
8.	Father Thomas Kocherry, Coordinator, World Forum of Fish Harvesters and Fish Workers (WFF), Valiathura, Thiruvananthapuram.	Member
9.	Shri Bal Mane, President, Ratnagiri District Fishermen's Association, Ratnagiri,	Member

10. Shri Shiva Kashinath Naik, Sarpanch Shioroda Kerwadi, Tehsil Vengurla, District Sindhudurg, Maharashtra.	Member
11. Shri Rajaram Gadhekar, Mukteshwar Sansthan, Apoogaon, Malad (West), Mumbai.	Member
12. Deputy Secretary, Impact Assessment, Ministry of Environment and Forests, New Delhi.	Member Secretary

II. The Authority shall have the power to take the following measures for protecting and improving the quality of the coastal environment and preventing, abating and controlling environmental pollution in coastal areas, namely:

(i) Co-ordination of actions by the State Coastal Zone Management Authorities and the Union Territory Coastal Zone Management Authorities under the said Act and the rules made thereunder, or under any other law which is relatable to the objects of the said Act.

(ii) Examination of the proposals for changes and modifications in classification of Coastal Regulation Zone areas and in the Coastal Zone Management Plans received from the State Coastal Zone Management Authorities and the Union Territory Coastal Zone Management Authorities, and making specific recommendations to the Central Government therefore.

(iii) (a) review of cases involving violations of

the provisions of the said Act and the rules made thereunder, or under any other law which is relatable to the objects of the said Act and, if found necessary, issue directions under section 5 of the said Act.

(b) Review of cases under (iii) (a) either suo-moto, or on the basis of complaint made by an individual, or a representative body or an organisation functioning in the field of environment.

(iv) File complaints, under section 19 of the said Act in cases of non-compliance of the directions issued by it under sub-paragraph (iii) (a) of paragraph II of the Order.

(v) To take action under section 10 of the said Act to verify the facts concerning the issue arising from sub-paragraphs (i), (iii), and (iii) of paragraph II of the Order.

III. The Authority shall provide technical assistance and guidance to the concerned State Government, Union Territory Government/Administrations, the State Coastal Zone Management Authorities, the Union Territory Coastal Zone Management Authorities, and other institutions/organisations as may be found necessary, in matters relating to the protection and improvement of the coastal environment.

IV. The Authority shall examine and accord its approval to area specific management plans, integrated Coastal Zone Management plans and modifications thereof submitted by the State Coastal Zone Management Authorities and the Union Territory Coastal Zone Management Authorities.

V. The Authority may advise the Central Government on policy, planning, research and development, setting up of Centres of Excellence and funding, in matters relating to Coastal Regulations Zone Management.

VI. The Authority shall deal with all environmental issue relating to Coastal Regulations Zone which may be referred to it by the Central Government.

VII. The Authority shall furnish report of its activities and the activities of the State Coastal Regulations Zone Management Authorities and Union Territory Coastal Zone Management Authorities at least once in six months to the Central Government.

VIII. The foregoing powers and functions of the Authority shall be subject to the supervision and control of the Central Government.

IX. the Authority shall have its headquarters at New Delhi.

X. Any matter specifically not falling within the scope and jurisdiction of the Authority as no constituted shall be dealt with by the statutory authorities concerned.

[F. No. 17011/18/96-IA-III]
K. Roy Paul, Additional, Secy.

ORDER

New Delhi, the 26th November, 1998

S.O. 992 (E).—In Exercise of the powers conferred by sub-sections (1) and (3) of section 3 of the Environment (Protection) Act, 1986 (29 of 1986) (hereinafter referred to as the said Act), the Central Government hereby constitutes an authority to be known as the Andaman and Nicobar Islands Coastal Zone Management Authority (hereinafter referred to as the Authority) consisting of the following persons, for a period of two years, with effect from the date of publication of this Order in the Official Gazette, namely:

1.	Chief Secretary, Andaman and Nicobar Administration, Andaman and Nicobar Islands, Port Blair.	Chairman
2.	Sh. W.G. Thambudurai, Chief Engineer and Administrator, Andaman Lakshadeep Harbour Works, Ministry of Surface Transport, Port Blair.	Member
3.	Secretary, Department of Environment, Andaman and Nicobar Islands, Port Blair.	Member
4.	Director, Department of Fisheries, Port Blair.	Member
5.	Director, Central Agriculture Research Institute, Port Blair.	Member
6.	Dr. P.S. N. Rao, Botanical Survey of India, Port Blair.	Member
7.	Conservator of Forests, Andaman and Nicobar Islands, Port Blair.	Member Secretary.

II. The Authority shall have the power to take the following measures for protecting and improving the quality of the coastal environment and preventing, abating and controlling environmental pollution in coastal areas of the Union Territory of the Andaman and Nicobar Islands, namely:

(i) Examination of proposals for changes/ modifications in classification of Coastal Regulation Zone areas and in the Coastal Zone Management Plan (CZMP) received from the Andaman and Nicobar Islands Administration, and making specific recommendations to the National Coastal Management Authority therefore.

(ii) (a) Inquiry into cases of alleged violations of the provisions of the said Act and the rules made thereunder, or under any other law which is relatable to the objects of the said Act and, if found necessary in a specific case, issuing directions under section 6 of the said Act, insofar as such directions are not inconsistent with any direction issued in that specific case by National Coastal Zone Management Authority or by the Central Zone Management Authority or by the Central Government;

(b) Review of cases involving violations of the provisions of the said Act and the rules made thereunder, or under any other law which is relatable to the objects of the said Act, and, if found necessary, referring such cases, with comments, for review to the National Coastal Zone Management Authority;

Provided that the cases under sub-paragraphs (ii) (a) and (ii) (b) of paragraph 2 may be taken up suo-moto, or on the basis of complaint made by an individual, or representative body, or an organisation.

(iii) Filing complaints under section 19 of the said Act in cases of non-compliance of the directions issued by it under sub-paragraph (ii) (a) of paragraph II of the Order.

(iv) To take action under section 10 of the said Act to verify the facts concerning the issues arising from sub-paragraph (i) and (ii) of paragraph II of this Order.

III. The Authority shall deal with environmental issues relating to Coastal Regulation Zone which may be referred to it by the Andaman and Nicobar Islands Administration, the National Coastal Zone Management Authority on the Central Government.

IV. The Authority shall identify ecologically sensitive areas in the Coastal Regulation Zone and formulate area-specific management plans for such identified areas.

V. The Authority shall identify coastal areas highly vulnerable to erosion/degradation, and formulate area-specific management plans for such identified areas.

VI. The Authority shall identify economically important stretches in the Coastal Regulation Zone and prepare Integrated Coastal Zone Management Plans for the same.

VII. The Authority shall submit the plans prepared by it under paragraphs IV, V, Vi above and modifications thereof the National Coastal zone Management Authority for examination and its approval.

VIII. The Authority shall ensure compliance of all specific conditions that are laid down in the approval Coastal Zone Management Plan and Andaman and Nicobar Islands.

IX. The Authority shall furnish report of its activities at least once in six months to the National Coastal Zone Management Authority.

X. The foregoing powers and functions of the Authority shall be subject to the supervision and control of the Central Government.

XI. The Authority shall have its headquarters at Port Blair.

XII. Any matter specifically not falling within the scope and jurisdiction of the Authority as so constituted shall be dealt with by the statutory authorities concerned.

[F. No. 1701/18/96-1A-III]

K. Roy Paul, Addl. Secy.

ORDER

New Delhi, the 26th November, 1998

S.O. 993(E).—In exercise of the powers conferred by sub-section (1) and (3) of section 3 of the Environment (Protection) Act, 1986 (29 of 1986) (hereinafter referred to as the said Act), the Central Government hereby constitutes an authority to be known as the Andhra Pradesh Coastal Zone Management Authority (hereinafter referred to as the Authority)coasting of the following persons, for a period of two years, with effect from the date of publication of this Order in the Official Gazette, namely:

1. Principal Secretary —Chairman
   Environment, Forests and
   Science and Technology,
   Government of Andhra Pradesh,
   Hyderabad.

2. Secretary, —Member
   Department of Revenue
   Government of Andhra Pradesh
   Hyderabad.

3. Director, —Member
   National Remote Sensing Agency,
   Hyderabad.

4. Dr. M. Babu Rao, Retired Principal, College of Fisheries, ANGR Agriculture University. —Member

5. Dr. A.V. Raman, Head of the Department of Zoology College of Science and Technology Andhra University, Welfare. —Member

6. Member Secretary, Andhra Pradesh Pollution control Board, HUDA Complex, Hyderabad. —Member

7. Director, Shore Area Development Authority, Hyderabad. —Member Secretary

II. The Authority shall have the power to take the following measures for prosecuting and improving the quality of the coastal environment and preventing, abating and controlling environmental pollution in areas of the State of Andhra Pradesh, namely:

(i) Examination of proposals for changes/ modifications in classification of Coastal Regulation Zone area and in the Coastal Zone Management Plan (CZMP) received from they Andhra Pradesh State Government and making specific recommendations to the National Coastal Zone Management Authority therefore.

(ii) (a) Inquiry into cases of alleged violations of the provisions of the said Act and or the rules made thereunder, or under any other law which is relatable to the objects of the said Act and, if found necessary in a specific case, issuing directions under section 5 of the said Act, insofar as such directions are not inconsistent with any direction issued in that specific cases by the National Coastal Zone Management Authority or by the Central Government.

(b) Review of cases involving violations of the provisions of the said Act and the rules made thereunder, or under any often law which is relatable to the objects of the said Act, and, if found necessary referring such cases, with comments, for review to the National Coastal Zone Management Authority.

Provided that the cases under sub-paragraphs (ii) (a) and (b) of paragraph II may either be taken up suo-moto, or on the basis of complaint made by an individual, or a representative body, or an organisation.

(iii) Filing complaints, under section 19 of the said Act in cases of non-compliance of the directions issued by at under sub-paragraph (ii) (a) of paragraph (i) and (ii) of paragraph II of this Order.

(iv) To take action under section 10 of the said Act to verify the facts concerning the issues arising from sub-paragraphs (i) and (ii) of paragraph II of this Order.

III. The Authority shall deal with environmental issues relating to Coastal Regulation Zone which may be referred to it by the State Government, Andhra Pradesh the National Coastal Zone Management Authority or the Central Government.

IV. The Authority shall identify ecologically sensitive

areas in the Coastal Regulation Zone, and formulate area-specific management plans for such identified areas.

V. The Authority shall identify coastal areas highly vulnerable to erosion/degradation and formulate area-specific management plans for such identified areas.

VI. The Authority shall identify economically important stretches in Coastal Regulation Zone and prepare Integrated Coastal zone Management Plans for the same.

VII. The Authority shall submit the plans prepared by it under paragraphs IV, V, VI above and modifications thereof to the National Coastal Zone Management Authority for examination and its approval.

VIII. The Authority shall ensure compliance of all specific conditions that are laid down in the approved Coastal Zone Management Plan of Andhra Pradesh.

IX. The Authority shall furnish report of its activities at least once in six months to the National Coastal Zone Management Authority.

X. The foregoing powers and functions of the Authority shall be subject to the supervision and control of the Central Government.

XI. The Authority shall have its headquarters at Hyderabad.

XII. Any matter specifically not falling within the scope and jurisdiction of the Authority as so constituted shall dealt with by the statutory authorities concerned.

[F. No. 17011/18/96-1A-III]

K. Roy Paul, Ad. Secy.

ORDER

New Delhi, the 26th November, 1998

S.O. 993(E).—In exercise of the powers conferred by sub-sections (1) and (3) of section 3 of the Environment (Protection) Act, 1986 (29 of 1986) (hereinafter referred to as the said Act), the Central Government hereby constitutes an authority to be known as the Tamil Nadu Coastal Zone Management Authority (hereinafter referred to as the Authority) consisting of the following persons for a period of two years, with effect from the date of publication of this Order in the Official Gazette, namely:

1.	Secretary, Department of Environment, Government of Tamil Nadu, Chennai.	Chairman
2.	Director, Country and Town Planning, Government of Tamil Nadu, Chennai.	Member
3.	Member Secretary, Tamil Nadu Pollution Control Board, Chennai.	Member
4.	Dr. Ravindran, National Institute of Ocean Technology, Indian Institute of Technology, Chennai.	Member
5.	Dr. P.P. Vaidhyaraman, Rtd.-Director, CWPRS, Central Water and Power Research Station, Pune, (CWPRS)	Member

6. Dr. L. Kannan, Member
   Director,
   Central for Advanced Studies in Marine Biology,
   Anamalai University.

7. Director, Member Secretary
   Department of Environment
   Government of Tamil Nadu,
   Chennai.

II. The Authority shall have the power to take the following measures for protecting and improving the quality of the coastal environment and preventing, abating and controlling environmental pollution in coastal areas of the State of Tamil Nadu, namely:

(i) Examination of proposals for changes/ modifications in classification of Coastal Regulation Zone areas and in the Coastal Zone Management Plan (CZMP) received from the Tamil Nadu State Government and specific recommendations to the National Coastal Zone Management Authority therefore.

(ii) (a) Inquiry into cases of alleged violations of the provisions of the said Act and or the rules made thereunder, or any other law which is relatable to the objects of the said Act and, if found necessary in a specific case, issuing directions been under section 5 of the said Act insofar as such directions are not inconsistent with any direction issued in that specific case by the National Coastal Zone Management Authority or by the Central Government;

(b) Review of cases involving violations of the provisions of the said Act and the rules made thereunder, or under any other law which is relatable to tne objects of the said Act, and, if found necessary referring such cases, with comments, for review to the National Coastal Zone Management Authority.

Provided that the cases under sub-paragraphs (ii) (a) and (b) of paragraph II may either be taken up suo-moto, or on the basis of complaint made by an individual, or a representative body, or an organisation.

(iii) Filing complaints under Section 19 of the said Act in cases of non-compliance of the directions issued by it under sub-paragraph (ii) (a) of paragraph II of this Order.

(iv) To take action under section 10 of the said Act to verify, the facts concerning the issues arising from sub-paragraphs (i) and (ii) of paragraph II of this Order.

III. The Authority shall deal with environmental issues relating to Coastal Regulation Zone which may be referred to it by the Tamil Nadu State Government, the National Coastal Zone Management Authority or the Central Government.

IV. The Authority shall identify ecologically sensitive areas in the Coastal Regulation Zone, and formulate area specific management plans for such identified areas.

V. The Authority shall identify coastal areas highly vulnerable to erosion/degradation, and formulate area specific management plans for such identified areas.

VI. The Authority shall identified economically important stretches in the Coastal Regulation Zone and prepare Integrated Coastal Zone Management Plans for the same.

VII. The Authority shall ensure compliance of all specific conditions that are laid down in the approved Coastal Zone Management Plan of Tamil Nadu.

IX. The Authority shall furnish report of its activities at least once in six months to the National Coastal Zone Management Authority.

X. The foregoing powers and functions of the Authority shall be subject to the supervision and control of the Central Government.

XI. The Authority shall have its headquarters at Chennai.

XII. Any matter specifically not falling within the scope and jurisdiction of the Authority as so constituted shall dealt with by the statutory authority concerned.

[F. No. 17011/18/96-1A-III]

K. Roy Paul, Addl. Secy.

ORDER

New Delhi, the 26th November, 1998

S.O. 995(E).—In exercise of the powers conferred by sub-section (1) and (3) of section 3 of the Environment (Protection) Act, 1986 (29 of 1986) (hereinafter referred to as the said Act), the Central Government hereby constitutes an authority to be known as the Goa Coastal Zone Management Authority (hereinafter referred to as the Authority) consisting of the following persons, for a period of two years with effect from the date of publication of this Order in the Official Gazette, namely:

1. Secretary —Chairman
   Department of Environment,
   Panjim.

2. Chief Town Planner, —Member
   Town and Country Planning Office,
   Panjim.

3. Shri Ashok Kumar, —Member
Regional controller of Mines,
Indian Bureau of Mines,
Panjim

4. Director, —Member
Department of Tourism,
Panjim.

5. Dr. Arvinda Untawale, —Member
National Institute of Oceanography,
Dona Paula.

6. Prof. Leela Bhosle, —Member
Head of Department,
University of Kolhapur.

7. Director —Member Secretary
Department of Science, Technology and Environment, Panjim.

II. The Authority shall have the power to take the following measures for protecting and improving the quality of the coastal environment and preventing abating and controlling environmental pollution in coastal areas of the State of Goa, namely:

(i) Examination of proposals or changes/ modifications in classification of Coastal Regulation Zone areas and in the Coastal Zone Management Plan (CZMP) received from the Goa State Government and making specific recommendations to the National Coastal Zone Management Authority therefore.

(ii) (a) Inquiry into cases of alleged violations of the provisions of the said Act and/or the rules made thereunder, or under any other law which is relatable to the objects of the said Act and, if found necessary in a specific case, issuing directions under section 5 of the said Act insofar as such direction are not inconsistent with any direction issued in that specific case by the National Coastal Zone Management Authority or by the Central Government;

(b) Review of Cases involving violations of the provisions of the said act and the rules made thereunder, or under any other law which is relatable to the objects of the said Act, and, if found necessary referring such cases, with comments, for review to the National Coastal Zone Management Authority;

Provided that the cases under sub-paragraphs (ii) (a) and (ii) (b) of paragraph II may be taken up suo-moto, or on the basis of complaint made by an individual, or a representative body, or an organisation.

(iii) Filing complaints, under section 19 of the said Act in cases of non-compliance of the directions issued by it under sub-paragraph (ii) (a) of paragraph II of this Order.

(iv) To take action under section 10 of the said Act to verify the facts concerning the issues arising from sub-paragraphs (i) and (ii) of paragraph II of this Order.

III. The Authority shall deal with environmental issues relating to Coastal Regulation Zone which may be referred to it by the Goa State Government, the National Coastal Zone Management Authority or the Central Government.

IV. The Authority shall identify ecologically sensitive

ares in the Coastal Regulation Zone, and formulate area-specific management plans for such identified areas.

V. The Authority shall identify coastal areas highly vulnerable to erosion/degradation, and formulate area-specific management plans for such identified areas.

VI. The Authority shall identify economically important stretches in the Coastal Regulation Zone and prepare Integrated Coastal Zone Management Plans for the same.

VII. The Authority shall submit the plans prepared by it under paragraph IV, V, VI above and modifications thereof to the National Coastal Zone Management Authority for examination and its approval.

VIII. The Authority shall ensure compliance of all specific conditions that are laid down in the approved coastal Zone Management Plan of Goa.

IX. The Authority shall furnish report of its activities at least once in six months to the National Coastal Zone Management Authority.

X. The foregoing powers and functions of the authority shall be subject to the supervision and control of the Central Government.

XI. The Authority shall have its headquarters a Panaji.

XII. Any matter specifically not falling within the scope and jurisdiction of the Authority as so instituted shall be dealt with by the statutory authorities concerned.

[F. No. 17011/18/96/1A-III]

K. Roy Paul Addl. Secy.

ORDER

New Delhi, the 26th November, 1998

S.O. 996 (E).—In exercise of the powers conferred by sub-sections (1) and (3) of section 3 of the Environment (Protection) Act 1986 (29 of 1986) (hereinafter referred to as the said Act), the Central Government hereby constitutes an authority to be known as the Pondicherry Coastal Zone Management Authority (hereinafter referred to as the Authority) consisting of the following persons, for a period of two years with effect from the date of publication of this Order in the Official Gazette, namely:

1.	Secretary Department of Environment, Pondicherry.	—Chairman
2.	Director, Department of Fisheries, Pondicherry.	—Member
3.	Chief Town Planner, Town and Country planning Department.	—Member
4.	Dr. R. Mahadevan, National Institute of Ocean Technology, Indian Institute of Technology, Chennai.	—Member
5.	Dr. L. Kannan, Director, Centre for Advanced Studies in Marine Biology, Anamalai University.	—Member
6.	Member Secretary, Pondicherry Pollution Control Committee, Pondicherry.	—Member Secretary

II. The Authority shall have the power to take the following measures for protecting and improving the quality of the coastal environment and preventing, abating and controlling environmental pollution in coastal areas of the Union Territory of Pondicherry, namely:

following:

(i) Examination of proposals or changes/ modifications in classification of Coastal Regulation Zone areas and in the Coastal Zone Management Plan (CZMP) received from the Pondicherry Administration and making specific recommendations to the National Coastal Zone Management Authority therefore.

(ii) (a) Inquiry into cases of alleged violations of the provisions of the said Act and the rules made thereunder, or under any other law which is relatable to the objects of the said Act and, if found necessary in a specific case, issuing directions under section 5 of the said Act insofar as such directions are not inconsistent with any directions issued in that specific case by the National Coastal Zone Management Authority or by the Central Government;

(b) Review of cases involving violations of the provisions of the said Act and the rules made thereunder, or under any other law which is relatable to the objects of the said Act, and, if found necessary referring such cases, with comments, for review to the National Coastal Zone Management Authority:

Provided that the cases under sub-paragraphs (ii) (a) and (ii) (b) of paragraph II may be taken up *suo-moto*, or on the basis of complaint made by any individual, representative body, or an organisation.

(iii) Filing complaints, under section 19 of the said Act in cases of non-compliance of the directions issued by it under sub-paragraph (ii) (a) of paragraph II of this Order.

(iv) To take action under section 10 of the said Act to verify the facts concerning the issues arising from sub-paragraphs (i) and (ii) of paragraph II of this Order.

III. The Authority shall deal with environmental issues relating to Coastal Regulation Zone which may be referred to it by the Pondicherry Administration, the National Coastal Zone Management Authority on the Central Government.

IV. The Authority shall identify ecologically sensitive areas in the Coastal Regulation Zone, and formulate area-specific management plans for such identified areas.

V. The Authority shall identify coastal areas highly vulnerable to erosion/degradation, and formulate area-specific management plans for such identified areas.

VI. The Authority shall identify economically important stretches in the Coastal Regulation Zone and prepare Integrated Coastal Zone Management Plans for the same.

VII. The Authority shall submit the plans prepared by it under paragraphs IV, V, VI above and modifications thereof to the National Coastal Zone Management Authority for examination and its approval.

VIII. The Authority shall ensure compliance of all specific conditions that are laid down in the approved Coastal Zone Management Plan of Pondicherry.

IX. The Authority shall furnish report of its activities at

least once in six months to the National Coastal Zone Management Authority.

X. The foregoing powers and functions of the Authority shall be subject to the supervision and control in the Central Government.

XI. The Authority shall have its headquarters at Pondicherry.

XII. Any matter specifically not falling within the scope and jurisdiction of the Authority as so constitute shall be death with by the statutory authorities concerned.

[F. No. 17011/18/96-1A-III]

K. Roy Paul, Addl. Secy.

ORDER

New Delhi, the 26th November, 1998

S.O. 997/(E).—In exercise of the powers conferred by sub-sections (1) and (3) of section 3 of the Environment (Protection) Act, 1986 (29 of 1986) (hereinafter referred to as the said Act), the Central Government hereby constitutes an authority to be known as the West Bengal Coastal Zone Management Authority (hereinafter referred to as the Authority) Consisting of the following persons, for a period of two years, with effect from the date of publication of this Order in the official Gazette, namely:

1. Secretary — Chairman
   Department of Environment,
   Government of West Bengal,
   Calcutta.

2. Director — Member
   Department of Fisheries
   Government of West Bengal,
   Calcutta.

3.	Principal Chief Conservator of Forests, Department of Forests Government of West Bengal.	Member
4.	Sh. Anil Varun Biswas, Centre for Study for Man and Environment, Department of Geology, University of Calcutta.	
5.	Dr. L.K. Banarjee, Scientist S.F. Botanical Survey of India, Calcutta.	Member
6.	Dr. A.K. Ghosh, Zoological Survey of India	Member
7.	Member Secretary, West Bengal Pollution Control Board.	Member Secretary

II. The Authority shall have the power to take the following measures for protecting and improving the quality of the coastal environment and preventing, abating and controlling environmental pollution in coastal areas of the State of West Bengal, namely:

(i) Examination of proposals for changes/ modifications of classification of Coastal Regulation Zone areas and in the Coastal Zone Management Plan (CZMP) received from the West Bengal State Government and making specific recommendations to the National Coastal Zone Management Authority therefore.

(ii) (a) Inquiry into cases of alleged violations of the provisions of the said Act and or the rules made thereunder, or any other law for the time being in force which is relatable to the objects of the said Act and, if found necessary in a specific case, issuing directions under section 5 of the said Act insofar as such directions are not inconsistent with any direction issued in that specific case by the National Coastal Zone Management Authority or by the Central Government.

(b) Review of cases involving violations of the provisions of the said Act and the rules made thereunder, or under any other law which is relatable to the objects of the said Act, and, if found necessary referring such cases, with comments, for review to the National Coastal Zone Management Authority;

Provided that the cases under sub-paragraph (ii) (a) and (ii) (b) of paragraph II may either be taken up suo-moto, or on the basis of complaint made by an individual, or a representative body, or an organisations.

(iii) Filing complaints, under section 19 of the said Act in cases of non-compliance of the direction issued by it under sub-paragraph (ii) (a) of paragraph II of this Order.

(iv) To take action under section 10 of the said Act to verify the facts concerning the issues arising from sub-paragraphs (i) and (ii) of paragraph II of this Order.

III. The Authority shall deal with environmental issues relating to Coastal Regulation Zone which may be referred to it by the West Bengal State Government, the National Coastal Zone Management Authority or the Central Government.

IV. The Authority shall identify ecologically sensitive areas in the Coastal Regulation Zone, and formulate area-specific management plans for such identified areas.

V. The Authority shall identify coastal areas lightly vulnerable to erosion/degradation, and formulate area specific management plans for such identifies areas.

VI. The Authority shall identify economically important stretches in the Coastal Regulation Zone and prepare Integrated Coastal Zone Management Plan or the same.

VII. The Authority shall submit the plans prepared by it under paragraphs IV, V, VI above and modifications thereof the National Coastal Zone Management Authority for examination and approval.

VIII. The Authority shall ensure compliance of all specific conditions that are laid down in the approved Coastal Zone Management Authority.

IX. The Authority shall furnish report of its activities at least once in six months to the National Coastal Zone Management Authority.

X. The foregoing powers and functions of the Authority shall be subject to the supervision and control of the Central Government.

XI. The authority shall have its headquarters at Calcutta.

XII. Any matter specifically not falling within the scope and jurisdiction of the Authority as so constituted shall be dealt with by the statutory authorities concerned.

[F. No. 17011/18/96-1A-III]

K. Roy Paul, Addl. Secy.

ORDER

New Delhi, the 26th November, 1998

S.O. 998(E).—In exercise of the powers conferred by sub-section (1) and (3) of section 3 of the Environment (Protection) Act, 1986 (29 of 1986) (hereinafter referred to as the said Act), the Central Government hereby continues an authority to be known as the Daman and Diu Islands Coastal Zone Management Authority (hereinafter referred to as the Authority) consisting of the following persons, for a period of two years, with effect from the date of publication of this Order in the Official Gazette, namely:

1.	Administrator, Daman and Diu, Dadar and Nagar Haveli, Secretariat, Moti Daman.	Chairman
2.	Executive Engineer, Public Works Department, Moti Daman.	Member
3.	Chief Conservator of Forests, Moti Daman.	Member
4.	Director, Space Application Centre, Ahmadabad.	Member
5.	Director, Central Institute of Fisheries Education, Mumbai	Member
6.	Member Secretary, Pollution Control Committee, Moti Daman.	Member Secretary

II. The Authority shall have the power to take the following measures of protecting and improving the quality of the coastal environment and preventing, abating and controlling environmental pollution in coastal areas of the Union Territory of the Daman and Diu, namely:

(i) Examination of proposals for changes/ modifications in classification of Coastal Regulation Zone areas and in the Coastal Zone Management Plan (CZMP) received from the Daman and Diu Administration, and making specific recommendations to the National Coastal Zone Management Authority therefore.

(ii) (a) Inquiry into cases of alleged violations of the provisions of the said Act and the rules made thereunder, or under any other law which is relatable to the objects of the said Act and, if found necessary in a specific case, issuing directions under section 5 of the said Act, insofar as such directions are not inconsistent with any direction issued in that specific case by the National Coastal Zone Management Authority or by the Central Government.

(b) Review of cases involving violations of the provisions of the said Act and the rules made thereunder, or under any other law which is relatable to the objects of the said Act, and, if found necessary, referring such cases, with comments, for review to the National Coastal Zone Management Authority.

Provided that the cases under sub-paragraphs (ii) (a) and (ii) (b) of paragraph II may either be taken up suo-moto, or on the basis of complaint made by an individual, or a representative body, or an organisation.

(iii) Filing complaints, under section 19 of the said Act in cases of non-compliance of the directions issued by it under sub-paragraph (ii) (a) of paragraph II of this Order.

(iv) To take action under section 10 of the said Act to verify the facts concerning the issues arising from sub-paragraphs (i) and (ii) of paragraph II of this Order.

III. The Authority shall deal with environmental issues relating to Coastal Regulation Zone which may be referred to it by the Daman and Diu Administration, the National Coastal Zone Management Authority or the Central Government.

IV. The Authority shall identify ecologically sensitive areas in the Coastal Regulation Zone, and formulate area-specific management for such identified areas.

V. The authority shall identify coastal areas highly vulnerable to erosion/degradation, and formulate area-specific management plans for such identified areas.

VI. The Authority shall identify economically important stretches in the Coastal Regulation Zone and prepare Integrated Coastal Zone Management Plan for the same.

VIII. The Authority shall submit the plans prepared by it under paragraph IV, V, VI above and modifications thereof to the National Coastal Zone Management Authority for examination and its approval.

VIII. The Authority shall ensure compliance of all specific conditions that are laid down in the approved Coastal Zone Management Plan of Daman and Diu.

IX. The Authority shall furnish report of its activities at least once in six months to the National Coastal Zone Management Authority.

X. The foregoing powers and functions of the Authority shall be subject to the supervision and control of the Central Government.

XI. The Authority shall have its headquarters at Moti Daman.

XII. Any matter specifically not falling within the scope and jurisdiction of the Authority as so constituted shall be dealt with by the statutory authorities concerned.

[F. No. 17011/18/96-1A-III]
K. Roy Paul, Addl. Secy.

ORDER

New Delhi, the 26th November, 1998

S.O. 999(E).—In exercise of the powers conferred by sub-section (1) and (3) of section 3 of the Environment (Protection) Act, 1986 (29 of 1986) (hereinafter referred to as the said Act), the Central Government hereby constitutes an authority to be known as the Gujarat Coastal Zone Management Authority (hereinafter referred to as the Authority) consisting of the following persons, for a period of two years, with effect from the date of publication of this Order in the Official Gazette, namely;

1. Secretary
   Environment and Forests Department,
   Government of Gujarat. — Chairman

2. Commissioner
   Department of Industries
   Government of Gujarat — Member

3. Principal Chief Conservator of Forests
   and Wild Live
   Gandhi Nagar — Member

4. Prof. Nikhil Desai — Member
   Department of Geology
   M.S. University of Geology,
   Vadodara.

5. Sh. K.B. Jain — Member
   Director
   Centre for Environment and Planning
   Technology School and Architecture,
   Ahmedabad.

6. Prof. Anil Gupta, — Member
   Indian Institute of Management,
   Ahmedabad.

7. Director, — Member Secretary
   Department of Environment,

II. The Authority shall have the power to take the following measures for protecting and improving the quality of the coastal environment and preventing, abating and controlling environment pollution of coastal areas of the State of Gujarat namely:

(i) Examination of proposals for changes/ modifications in classification of Coastal Regulation Zone areas and in Coastal Zone Management Plan (CZMP) received from the Gujarat State Government and making specific recommendations to the National Coastal Zone Management Authority therefore.

(ii) (a) Inquiry into cases of alleged violations of the provisions of the said Act and the rules made thereunder, or under any other law which is relatable to the objects of the said Act and, if found necessary in a specific case, issuing directions under section 5 of the said Act, insofar as such directions are not inconsistent with any direction issued in that specific case by the National Coastal Zone Management Authority or by the Central Government;

(b) Review of cases involving violations of the provisions of the said Act and the rules made thereunder, or under any other law which is relatable to the objects of the said Act, and, if found necessary, referring such cases, with comments, for review to the National Coastal Zone Management Authority:

Provided that the cases under sub-paragraphs (ii) (a) and (ii) (b) of paragraph II may either be taken up suo-moto, or in the basis of complaint made by an individual, or a representative body, or an organisation.

(iii) Filing complaints under section 19 of the said Act in cases of non-compliance of the directions issued by it under sub-paragraph (ii) (a) of paragraph II of this order.

(iv) To take action to verify the facts concerning the issues arising from sub-paragraphs (i) and (ii) of the paragraph II of this order.

III. The Authority shall deal with environmental issue relating to Coastal Regulation Zone which be referred to it by the State Government of Gujarat the National Coastal Zone Management Authority or the Central Government.

IV. The Authority shall identify ecological sensitive areas in the Coastal Regulation Zone, and formulate area-specific management plans for such identified areas.

V. The Authority shall identify, coastal areas highly vulnerable to erosion/degradation, and formulate area-specific management plans for such identified areas.

VI. The Authority shall identify economically important stretches in the Coastal Regulation Zone and prepare Integrated Coastal Zone Management Plans for the same.

VII. The Authority shall submit the plans prepared by it under paragraphs IV, V, VI above and modification thereof to the National Coastal Zone Management Authority for examination and its approval.

VIII. The Authority shall ensure compliance of all specific conditions that are laid down in the approved Coastal Zone Management Plan of Gujarat.

IX. The Authority shall furnish a progress report of its activities at least once in six months to the National Coastal Zone, Management Authority.

X. The foregoing powers and functions of the Authority shall be subject to the supervision and control of the Central Government.

XI. The Authority shall have its headquarters at Gandhinagar.

XII. Any matter specifically not falling within the scope and jurisdiction of the Authority as so constituted shall be dealt with by the statutory authorities concerned.

[F. No. 17011/18/96-1A-III]

K. Roy Paul, Addl. Secy.

MINISTRY OF ENVIRONMENT AND FORESTS NOTIFICATION

New Delhi, the 12th February, 1999

S.O.104 (E). — Whereas by notification of the Government of India in the Ministry of Environment and Forests number S.O. 1001(E), dated the 26th November, 1998 (hereinafter referred to as the said notification, the Central Government constituted an authority to be known as the Kerala Coastal Zone Management Authority (hereinafter referred to as the said Authority).

And whereas, the State Government of Kerala had drawn attention of the Central Government to the need to modify the composition of the said Authority;

And whereas, the matter has been examined by the Government of India in the Ministry of Environment and Forests;

And whereas, the Central Government is of the opinion that the said notification should be amended.

2. Now, therefore, in exercise of the powers conferred by sub-section (1) and clause (v) of sub-section (2) of section 3 of the Environment (Protection) Act, 1986 (29 of 1986) read with sub-rule (3) and (4) of rule 5 of the Environment (Protection) Rules, 1986, the Central Government hereby makes the following amendments in paragraph I of the said notification, namely:

(i) For the words "Secretary, Department of Health and Family Welfare" the words "Chairman, Science, Technology and Environment Department and Ex-Officio Secretary to the" shall be substituted;

(ii) For the words "Department of Revenue" the words "Department of Fisheries" shall be substituted;

(iii) For the words "Central for Earth Sciences and Studies" the words "Centre for Earth Science Studies" shall be substituted;

(iv) For the word "Centre" the word "Central" shall be substituted;

(v) For the words "Member Secretary, Kerala State Pollution Control Board" the words "Secretary, Local Government" shall be substituted.

[No. Z-17011/1998-1A-III]
V. RAJAGOPALAN. Jt. Secy.

APPENDIX—VI

MODEL STATE DISASTER MANAGEMENT ACT

STATE DISASTER MANAGEMENT ACT
(DRAFT OF A MODEL ACT FOR THE STATE)

An Act to ensure efficient and effective management of disaster to achieve a greater co-ordination and responsiveness in respect of prevention, reduction ana mitigation of disaster and preparedness programmes for the same to provide for better rescue, relief and rehabilitation of the victims of such disaster and for matters connected therewith or incidental thereto.

Be it enacted by Vidhan Sabha (Legislative Assembly) in the Fifty First Year of the Republic of India as follows:-

CHAPTER - I

PRELIMINARY

1. Short Title Extent and Commencement

(i) The Act may be called State Disaster Management Act, 2000.

(ii) It extends to the whole of the State.

(iii) It shall come into force on such date as the State Government may, by notification in the official Gazette, appoint in this behalf.

2. Definitions

In the Act, unless the context otherwise requires

(i) "Disaster" means a catastrophe, calamity or mishap, a grave occurrence, which causes loss of life, human suffering, damage to and destruction of property, and/or degradation of environment and/or which disrupts the normal functioning of societies, Government and/or communities and/or adversely affects individuals and families with severity and it includes any or more of the occurrences mentioned in Schedule-1

(ii) "The State Government" means the Government of the State of

(iii) "Public Servant" shall have the same meaning assigned to that term in Section 21 of the Indian Penal Code.

(iv) "Life" means Human and Animal Life.

(v) "State" means the State of............................

(vi) "Local Bodies" shall have same meaning as defined in Panchayat Act and Urban Local Bodies Act of the State.

(vii) "Act" means State Disaster Management Act.

(viii) "Notification" means a notification published in the official gazette,

(ix) "Prescribed" means prescribed by the Rules made under the Act

(x) "District' means a Revenue District in the State.

(xi)"District Magistrate" includes Collector and/or Deputy Commissioner. Incharge of a district by whatever nomenclature he may be called.

(xii) "DRC" means District Relief Commissioner who is the District Magistrate so designated by the State Government.

(xiii) "SRC" means State Relief Commissioner, the Officer not below the rank of Secretary to the State Government so designated by the State Government.

(xiv) "STC" means Standing Technical Committee, the Committee constituted by the State Government Under Section 4 (iii) by this Act.

(xv) "Relief Operations" includes any action or step or measure taken, assistance given or support rendered or succour delivered, at any time, before, during or after disaster towards preventing, easing, alleviating, mitigating any suffering or hardship or pain or injury or distress arising out of or relatable to a disaster.

(xvi) "Imprisonment" shall mean imprisonment of either description as defined in Indian Penal Code 1860.

CHAPTER - II

3. Principal Authorities for Disaster Management

The Principal Authorities for the purpose of carrying out the objects of this Act and operationalising its provisions and the rules made thereunder shall be as specified below.

(i) The State Government

(ii) Standing Technical Committee (STC)

(iii) An Officer of the State Government not below the rank of the Secretary shall be appointed to be the State Relief Commissioner (SRC) and he shall be placed in-charge of the relief operations throughout the State,

(iv) District Magistrate shall be designated, as District Relief Commissioner (DRC) and he shall be responsible for relief operations within the district.

4. Powers and Responsibilities of the State Government

(i) Subject to the provisions of this Act, the State Government shall have the power to take all such measures, as it deems necessary or expedient for the purpose of preventing and managing disaster.

(ii) In particular and without prejudice to the generality of the provisions of sub section (i), such measures may include measures with respect to all or any of the following matters, namely,

(a) co-ordination of actions by the State Government, officers, officials and other authorities and NGOs, under this Act or rules made thereunder or under any other law for the time being in force which is relatable to the objects of this Act.

(b) Planning and execution of a Statewide programme for prevention, management and mitigation of Disaster.

(c) Laying down procedures and safeguards for the prevention of Disaster.

(d) Collection and dissemination of information in respect of matters relating to Disasters including suo motto propagation of vital information affecting the public.

(e) Preparation of manuals, codes, or guidelines relating to prevention, management and mitigation of Disaster.

(iii) The State Government shall constitute a Standing Technical Committee for the purpose of facilitating procurement related to disaster management and ensuring the quality of materials, equipments and services to be procured in connection therewith.

(iv) State Government shall exercise supervision and control over the STC, SRC and DRC.

(v) It shall be the duty of the State Government to

(a) to notify the disaster prone areas for the general information of the public and also for the purpose of implementation of the provisions of the Act or Rules made thereunder.

(b) such notification shall be issued once in three years or at such shorter interval whenever the circumstances so warrant.

(vi) The State Government shall draw up a plan for relief in advance and ensure that the concerned officials and local inhabitants are given adequate training for the successful execution of the plan.

(vii) The State Government shall declare an area where a disaster has occurred to be a "disaster affected" area as early as possible and shall denotify the same as soon as disaster ceases, both within a period of time prescribed in this behalf.

(viii) Notwithstanding anything contained in any other law but subject to the provisions of this Act, the State Government, may in exercise of its powers and performance of its functions under this Act, issue directions in writing to any person, officer, or authority and such person, officer, or authority shall be bound to comply with such directions.

5. Duties and Functions of the Standing Technical Committee

(i) The Standing Technical Committee shall

(a) identify such materials, equipments and services as are essential for Disaster Management for any or more of the purposes specified in Sub Clauses a—I, of Clause (i) of section 16.

(b) *ensure the quality and standard of such materials, equipments and services by appropriate certification.*

(c) *for the purpose of facilitating purchase and avoiding delay, select suitable suppliers and enter into rate contracts with them, the facility of which may be availed by State Relief Commissioner, District Relief Commissioner or any other agency so authorised.*

(ii) *In special circumstances to be prescribed in this behalf, it shall be lawful for the Standing Technical Committee to relax or to waive, by general or special orders, to dispense with the ordinary procedures and routine formalities for the purpose of procurement of such materials, equipments and services.*

6. Duties and Functions of the State Relief Commissioner and District Relief Commissioner.

(i) The SRC and the DRC shall be placed in charge of

and be responsible for disaster management operations within the local limits of the State and the District respectively.

(ii) State Relief Commissioner / District Relief Commissioner shall supervise, coordinate, discharge the responsibilities and perform functions within their respective territorial, jurisdiction, as mentioned hereinunder -

(a) to draw up disaster management plans in respect of their territorial jurisdictions for prevention, reduction, preparedness, mitigation, response, warning, emergency operations, rescue, evacuation, relief, recovery and rehabilitation, and to update the same.

(b) to organise training programmes and exercises.

(c) To issue timely warnings to state and local officials and also to the people likely to be affected by any disaster regarding risks and hazards.

(d) To utilise the services or facilities of local Bodies, including Panchayats and Gram Sabhas.

(e) To seek support/assistance from any Institution, organisation, authority, both Government as well as Non-Government and to identify essential functionaries as may be prescribed.

(f) To provide public health and safety information including dissemination of such information.

(g) To adopt health and safety measures including constructing temporary bridges.

(h) To arrange for distribution of medicine, food and other consumable supplies and emergency assistance.

(i) To strive earnestly to save lives and to protect properties.

(j) To strive earnestly to protect and improve the natural environment including forest, flora and fauna.

(k) To endeavor earnestly to ensure at least a minimum standard of relief and rehabilitation as may be prescribed in this behalf.

(l) The State Relief Commissioner shall ensure that medicines and relief equipments are stored at convenient places so that at times of crisis they could be reached to the needy at a short notice. The State Relief Commissioner shall periodically review the validity and availability of medicines, so as to make them readily available in proper condition.

(m) State Relief Commissioner / District Relief Commissioner shall monitor the registration of all daily wage earners to be carried out by their respective employers in disaster prone area so as to facilitate identification of migratory labourers at times of disaster.

(n) State Relief Commissioner / District Relief Commissioner shall enlist volunteers for HAM (Help All Mankind) and other essential requirements and utilise their services.

(o) State Relief Commissioner / District Relief Commissioner shall make a first report to the next higher authority as prescribed within 24 hours of the occurrence of a disaster, and a weekly report till the disaster continues and a detailed final report of the disaster soon after the cessation of the disaster.

(p) They shall submit an Annual Report (Financial Year) as prescribed regarding the disasters occurring and management thereof within their jurisdictions by the end of the month of June of the following year, to the next higher authority.

7. Powers of State Relief Commissioner and District Relief Commissioner

(i) it shall be lawful for the State Relief Commissioner/ District Relief Commissioner or any of his nominees, duly authorised in this behalf

(a) to requisition the services of any aduit private individual and to assign to him such responsibility, consistent with his age and ability, as may be deemed fit and proper, for the purpose of carrying out the objectives of this Act and translating its provisions into actions.

(b) to requisition men, material, building and transport from any Government organisation, department, corporations, companies, public sector undertakings, and the like, functioning within his jurisdiction, with a view to operationalise the Act and the persons in charge of such organisations, departments, corporations, companies, public sector undertaking, shall be bound to comply with the requisition made in this behalf.

(ii) Whoever being called upon in writing by the State Relief Commissioner or District Relief Commissioner to comply with such requisition, without reasonable excuse, refuses or neglects to do so, shall be deemed to have committed an offence, punishable u/s 187 of the Indian Penal Code.

(iii) *It shall be lawful for the State Relief Commissioner or District Relief Commissioner or for any other person authorised by general or special order of the State Relief*

Commissioner/District Relief Commissioner in his behalf, to enter into or upon any building or land with or without assistants or workmen in order to make any inquiry, inspection, measurement, valuation or survey or to execute any work, which is authorised by the Act. or to see whether the provisions of the Act were complied with.

(iv) *It shall be lawful for any person, authorised by or under the Act to make any entry into any place, to open or cause to be opened, any door, gate or other barrier in saving lives and/or properties, if he considers the opening thereof necessary for the purpose of such entry; and if the owner or occupier is absent, or being present, refuses to open such door, gate or barrier for any or more of the purposes specified below:*

(a) Removal of Debris
(b) Conduct of search and rescue operations
(c) Providing Emergency shelter and/or services
(d) Provisioning of food, medicine and other essential needs
(e) Demolition of unsafe structure which may endanger the public
(f) Warning of further risk and hazards.
(g) Dissemination of information including do's and don'ts
(h) Rendering technical safety advice
(i) Reduction of all immediate threats to life and public health and safety,
(j) Constructing temporary bridges for emergency evacuation.

(v) (a) It shall be the responsibility of the State Relief Commissioner and/or District Relief Commissioner to make adequate arrangements for evacuation of the inhabitants before, during and after the disaster strikes and for the purpose, they shall be competent to give appropriate direction for evacuation.

(b) In the event of such direction being disobeyed, it shall be lawful for the SRC/DRC or such authority as may be empowered in his behalf to use such amount of force as may be necessary for effecting the evacuation of inhabitants before, during and after the disaster strikes.

(c) *Wilful violation of such directions shall constitute an offence under this Act.*

8. Role of Police in Disaster Management

(i) Under the overall supervision of the SRC, the Police of the State shall be geared effectively and adequately to reach the site of disaster immediately with a view to carrying out relief ana rescue operations.

(ii) Under the overall supervision or" DRC, it shall be the responsibility of the Superintendent of Police in-charge of the District to ensure that the police personnel of adequate strength reach the site of Disaster immediately with a view to carrying out rescue and relief operations. Each of them may be utilised during the disaster period for giving warnings, supervising relief operations, providing relief and rehabilitating people.

(iii) The Police communication system, for instance, wireless etc. shall be made available, free of charge, for being used for transmission and receipt of messages in connection with disaster.

(iv) *The Director General of Police shall make suitable provisions for the following:*

(a) Police wireless system/communication system must be always in good working condition.

(b) Police personnel should be identified, and given adequate training for the purposes of disaster management so that at times of crisis their services may be readily and properly utilised.

(c) Essential elements of disaster management should be incorporated in the training at entry point of service to all police personnel.

(d) A code of conduct shall be prescribed for the Police personnel to be observed strictly by them in any Disaster situation and the contents thereof shall be notified for the general information of the public.

(e) It shall be the duty of every police personnel to rush to the aid of any person in need of help in a disaster situation.

(f) It shall be the duty and responsibility of the police personnel deployed for such relief operations to prevent commission of cognizable offences including all offences against property, human body and public tranquility.

9. Rold of Fire Service, Home Guard and Civil Defence Personnel in Disaster Management

Under overall supervision of the SRC/ DRC,

(i) It shall be the responsibility of the Chief of each of the aforesaid organisation to ensure that their personnel of adequate strength reach the site of Disaster immediately with a view to carrying out rescue and relief operations. Each of them may be utilised during the disaster period for giving warnings, supervising relief operations, providing relief and rehabilitating people.

(ii) The aforesaid organisations shall be geared effectively and adequately so that its personnel may reach the site of disaster immediately with a view to carrying out relief and rescue operations.

(iii) The communication system of the above said organisations, for instance, wireless etc. shall be made available, free of charge, for being used for transmission and receipt of messages in connection with disaster.

(iv) The Chief of the. Organisations shall make suitable provisions for the following:

(a) wireless system/communication system must be always in good working condition.

(b) personnel should be identified, and given adequate training for the purposes of disaster management so that at times of crisis their services may be readily and properly utilised.

(c) Essential elements of disaster management should be incorporated in the training at entry point of service to all personnel.

(d) It shall be the duty of every person to rush to the aid of any person in need of help in a disaster situation.

(e) A code of conduct shall be prescribed for the personnel to be observed strictly by them in any Disaster situation and the contents thereof shall be notified for the general information of the public.

10. Duties of Local Bodies and Other Agencies

(i) Each Municipal Local Body shall prepare a Disaster Management plan to meet adequately the requirements of the locality concerned.

(ii) Each Factory as defined under the Factories Act 1948, each of the authorities, undertakings and enterprises, as may be prescribed, shall have a disaster management plan in conformity with the disaster management plan of local authorities / district administration and consistent with the laws made in this behalf.

(iii) Such local bodies, factories, authorities, undertakings, enterprises shall be responsible for effective implementation of the plans drawn up by them in this behalf.

11. Financial Arrangements

All civil works, equipment purchases, and training activities for prevention and reduction of Disaster shall be treated as developmental projects and the expenditure on such accounts shall be the first charge on the plan funds.

12. Insurance

(i) *The state government by making rules, shall make life and property insurance mandatory for the persons residing in the recurrent disaster prone areas; for example the coastal belts, the flood prone areas, the areas near the nuclear, chemical and hazardous industries, large congregations as may be specified under the rules.*

(ii) *It shall be lawful for the State Government to use Panchayats for carrying out the insurance contracts with the insurance companies. Further, local inhabitants, including landless / shelterless, who are living below the poverty line shall be identified and their insurance premium shall be paid by the State.*

(iii) Every property owner in the disaster prone areas prescribed shall be under a legal obligation to get his property insured as per the local standards, expeditiously, failing which no claim for compensation shall be entertained.

13. Communication

It shall be lawful for any of the principal authorities namely, State Government, State Relief Commissioner and District Relief Commissioner to use or cause to be used all media like Doordarshan, Cable TVs, All India Radio, FM Radios, Internet, cinema halls and similar communication channels for broadcasting news and disseminating information regarding disasters.

14. Severity of Disaster

(i) As soon as the disaster has occurred, the State Government shall make a report to the Central

Government giving out the essential details which would include among other things, the extent of damage to and destruction of properties and loss of life, etc.

(ii) Whenever the situation so warrants, the State Government may seek assistance from the Central Government in such form and to such extent as may be deemed necessary.

(iii) *On receipt of such request from the State Government, the Central Government may make appropriate arrangements for relief and rescue operations and if considered necessary, depute a team of experts to assess the gravity of the Disaster and extent of damage and destruction.*

(iv) The Central Government may with due regard to the nature and gravity of the Disaster, including the extent of damage and destruction, release such funds as may be deemed appropriate.

(v) *On receipt of financial assistance from the Central Government, the State government shall be accountable to the Central Government for proper utilisation of funds and for submitting full accounts thereof.*

15. Training

Key functionaries belong to police force, fire service, civil defence, home guard organisation and selected members of the public shall be trained regularly and in case of necessity, their services *may be requisitioned at short notice.*

16. Obligation to Assist Relief Officials

(i) Every citizen shall be bound to assist the State and/or District Relief Commissioner or such other public servant entrusted with or engaged in Disaster Management work as may be authorised by him in this behalf reasonably demanding his aid for the purpose of disaster management which includes among other things:

(a) Prevention
(b) Reduction
(c) Preparedness
(d) Mitigation
(e) Response
(f) Warning
(g) Emergency Operations
(h) Rescue
(i) Evacuation
(j) Relief
(k) Recovery
(l) Rehabilitation

(ii) *Any person, who without reasonable cause, refuses or neglects to perform such public duty, when called upon to do so by an order in writing delivered or tendered to him, shall be deemed to have committed an offence punishable under section 187 of the Indian Penal Code.*

17. Non-discrimination in Disaster Management

All principal authorities shall ensure that the distribution of supplies, the process of application and other relief and assistance activities are accomplished in an equitable and impartial manner without discrimination on the grounds of race, colour, religion, caste, sex, age, region, language, economic status or political affiliation.

CHAPTER - III

LIABILITIES AND LEGAL PROCEEDINGS

18. Offences

(i) Wilfull violation of any duty imposed by the Act or Rules made *thereunder shall be deemed to be an offence.*

(ii) Such offence shall be punishable with imprisonment for a term not exceeding six months or with fine which may extend Rs. 5000/- or with both.

19. Penalty for Contraventions of the Provisions of the Act and the Rules, Orders and Directions

(i) Whoever fails to comply with or contravenes of any of the provisions of this Act or the rules made thereunder or orders or directions issued in this behalf shall in respect of each such failure or contravention be guilty of an offence against this Act.

(ii) Such offence shall be punishable with imprisonment of either description, simple or rigorous, for a term, which may extend to six months or with fine, which may extend to Rs. 5000/- or with both.

(iii) Notwithstanding anything contained in the Criminal Procedure Code, 1973 no court inferior to that of Metropolitan Magistrate or a *Judicial Magistrate of First Class, shall try any offence under this Act.*

20. Offences Committed by the Governemnt Department/ Agency

(i) Where an offence under this Act has been committed by any department of Government, the Head of the Department or Office shall be deemed to be guilty of the offence and shall be liable to be proceeded against and punished accordingly, provided that, nothing contained in this section shall render such Head liable to punishment if he proves that the offence was committed without his knowledge or that he exercised due diligence to prevent this commission of such offence.

(ii) Notwithstanding anything contained in sub section (i), where an offence under this Act has been committed by a Department of Government and it is proved that the offence has been committed with the consent or connivance of /or is attributable to any neglect on the part of any officer or official other than that of the Head of the Department or office, such officer or official shall also be deemed to be guilty of that offence and shall be liable to be proceeded against and punished accordingly.

21. Civil Liability for Misuse of Funds

(i) Any official/functionary entrusted with or engaged in any relief and/or rescue operation, if found responsible, directly or indirectly, for loss of public money or damage to public property shall be liable for recovery of funds which shall be to the tune of 150 per cent of the total loss / damage caused.

(ii) An amount to the tune of 150 per cent of the embezzled / misappropriated amount shall be recovered and a penalty in cash shall be imposed on such official/ functionary without prejudice to any other legal proceedings or criminal prosecution that may be launched against him.

(iii) The Competent Authority for imposing such penalty for loss of public money and damage to public property shall be as prescribed.

22. Previous Sanction of the Government or the District Magistrate Necessary

(i) No prosecution shall be instituted against any person other than a public servant not removable from his office save by or with the sanction of the government in respect of any offence under the Act without the previous sanction of the District Magistrate.

(ii) When any public servant not removable from his office save by or with the sanction of the Government is accused of any offence alleged to have been committed by him while acting or purporting to act in the discharge of his official duty under the Act, no court shall take cognizance of such offence except with the previous sanction:-

(a) In the case of a public servant who is employed or, as the case may be, was at the time of commission of the alleged offence employed, in connection with the affairs of the Union, of the Central Government;

(b) In the case of a public servant who is employed or, as the case may be, was at the time of commission of the alleged offence employed, in connection with the affairs of the State, of the State Government.

CHAPTER - IV

MISCELLANEOUS

23. Protection of Action Taken in Good Faith

No suit, prosecution or other legal proceeding shall lie against any person for anything, which is in good faith done or intended to be done under the Act.

24. Bar of Jurisdiction

No Civil Court shall have jurisdiction to entertain any suit or proceeding in respect of anything done, action taken or order or direction issued by the State Government or any other authority or officer in pursuance of any power conferred by or in relation to its or his functions under the Act.

25. Effect of other Laws

(i) Subject to the provisions of sub-section (ii), the provisions of the Act and the Rules or orders made there under shall have effect, notwithstanding anything inconsistent therewith contained in any enactment other than the Act.

(ii) Where any act or omission constitutes an offence punishable under the Act and also under any other Act, then the offender found guilty of such offence shall be liable to be punished under the other Act and not under the Act.

26. Power to Make Rules

(i) The State Government may make rules to carry out the purposes and objects of this Act.

(ii) All Rules made by the State Government under this Act shall be published in the official gazette and on such publication, shall have effect as if enacted under this Act.

(iii) Every Rule made by the State Government under this Act shall be laid, as soon as may be after it is made, before the State Legislature.

SCHEDULE-I

LIST OF DISASTERS IDENTIFIED BY THE HIGH POWERED COMMITTEE

I. Water and Climate Related Disasters

1. Floods and Drainage Management
2. Cyclones
3. Tornadoes and Hurricanes
4. Hailstorm
5. Cloud Burst
6. Thunder and Lightning
7. Snow Avalanches
8. Heat Wave and Cold Wave
9. Sea Erosion
10. Droughts

II. Geologically related Disasters

1. Earthquakes
2. Landslides and Mudflows
3. Dam Bursts
4. Mine Fires

III. Chemical, Industrial & Nuclear related Disasters

1. Chemical and Industrial Disasters
2. Nuclear Disasters

IV. Accident related Disasters

1. Urban Fires
2. Village Fire
3. Forest Fires
4. Electrical Disasters & Fires
5. Serial Bomb Blasts
6. Oil Spill
7. Festival related Disasters
8. Air, Road and Rail Accidents
9. Boat Capsising
10. Mine Flooding
11. Major Building Collapse

V. Biologically related Disasters

1. Biological Disasters and Epidemics
2. Pest Attacks
3. Cattle Epidemics
4. Food Poisoning

APPENDIX—VII

THE ENVIRONMENT (PROTECTION) ACT, 1986

[23rd May, 1986]

An Act to provide for the protection and improvement of environment and for matters connected there with:

Whereas the decisions were taken at the United Nations Conference on the Human Environment held at Stockholm June. 1972 in which India participated, to take appropriate steps for the protection and improvement of human environment;

And whereas it is considered necessary further to implement the decisions aforesaid in so far as they relate to the protection and improvement of environment and the prevention of hazards to human beings, other living creatures, plants and properly;

Be it cnacted by Parliament in the Thirty-seventh Year of the Republic of India as follows:-

PRELIMINARY

I. Short title, extent and commencement- (1) This Act may be called the Environment (Protection) Act. 1986.

(2) It extends to the whole of India.

(3) It shall come into force on such dale as the Central Government may, by notification in the Official Gazette, appoint and different dales may be appointed for different provisions of this Act and for different areas.

2. Definitions - In this Act. unless the context other wise requires-

(a) "environment" includes water, air and land and the inter-relationship which exists among and between water, air and land, and human beings, other living creatures, plants, micro-organism and property;

(b) "environmental pollutant" means any solid. 1iquid or gaseous substance present in such concentration as may he, or tend to be injurious to environment;

(c) "environmental pollution" means the presence in the environment of any environmental pollutant;

(d) "handling", in relation to any substance, means the manufacture, processing, treatment, package, storage, transportation, use. collection, destruction. conversion, offering for sale, transfer or the like of such substance;

(e) "hazardous substance" means any substance or preparation which, by reason of its chemical or physico-chemical properties or handling is liable to cause harm to human beings, other living creatures, plant, micro-organism. property or the environment;

(f) "occupier", in relation to any factory or premises, means a person who has control over the affairs of the factory or the premises and includes in relation to any substance, the person in possession of the substance;

(g) "prescribed" means prescribed by rules made under this Act.

GENERAL POWERS OF THE CENTRAL GOVERNMENT

3. Power of Central Government to take measures to protect and improve environment.- (1) Subject to the provisions of this Act. the Central Government, shall have the power to take all such measures as it deems necessary or expedient for the purpose of protecting and improving the quality of the environment and preventing controlling and abating environmental pollution.

(2) In particular, and without prejudice to the generality of the provisions of sub-section (1), such measures

may include measures with respect to all or any of the following matters, namely:-

(i) co-ordination of actions by the State Governments, officers and other authorities,-

(a) under this Act, or the rules made thereunder, or

(b) under any other law for the time being in force which is relatable to the objects of this Act;

(ii) planning and execution of a nation-wide programme for the prevention, control and abatement of environmental pollution;

(iii) laying down standards for the quality of environment in its various aspects;

(iv) laying down standards for emission or discharge of environmental pollutants from various sources whatsoever;

Provided that different standards for emission or discharge may be laid down under this clause from different sources having regard to the quality or composition of the emission or discharge of environmental pollutants from such souces;

(v) restriction of areas in which any industries, operations or processes or class of industries, operations or processes shall be carried out or shall not be carried out subject to certain safeguards;

(vi) laying down procedures and safeguards for the prevention of accidents which may cause environmental pollution and remedial measures for such accidents;

(vii) laying down procedures and safeguards for the handling of hazardous substances;

(viii) examination of such manufacturing processes, materials and substances as are likely to cause environmental pollution;

(ix) carrying out and sponsoring investigations and research relating to problems of environmental pollution;

(x) inspection of any premises, plant, equipment, machinery, manufacturing or other processes materials or substances and giving, by order, of such directions to such authorities, officers or persons as it may consider necessary to take steps for the prevention, control and abatement of environmental pollution;

(xi) establishment or recognition of environmental laboratories and institutes to carry out the functions entrusted to such environmental laboratories and institutes under this Act;

(xii) collection and dissemination of information in respect of matters relating to environmental pollution;

(xiii) preparation of manuals, codes or guides relating to the prevention, control and abatement of environmental pollution;

(xiv) such other matters as the Central Government deems necessary or expedient for the purpose of securing the effective implementation of the provisions of this Act.

(3) The Central Government may, if it considers it necessary or expedient so to do for the purpose of this Act, by order, published in the Official Gazette, constitute an authority or authorities by such name or names as may be specified in the order for the purpose of exercising and performing such of the powers and functions, (including the power to issue directions under section 5) of the Central Government under this Act and for taking measures with respect

to such of the matters referred to in sub-section (2) as may be mentioned in the order and subject to the supervision and control of the Central Government and the provisions of such order, such authority or authorities may exercise the powers or perform the functions or take the measures so mentioned in the order as if such authority or authorities has been empowered by this Act to exercise those powers or perform those functions or take such measures.

4. **Appointment of Officers and their powers and functions.** - (1) Without prejudice to the provisions of sub-sections (3) of section 3. the Central Government may appoint officers with such designation as it thinks fit for the purposes of this Act and may entrust to them such of the powers and functions under this Act as it may deem fit.

(2) The officers appointed under sub-section (1) shall he subject to the general control and direction of the Central Government or, if so directed by that Government, also of the authority or authorities, if any, constituted under sub-section (3) of section 3 or of any other authority or officer.

5. **Power to give directions.** - Notwithstanding anything contained in any other law but subject to the provisions of this Act. the Central Government may, in the exercise of its powers and performance of its functions under this Act, issue directions in writing to any person, officer or any authority and such person. officer or authority shall be bound to comply with such directions.

Explanation For the avoidance of doubts, it is hereby declared that the power to issue directions under this section includes the power to direct-

(a) the closure, prohibition or regulation of any industry, operation or process; or

(b) stoppage or regulation of the supply of electricity or water or any other service.

6. Rules to regulate environment pollution.- (1) The Central Government may, by notification in the Official Gazette, make rules in respect of all or any of the matters referred to in section 3.

(2) In particular, and without prejudice to the generality of the foregoing power, such rules may provide for all or any of the following matters, namely:-

(a) the standards of quality of air, water or soil for various areas and purposes;

(b) the maximum allowable limits of concentration of various environmental pollutants (including noise) for different areas;

(c) the procedures and safeguards for the handling of hazardous substances;

(d) the prohibition and restrictions on the handling of hazardous substances in different areas;

(e) the prohibition and restriction on the location of industries and the carrying on process and operations in different areas;

(f) the procedures and safeguards for the prevention of accidents which may cause environmental pollution and for providing for remedial measures for such accidents.

PREVENTION, CONTROL, AND ABATEMENT OF ENVIRONMENTAL POLLUTION

7. Persons carrying on industry operation, etc, not to allow emission or discharge of environmental pollutants in excess of the standards.- No person carrying on any industry, operation or process shall discharge or emit or permit to be discharged or emitted any environmental pollutants in excess of such standards as may be prescribed.

8. Persons handling huzardous substances to comply with procedural safeguards. - No person shall handle or cause to be handled any hazardous substance except in accordance with such procedure and after complying with such safeguards as may be prescribed.

9. Furnishing of information to authorities and agencies in certain cases.-(1) Where the discharge of any environmental pollutant in excess of the prescribed standards occurs or is apprehended to occur due to any accident or other unforeseen act or event, the person responsible for such discharge and the person in charge of the place at which such discharge occurs or is apprehended to occur shall be bound to prevent or mitigate the environmental pollution caused as a result of such discharge and shall also forthwith-

(a) intimate the fact of such occurrence or apprehension of such occurrence; and

(b) be bound, if called upon, to render all assistance, to such authorities or agencies as may be prescribed.

(2) On receipt of information with respect to the fact or apprehension of any occurrence of the nature referred to in sub-section (1). whether through intimation under that sub-section or otherwise, the authorities or agencies referred to in sub-section(l) shall, as early as practicable, cause such remedial measures to be taken as are necessary to prevent or mitigate the environmental pollution.

(3) The expenses, if any, incurred by any authority or agency with respect to the remedial measures referred to in sub-section (2), together with interest (at such reasonable rate as the Government may, by order, fix) from the date when a demand for the expenses is made until it is paid, may be recovered by such authority or agency from the person concerned as arrears of land revenue or of public demand.

10. **Powers of entry and inspection**.- (1) Subject to the provisions of this section, any person empowered by the Central Government in this behalf shall have a right to enter, at all reasonable times with such assistance as he considers necessary, any place-

(a) for the purpose of performing any of the functions of the Central Government entrusted to him;

(b) for the purpose of determining whether and if so in what manner, any such functions are to be performed or whether any provisions of this Act or the rules made thereunder or any notice, order, direction or authorisation served, made, given or granted under this Act is being or has been complied with;

(c) for the purpose of examining and testing any equipment, industrial plant, record, register, document or any other material object or for conducting a search of any building in which he has reason to believe that an offence under this Act or the rules made thereunder has been or is being or is about to be committed and for seizing any such equipment, industrial plant, record, register, document or other material object if he has reason to believe that it may furnish evidence of the commission of an offence punishable under this Act or the rules made thereunder or that such seizure is necessary to prevent or mitigate environmental pollution.

(2) Every person carrying on any industry, operation or process of handling any hazardous substance shall be bound to render all assistance to the person empowered by the Central Government under sub-section (1) for carrying out the functions under that sub-section and if he fails to do so without any

reasonable cause or excuse, he shall be guilty of an offence under this Act.

(3) If any person wilfully delays or obstructs any persons empowered by the Central Government under sub-section (1) in the performance of his functions, he shall be guilty of an offence under this Act.

(4) The provisions of the Code of Criminal Procedure, 1973, or, in relation to the State of Jammu and Kashmir, or an area in which that Code is not in force, the provisions of any corresponding law in force in that Slate or area shall, so far as may be, apply to any search or seizures under this section as they apply to any search or seizure made under the authority of a warrant issued under section 94 of the said Code or as the case may be. under the corresponding provision of the said law.

11. **Power to take sample and procedure to be followed in connection therewith.** - (1) The Central Government or any officer empowered by it in this behalf, shall have power to take, for the purpose of analysis, samples of air, water, soil or other substance from any factory, premises or other place in such manner as may be prescribed.

(2) The result of any analysis of a sample taken under sub-section (1) shall not he admissible in evidence in any legal proceeding unless the provisions of sub-sections (3) and (4) are complied with.

(3) Subject to the provisions of sub-section (4), the person taking the sample under sub-section (1) shall -

(a) serve on the occupier or his agent or person in charge of the place, a notice, then and there, in such form as may he prescribed. of his intention to have it so analysed;

(b) in the presence of the occupier or his agent or person, collect a sample for analysis;

(c) cause the sample to he placed in a container or containers which shall he marked and sealed and shall also be signed both by the person taking the sample and the occupier or his agent or person;

(d) send without delay, the container or the containers to the laboratory established or recognised by the Central Government under section 12.

(4) When a sample is taken for analysis under sub-section (1) and the person taking the sample serves on the the occupier or his agent or person, a notice under clause (a) of sub-section (3). then.-

(a) in a case where the occupier, his agent or person wilfully absents himself, the person taking the sample shall collect the sample for analysis to he placed in a container or containers which shall be marked and sealed and shall also be signed by the person taking the sample, and

(b) in a case where the occupier or his agent or person present at the time of taking the sample refuses to sign the marked and sealed container or containers of the sample as required under clause (c) of sub-section (3). the marked and sealed container or containers shall be signed by the person taking the samples.

and the container or containers shall be sent without delay by the person taking the sample for analysis to the laboratory established or recognised under section 12 and such person shall inform the Government Analyst appointed or recognised under section 13 in writing, about the wilfull absence of the occupier or his agent or person, or as the case-may be, his refusal to sign the container or containers.

12. Environmental laboratories.- (1) The Central Government may, by notification in the Official Gazette.-

(a) establish one or more environmental laboratories;

(b) recognise one or more laboratories or institutes as environmental laboratories to carry out the functions entrusted to an environmental laboratory under this Act.

(2) The Central Government may, by notification in the Official Gazette, make rules specifying-

(a) the functions of the environmental laboratory;

(b) the procedure for the submission to the said laboratory of samples of air, water, soil or other substance for analysis or tests, the form of the laboratory report thereon and the fees payable for such report;

(c) such oilier mailers as may be necessary or expedient to enable that laboratory to carry out its function.

13. Government Analysts - The Central Government may by notification in the Official Gazette, appoint or recognise such persons as it thinks fit and having the prescribed qualifications to be Government Analysts for the purpose of analysis of samples of air, water, soil or other substance sent for analysis to any environmental laboratory established or recognised under sub-section (1) of section 12.

14. Reports of Government Analysts - Any document purporting to be a report signed by a Government analyst may be used as evidence of the facts stated therein in any proceeding under this Act.

15. Penalty for contravention of the provisions of the Act and the rules, orders and directions. - (1) Whoever fails to comply with or contravenes any of the provisions of this

Act, or the rules made or orders or directions issued thereunder, shall, in respect of each such failure or contravention, be punishable with imprisonment for a term which may extend to five years with fine which may extend to one lakh rupees, or with both, and in case the failure or contravention continues, with additional fine which may extend to five thousand rupees for every day during which such failure or contravention continues after the conviction for the first such failure or contravention.

(2) If the failure or contravenlion referred to in sub-section (I) continues beyond a period of one year after the date of conviction, the offender shall be punishable with imprisonment for a term which may extend to seven years.

16. Offences by companies. (1) Where any offence under this Act has been committed by a company, every person who. at the time the offence was committed, was directly in charge of, and was responsible to, the company for the conduct of the business of the company, as well as the company, shall be deemed to be guilty of the offence and shall he liable to be proceeded against and punished accordingly:

Provided that nothing contained in this sub-section shall render any such person liable to any punishment provided in this Act. if he'proves that the offence was committed without his knowledge or that be exercised all due diligence to prevent the commission of such offence.

(2) Not withstanding anything contained in sub-section (1), where an offence under this Act has been committed by a company and it is proved that the offence has been committed with the consent or connivance of. or is attributable to any neglect on the part of any director, manager, secretary or other officer of the company, such director, manager, secretary or other officer shall also deemed to be guilty of that

offence and shall be liable to be proceeded against and punished accordingly.

Explanation - For the purpose of this section -

(a) "company" means any body corporate and includes a firm or other association of individuals;

(b) "director", in relation to a firm, means a partner in the firm.

17. Offenees by Government Departments. (1) Where an offence under this Act has been committed by any Department of Government, the Head of the Department shall be deemed to be guilty of the offence and shall be liable to he proceeded against and punished accordingly:

Provided that nothing contained in this section shall render such Head of the Department liable to any punishment if he proves that the offence was committed without his knowledge or that he exercise all due diligence to prevent the commission of such offence.

(2) Notwithstanding anything contained in sub-section.- (1) where an offence under this Act has been committed by a Department of Government and it is proved that the offence has been committed with the consent or connivance of. or is attributable to any neglect on the part of any officer, other than the Head of the Department, such officer shall also be deemed to be guilty of that offence and shall be liable to be proceeded against and punished accordingly.

MISCELLANEOUS

18. Protection of action taken in good faith. - No suit, prosecution or other legal proceeding shall lie against the Government or any officer or other employee of the Government or any authority constituted under this Act or any member, officer or other employee of such authority in respect of anything which is done or intended to be done in good faith in pursuance of this Act or the rules made or orders or directions issued thereunder.

19. Cognizance of offences. - No court shall lake cognizance of any offence under this Act except on a complaint made by-

(a) the Central Government or any authority or officer authorised in this behalf by that Government, or

(b) any person wh has given notice of not less than sixty days, in the manner prescribed, of the alleged offence and of his intention to make a complaint, to the Central Government or the authority or officer authorised aforesaid.

20. Information, reports or returns. -The Central Government may, in relation to its function under this Act, from time to time, require any person, officer. State Government or authority to furnish to it or any statistics, accounts and other information and such person, officer. State Government or other authority shall be bound to do so.

21. Members, officers and employees of the authority constituted under section 3 to be public servants - All the members of the authority, constituted, if any in pursuance of any provisions of this Act or the rules made or orders or directions issued thereunder shall be deemed to be public servants within the meaning of section 21 of the Indian Penal Code (45 of 1860).

22. Bar of Jurisdiction- No civil court shall have jurisdiction to entertain any suit or proceeding in respect of anything done, action taken or order or direction issued by the Central Government or any other authority or officer in pursuance of any power conferred by or in relation to its or his functions under this Act.

23. Powers to delegate. - Without prejudice to the provisions of sub-section (3), the Central Government may, by notification in the Official Gazette, delegate, subject to such conditions and limitations as may be specified in the notifications, such of its powers and functions under this Act [except, the powers to constitute an authority under sub-section (3) of section 3 and to make rules under section 25] as it may deem necessary or expedient, to any officer. State Government or authority.

24. Effect of other laws.- (1) Subject to the provisions of sub-section (2) the provisions of this Act and the rules or orders made therein shall have effect notwithstanding anything inconsistent therewith contained in any enactment other than this Act.

(2) Where any act or omission constitutes an offence punishable under this Act and also under any other Act then the offender found guilty of such offence shall be liable to be punished under the other Act and not under this Act.

25. Power to make rules. - (1) The Central Government may, by notification in the Official Gazette, make rules for carrying out the pu poses of this Act.

(2) In particular, and without prejudice to the generality of the foregoing power, such rules-may provide for all or any of the following matters, namely-

(a) the standards in excess of which environmental pollutants shall not be discharged or emitted under section 7;

(b) the procedure in accordance with and the safeguards in compliance with which hazardous substances shall be handled or caused to be handled under section 8;

(c) the authorities or agencies to which intimation

of the fact of occurrence or apprehension of occurrence of the discharge of any environmental pollutant in excess of the prescribed standards snall be given and to whom all assistance shall be bound to rendered under sub-section (1) of section 9;

(d) the manner in which samples of air, water, soil or other substance for the purpose of analysis shall be taken under sub-sect ion (1) of section II;

(e) the form in which notice of intention to have a sample analysed shall be served under clause (a) of sub section (3) of section 11;

(f) the functions of the environmental laboratories, the procedure for the submission to such laboratories of samples of air, water, soil and other substances for analysis or test; the form of laboratory report; the fees payable for such, report and other matters to enable such laboratories to carry out their functions under sub-section (2) of section 12;

(g) the qualifications of Government Analyst appointed or recognised for the purpose of analysis of samples of air, water, soil or other substances under section 13;

(h) the manner in which notice of the offence and the intention to make a complaint to the Central Government shall be given under clause (b) of section 19;

(i) the authority or officer to whom any reports, returns, statistics accounts and other information shall be furnished under section 20;

(j) any other matter which is required to be, or may be, prescribed.

26. Rules made under this Act to be laid before Parliament. -Every rule made under this Act shall be laid, as soon as may be after it is made, before each House of Parliament, while it is in session, for a total period of thirty days which may be comprised in one session or in two or more succcessive sessions, and if, before the expiry of the immediately following the session or the successive sessions aforesaid, both Houses agree in making any modification in the rule or both Houses agree that the rule should not be made, the rule shall thereafter have effect only in such modified form or be of no effect, as the case may be; so, however, that any such modification or annulment shall be without prejudice to the validity of anything previously done under that rule.

APPENDIX—VIII

HAZARDOUS WASTES (MANAGEMENT AND HANDLING) RULES, 1989[1]

In exercise of the powers conferred by section 6, 8 and 25 of the Environment (Protection) Act, 1986 (29 of 1986), the Central Government hereby makes the following rules, namely,-

1. Short Title and Commencement

(1) These rules may be called the Hazardous Wastes (Management and Handling) Rules, 1989.

(2) They shall come into fore on the dale of their publication in the Official Gazette.

2. Application

These rules shall apply to hazardous wastes as specified in the Schedule and shall not apply to,-

(a) waste water and exhaust gases as covered under the provisions of the Water (Prevention and Control of Pollution) Act, 1974 (6 of 1974), and the Air (Prevention and Control of Pollution) Act, 1981 (14 of 1981), and rules made thereunder;

(b) wastes arising out of the operation from ships beyond five kilometres as covered under the provisions of the Merchant Shipping Act, 1958 (44 of 1958), and the rules made thereunder;

(c) radio active wastes as covered under the provisions of the Atomic Energy Act, 1962 (33 of 1962), and rules made thereunder.

3. Definitions

In these rules, unless the context otherwise requiries,

(a) "Act" means the Environment (Protection) Act, 1986 (29 of 1980);

(b) "applicant" means a person or an organisation that applies, in Form I, for granting of authorisation to perform specific activities connected with handling of hazardous wastes;

(c) "authorisation" means permission for collection, reception, treatment, transport, storage and disposal of hazardous wastes, granted by the competent authority in Form 2;

(d) "authorised person" means a person or an organisation authorised by the competent authority to collect, treat, transport, store or dispose of hazardous wastes in accordance with the guidelines to be issued by the competent authority from time to time;

(e) "export" with its grammatical variations and cognate expressions, means taking out of India to a place outside India;

(f) "export" means any person under the jurisdiction of the exporting country who exports hazardous wastes and the exporting country itself, which exports hazardous wastes;

(g) "facility" means any location wherein the processes incidental to the waste generation, collection, reception, treatment, storage and disposal are carried out;

(h) "Form" means Form appended to these rules;

(i) "hazardous wastes" means categories of wastes specified in the Schedules;

(j) "hazardous wastes site" means a place for collection, reception, treatment, storage and disposal of hazardous wastes which has been duly approved by the competent authority;

(k) "import", with its grammatical variations and cognate expressions, bringing into India from a place outside India;

(l) "importer" means an occupier or any person who imports hazardous waste;

(m) "operator of a facility" means a person who owns or operates a facility for collection, reception, treatment, storage and disposal of hazardous waste;

(n) "Schedule" means the Schedule appended to these rules;

(o) "State Pollution Control Board" means the Board appointed under sub-section (1) of section 4 of the Water (Prevention and Control of Pollution Act, 1974 (6 of 1974) and under section 4 of the Air (Prevention and Control of Pollution) Act, 1981 (14 of 1981);

(p) "transboundary movement" means any movement of hazardous wastes or other wastes from an area under the national jurisdiction of one country to or through an area under the national jurisdiction of another country to or through an area not under the national jurisdiction of any country, provided at least two countries are involved in the movement;

(q) the words and expressions used in these rules and not defined but defined in the Act, shall have the meanings respectively assigned to them in the Act.

4. Responsibility of the Occupier for Handling of Wastes

(1) The occupier generating hazardous wastes listed in column (2) of the Schedule in quantities equal to or exceed ing the limits given in column (3) of the said Schedule, shall take all practical steps to ensure that such wastes are properly handled and disposed of without any adverse, effects which may result for such wastes and the occupier shall also be responsible for proper collection, reception, treatment, storage and disposal of these wastes either himself or through the operator of facility.

(2) The occupier or any other person acting on his behalf

who intends to get his hazardous waste treated by the operator of a facility under sub-rule (1) shall give to the operator of a facility such information as may be specified by the [2][State Pollution Control Board or Committee].

5. Grant of Authorisation for Handling Hazardous Wastes

(1) Hazardous wastes shall be collected, treated, stored and disposed of only in such facilities as may be authorised for this purpose.

(2) Every occupier generating hazardous wastes and having a facility for collection, reception, treatment, transport, storage and disposal of such wastes shall make an application in Form 1 to the [2][State Pollution Control Board or Committee for the grant of authorisation for any of the above activities:

Provided that the occupier not having a facility for the collection, reception, treatment, transport, storage and disposal of hazardous wastes shall make an application to the State Pollution Control Board in Form I for the grant of authorisation within a period of six months from the dale of commencement of these rules.

(3) Any person who intends to be an operator of a facility for the collection, reception, treatment, transport, storage and disposal of hazardous wastes, shall make an application in Form I to the [State Pollution Control Board or Committee for] the grain of authorisation for any of the above activities:

Provided that the operator engaged in the business of collection, reception, treatment, transport, storage and disposal of hazardous wastes shall make an application to the State Pollution Control Board in Form I for the grant of authorisation within a period of six months from the date of commencement of these rules.

(4) The [3][State Pollution Control Board or Committee] shall not issue an authorisation unless it is satisfied that the operator of a facility or an occupier, as the case may be, possesses appropriate facilities, technical capabilities and equipment to handle hazardous wastes safely.

(5) The authorisation to operate a facility shall be issued in Form 2 and shall be subject to conditions laid down therein.

(6) (i) An authorisation granted under this rule shall, unless sooner suspended or cancelled, be in force fora period of two years from the date of issue or from the date of renewal.

(ii) An application for the renewal of an authorisation shall be made in Form I, before its expiry.

(iii) The authorisation shall continue to be in force until it is renewed or revoked.

(7) The [3][State Pollution Control Board or Committee] may, after giving reasonable opportunity of being heard to the applicant, refuse to gram any authorisation.

6. Power to Suspend or Cancel an Authorisation

(1) The [3][State Pollution Control Board or Committee] may cancel an authorisation issued under these rules or suspend it for such period as it thinks fit if, in its opinion, the authorised person has failed to comply with any of the conditions of the authorisation or with any provisions of the Act or these rules, after giving the authorised person an opportunity to show cause and after recording reasons therefor.

(2) Upon suspension or cancellation of the authorisation and during the pendency of an appeal under rule 12, the [3][State Pollution Control Board or Committee] may give directions to the persons whose authorisation

has been suspended or cancelled for the safe storage of the hazardous wastes, and such person shall comply with such directions.

7. Packaging, Labelling and Transport of Hazardous Wastes

(1) Before hazardous waste is delivered at the hazardous wastes site, the occupier or operator of a, facility shall ensure that the hazardous waste is packaged in a manner suitable for storage and transport and the labelling and packaging shall be easily visible and be able to withstand physical conditions and climatic factors.

(2) Packaging, labelling and transport of hazardous wastes shall be in accordance with the provisions of the rules issued by the Central Government under the Motor Vehicles Act. 1988, and of her guidelines issued from time to time.

8. Inventory of Disposal Sites

(1) The State Government or a person authorised by it shall undertake a continuing programme to identify the sites and compile and publish periodically an inventory of disposal sites within the State for the disposal of hazardous wastes.

(2) The State Government or a person authorised by it shall undertake an environmental impact study before identifying a site as waste disposal site in the State.

(3) The State Government or a person authorised by it shall under take a continuing programme to compile and publish an inventory of sites within the State at which hazardous wastes have at any time been stored or disposed of and such inventory shall contain, besides the location and description, information relating to the amount, nature and toxicity of hazarous wastes at each such site as may be associated with such site.

9. Records and Returns

(1) The occupier generating hazardous waste and operator of a facility for collection, reception, treatment, transport, storage and disposal of hazardous waste shall maintain records of such operations in Form 3.

(2) The occupier and operator of a facility shall send annual returns to the [4][State Pollution Control Board or Committee] in Form 4.

10. Accident Reporting and Follow-Up

Where an accident occurs at the facility or on a hazardous waste site or during transportation of hazardous wastes, the occupier or operator of a facility shall report immediately to the [4] [State Pollution Control Board or Committee] about the accident in Form 5.

11. Import of Hazardous Wastes

(1) Import of hazardous wastes from any country to India shall not be permitted for dumping and disposal of such wastes. However, import of such wastes may be allowed for processing or reuse as raw material, after examining each case on merit by the [4][State Pollution Control Board or Committee] or by an officer authorised in this behalf.

(2) The exporting country or the exporter, as the case may be of hazardous wastes shall communicate in Form 6 to the Central Government (the Ministry of Environment and Forests) of the proposed transboundary movement of hazardous wastes.

(3) The Central Government shall, after examining the communication received under sub-rule (2) and on being satisfied that the import of such hazardous wastes is to be used for processing or reuse as raw material, gram permission for the import of such wastes subject to such conditions as the Central

Government may specify in this behalf and if, however, the Central Government is not satisfied with the communication received under sub-rule (2), it may refuse permission to import such hazardous wastes.

(4) Any importer importing hazardous wastes shall provide necessary information as to the type of hazardous wastes he is to import, in Form 6, to the concerned [4][State Pollution Control Board or Committee]/the Central Pollution Control Board in the case of Union Territories.

(5) The [4][State Pollution Control Board or Committee] shall examine the information received under sub-rule (4) and issue such instructions to the importer as it considers necessary.

(6) The Central Government or the [5][State Pollution Control Board or Committee] as the case may be, shall inform the concerned Port Authority to take appropriate steps regarding the safe handling of the hazardous wastes at the time of off-loading the same.

(7) Any person importing hazardous wastes shall maintain the records of the hazardous wastes imported as specified in Form 7 and the records so maintained shall be open for inspection by the [5][State Pollution Control Board or Committtee]/the Ministry of Environment and Forests/the Central Pollution Control Boards in the case of Union Territories or an officer appointed by them in this behalf.

12. Appeal

(1) An appeal shall lie, against any order of suspension or cancellation or refusal of an authorisation by the [5][State Pollution Control Board to the State Government or Committee to the Union Territory] and to the Ministry of Environment and Forests in the case of the Central Pollution Control Board.

(2) Every appeal shall be in writing and shall be accompanied by a copy of the order appealed against and shall be presented within thirty days of the order passed.

REFERENCES

1. Vide Notification No. S.O. 594 (E), dated 28th July, 1989 published in Gazette of India, Extraordinary, Pt. II. sec. 3(ii), dated 28th July, 1989.
2. Subs. by S.O. 625(E), dated 3rd September, 1996 (w.e.f. 3-9-1996).
3. Subs. by S.O. 625(E), dated 3rd September, 1996 (w.e.f. 3-9-1996).
4. Subs. by S.O. 625(E), dated 3rd September, 1996 (w.e.f. 3-9-1996).
5. Subs. by S.O. 625(E), dated 3rd September, 1996 (w.e.f. 3-9-1996).

APPENDIX—IX

THE MANUFACTURE, STORAGE, AND IMPORT OF HAZARDOUS CHEMICALS RULES, 1989[1]

In exercise of the powers conferred by Section 6, 8 and 25 of the Environment (Protection) Act, 1986 (29 of 1966), the Central Government hereby makes the following rules, namely.

1. Short Title and Commencement

(1) These rules may be called the Manufacture, Storage and import of Hazardous Chemicals Rules, 1989.

(2) They shall come into force on the date of their publication in the official Gazette.

2. Definitions

In these rules, unless the context otherwise requires,-

(a) "Act" means the Environment (Protection) Act, 1986 (29 of 1986);

(b) "Authority" means an authority mentioned in Column 2 of Schedule 5;

(c) "export" with its grammatical variations and cognate expression, means taking out of India to a place outside India;

(d) "exporter" means any person under the jurisdiction of the exporting country and includes the exporting country who exports hazardous chemical;

(e) "hazardous chemical" means-

   (i) any chemical which satisfies any of the criteria laid down in Part I of Schedule I and is listed in Column 2 of Part II of this Schedule;

   (ii) any chemical listed in Column 2 of Schedule 2;

   (iii) any chemical listed in Column 2 of Schedule 3;

(f) "import" with its grammatical variations and cognate expression, means bringing into India from a place outside India;

(g) "importer" means an occupier or any person who imports hazardous chemicals;

(h) "industrial activity" means-

  (i) an operation of process carried out in an industrial installation referred to in Schedule 4 involving or likely to involve one or more or hazardous chemicals and includes on-site storage or on-site transport which is associated with that operation or process, as the case may be; or

  (ii) isolated storage; or

  (iii) pipeline;

(i) "isolated storage" means storage of a hazardous chemical, other than storage associated with an installation on the same site specified in Schedule 4 where that storage involves atleast the quantities of that chemical set out in Schedule 2;

(j) "major accident" means an occurrence including any particular major emission, fire or explosion involving one or more hazardous chemicals and resulting from uncontrolled developments in .he course of an industrial activity or due to natural events leading to serious effects both immediate or delayed, inside or outside the installation likely to cause substantial loss of life and property including adverse effects on the environments;

(k) "pipeline" means a pipe (together with any apparatus and works associated therewith) or system of pipes (together with any apparatus and work associated therewith) for the conveyance of a hazardous chemical other than a flammable gas as set out in Column 2 of Part II of Schedule 3 at a pressure of less than eight bars absolute the pipeline also includes inter-state pipe elines;

(l) "Schedule" means Schedule appended to these rules;

(m) "site" means any location where hazardous chemicals are manufactured or processed, stored, handled, used, disposed of and includes the whole of an area under the control of an occupier and includes pier, jetty or similar structure whether floating or not;

(n) "Threshold quantity" means,-

(i) in the case of a hazardous chemical specified in Column 2 of Schedule 2, the quantity of that chemical specified in the corresponding entry in Columns 3 & 4;

(ii) in the case of hazardous chemical specified in Column 2 of Part I of Schedule 3, the quantity of that chemical specified in the corresponding entry in Columns 3 & 4 of that part;

(iii) in the case of substances of a class specified in Column 2 of Part H of Schedule 3, the total quantity of all substances of that class specified in the corresponding entry in Column 3 & 4 of that part.

[2]3. Duties of Authorities

The concerned Authority shall,-

(a) inspect the industrial activity at least once in a calendar year

(b) except where such authority is the Ministry of Environment and Forests, annually report on the compliance of the rules by the occupiers to the Ministry of Environment and Forests through appropriate channel;

(c) Subject to the other provisions of these rules, the authority shall perform duties as specified in Column 3 of Schedule 5.

4. General Responsibility of the Occupier During Industrial Activity

(1) These rule shall apply to,-

(a) an industrial activity in which a hazardous chemical, which satisfies any of the criteria laid down in Part I of Schedule I and is listed in Column 2 of Part II of this Schedule is or may be involved; and

(b) isolated storage in which there is involved a threshold quantity of a hazardous chemical listed in Schedule 2 in Column 2 which is equal to or more than the threshold quantity specified in the Schedule for that chemical in Column 3 thereof.

(2) An occupier who has control of an industrial activity in term of sub-rule (I) shall provide evidence to show that he has,-

(a) identified the major accident hazards; and

(b) taken adequate steps to -

(i) prevent such major accidents and o limit their consequences to persons and the environment;

(ii) provide to the persons working on the site with the information, training and equipment including antidotes necessary to ensure their safely.

5. Notification of Major Accident

(1) Where a major accident occurs on a site or in a pipe line, the occupier shall [3][within 48 hours notify] the concerned authority as identified in Schedule 5 of that accident, and furnish thereafter to the concerned authority a report relating to the accidents in installments, if necessary, in Schedule 6.

(2) The concerned authority shall on receipt of the report in accordance with sub-rule (1) of this rule shall undertake a full analysis of the major accident and send the [3][requisite information within 90 days to the Ministry] of Environment and Forests through appropriate channel.

[3][(3) An occupier shall notify to the concerned Authority, steps taken to avoid any repetition of such occurrence on a site.]

[4](4) be concerned Authority shall compile information regarding major accidents and make available a copy of the same to the Ministry of Environment and Forest through appropriate channel].

(5) The concerned Authority shall in writing inform the occupier, of any lacunae which in its opinion needs to be rectified to avoid major accidents.]

6. Industrial Activity to Which Rules 7 to 15 Apply

(1) Rules 7 to 15 shall apply to,-

(a) an industrial activity in which there is involved a quantity of hazardous chemical listed in Column 2 of Schedule 3 which is equal to or more than the quantity specified in the entry for that chemical in Columns 3 & 4 (Rules 10-12 only for Column 4) and

(b) isolated storage in which there is involved a quantity of a hazardous chemical listed in Column 2 of Schedule 2 which is equal to or more than the quantity specified in the entry for that chemical in Column[4]

(2) For the purposes of rules 7 to 15,

(a) "new industrial activity" means an industrial activity which-

(i) commences after the date of coming into operation of these rules; or

(ii) if commenced before that date is an industrial activity in which a modification has been made which is likely to cover major accident hazards and that activity shall be deemed to have commenced on the date on which the modification was made;

(b) an "existing industrial activity" means an industrial activity which is not a new industrial activity.

7. Notification of Sites

(1) An occupier shall not undertake any industrial activity [5][unless he has been granted an approval for undertaking such an activity and has submitted] a written report to the concerned authority containing the particulars specified in Schedule 7 at least 3 months before commencing that activity or before such shorter time as the concerned authority may agree and for the purpose of this paragraph an activity in which subsequently there is or is liable to be a threshold quantity or more of an additional hazardous chemical shall be deemed to be a different activity and shall be notified accordingly.

[5](2) The concerned Authority within 60 days form the date of receipt of the report, shall approve the report submitted and on consideration of the report if it is of the opinion that contravention of the provisions of the Act of the rules made thereunder has taken place, it shall issue notice under rule 19.]

8. Updating of the site Notification Following Changes in the Threshold Quantity

Where an activity has been reported in accordance with rule 7(1) and the occupier makes a change in it (including an increase or decrease in the maximum threshold quantity of a hazardous chemical to which this rule applies which is or is liable to be at the site or in the pipeline or at the cessation of the activity) which affects the particulars specified in that report or any subsequent report made under this rule the occupier shall forthwith furnish a further report to the concerned authority.

9. Transitional Provisions

Where-

(a) at the date of coming into operation of these rules, an occupier is in control of an existing industrial activity which is required to be reported under rule 7(1); or

(b) within 6 months after that date an occupier commences any such new industrial activity;

it shall be a sufficient compliance with that rule if he reports to the concerned authority as per the particulars in Schedule 7 within 3 months after the date of coming into operation of these rules or within such longer time as the concerned authority may agree in writing.

10. Safety Reports

(1) Subjects to the following paragraphs of this rule, an occupier shall not undertake any industrial activity to which this rule applies, unless he has prepared a safety report on that industrial activity containing the information specified in Schedule 8 and has sent a copy of that report to the concerned authority al least ninety days before commencing that activity.

(2) In the case of a new industrial activity which an occupier commences, or by virtue of sub-rule (2) (a) (ii) of rule 6 is deemed to commence, within 6 months after coming into operation of these rules, it shall be a sufficient compliance with sub-rule (I) of this rule if the occupier sends to the concerned authority a copy of the report required in accordance with that

sub-rule within ninety days after the date of coming into operation of these rules.

[6][(3) In case of an existing industrial activity, the occupier shall prepare a safety report in consultation with the concern authority and submit the same within one year form the date of the commencement of the Manufacture, Storage and Import of Hazardous Chemicals (Amendment) Rules, 1994, to the concerned Authority.]

[7][(4) After the commencement of the Manufacture, Storage and Import of Hazardous Chemicals (Amendment) Rules, 1994, the occupiers of both the new and the existing industrial activities shall carry out an independent safety audit of the respective industrial activities with the help of an expert, not associated with such industrial activities.

(5) The occupier shall forward a copy of the auditor's report along with his comments, to the concerned Authority within 30 days after the completion of such Audit.

(6) The occupier shall update the safety audit report once a year by conducting a fresh safety audit and forward a copy of it with his comments thereon within 30 days to the concerned Authority.

(7) The concerned Authority may, if it deems fit, issue improvement notice under rule 19 within 45 days of the submission oft he said report].

11. Updating of Reports Under Rule 10

(1) Where an occupier has made a safety report in accordance with sub-rule (I) of rule 10 he shall not make any modification to the industrial activity to which that safely report relates which could materially

affect the particulars in that report, unless the has made a further report to take account of those modifications and has sent a copy of that report to the concerned authority at least 90 days before making those modifications.

(2) Where an occupier has made a report in accordance with rule 10 and sub-rule (1) of this rule and that industrial activity is continuing the occupier shall within three years of the date of the last such report, make a further report which shall have regard in particular to new technical knowledge which has affected the particulars in the previous report relating to safety and hazard assessment and shall within 30 days [8][***], send a copy of the report to the concerned authority.

[6]12. Requirements for Further Information to be Sent to the Authority

Where, in accordance with rule 10, an occupier has sent a safely report relating to an industrial activity to the concerned authority, the concerned authority may, by a notice served on the occupier, requires him to provide such additional information as may be specified in the notice, and occupier shall send that information to the cncerned Authority within 90 days.]

13. Preparation of On-Site Emergency Plan by the Occupier

(1) An occupier shall prepare and keep up-to-date [6][an on-site emergency plan containing details special in schedule 11 and detailing] how major accidents will be dealt with on the site on which the industrial activity is carried on and that plan shall include the name of the person who is responsible for safety on the site and the names of those who are authorised to take action in accordance with the plan in case of an emergency.

(2) The occupier shall ensure that the emergency plan prepared in accordance with sub-rule (I) takes into account any modification made in the industrial activity and that every person on the site who is affected by the plan is informed of its relevant provisions.

(3) The occupier shall prepare the emergency plan required under sub-rule (1).-

   (a) in the case of a new industrial activity, before that activity is commenced;

   (b) in the case of an existing industrial activity within 90 days of coming into operation of these rules.

[9][(4) The occupier shall ensure that a mock drill of the on-site emergency plan is conducted every six months;

(5) A detailed report of the mock drill conducted under sub-rule (4) shall be made immediately available to the concerned Authority.]

14. Preparation of Off-Site Emergency Plan by the Authority

(1) It shall be the duty of the concerned authority as identified in Column 2 of Schedule 5 to prepare and keep up-to-date [10][an adequate off-site emergency plan containing details specified in Schedule 12 and detailing] how emergencies relating to a possible major accident on that site will be dealt with and in preparing that plan the concerned authority shall consult the occupier, and such other persons as it may deem necessary.

(2) For the purpose of enabling the concerned authority to prepare the emergency plan required under sub-rule (1), the occupier shall provide the concerned authority with such information relating to the industrial activity under his control as the concerned

authority may require, including the nature, extent and likely effects off-site of possible major accidents and the authority shall provide the occupier with any information from the off-site emergency plan which relates to his duties under rule 13.

(3) The concerned authority shall prepare its emergency plan required under sub-rule (1),-

(a) in the case of a new industrial activity, before that activity is commenced;

(b) in the case of an existing industrial activity within six months of coming into operation of these rules.

[9][(4) The concerned authority shall ensure that a rehearsal of the off-site emergency plan is conducted at least once in a calendar year.]

15. Information to be Given to Persons Liable to be Affected by a Major Accident

(1) The occupier shall take appropriate steps to inform persons outside the site either directly or through District Emergency Authority who are likely to be in an area which may be affected by a major accident about-

(a) the nature of the major accident hazard; and

(b) the safety measures and the "Do's" and "Don'ts" which should be adopted in the event of a major accident.

(2) The occupier shall take the steps required under sub-rule (I) to inform persons about an industrial activity, before that activity is commenced, except, in the case of an existing industrial activity in which case the occupier shall comply with the requirements of sub-rule (I) within 90 days of coming into operation of these rules.

16. Disclosures of Information

(1) Where for the purpose of evaluating information notified under rule 5 or 7 to 15, the concerned authority discloses that information to some other person, that other person shall not use that information for any purpose except for the purpose of the concerned authority disclosing it, and before disclosing the information the concerned authority shall inform that other person of his obligations under this paragraph.

17. Collection, Development and Dissemination of Information

(1) This rule shall apply to an industrial activity in which a hazardous chemical which satisfies any of the criteria laid down in part I of Schedule I and is listed in Column 2 of Part II of this Schedule is or may be involved.

(2) An occupier, who has control of an industrial activity in term of sub-rule (1) of this rule, shall arrange to obtain or develop information in the form of safety data-sheet as specified in Schedule 9. The information shall be accessible upon request for reference.

(3) The occupier while obtaining or developing a safety data sheet as specified in Schedule 9 in respect of a hazardous chemical handled by him shall ensure that the information is recorded accurately and reflects the scientific evidence used in making the hazard determination. In case, any significant information regarding hazard of a chemical is available, it shall be added to the material safety data-sheet as specified in Schedule 9 as soon as practicable.

(4) Every container of a hazardous chemical shall be clearly labelled or marked to identify,-

(a) the contents of the container,

(b) the name and address of manufacturer or importer of the hazardous chemical;

(c) the physical, chemical and toxicological data as per the criteria given at Part I of Schedule 1.

(5) In terms of sub-rule (4) of this rule, where it is impracticable to label a chemical in view of the size of the container or the nature of the package, provision should be made for other effective means like tagging or accompanying documents.

18. Import of Hazardous Chemicals

(1) This rule shall apply to a chemical which satisfies any of the criteria laid down in Part I of Schedule I and is listed in Column 2 of Part II of this Schedule.

(2) Any person responsible for importing hazardous chemicals in India shall provide [11][before 30 days or as rasonably possible but not later than] the date of import to the concerned authorities as identified in Column 2 of Schedule 5 the information pertaining to-

(i) the name and address of the person receiving the consignment in India;

(ii) the port of entry in India;

(iii) mode of transport from the exporting country to India;

(iv) the quantity of chemical(s) being imported; and

(v) complete product safety information.

[12][(3) If the concerned authority at the State is satisfied that the chemical being imported is likely to cause major accident, it may direct the importer to take such safety measures as the concerned authority at the State may deem it appropriate.]

[13][3(A) In case the concerned Authority of the State is of the opinion that the chemical should not be imported on

safety or on environmental considerations, such Authority may direct stoppage of such import.]

(4) The concerned authority at the State shall simultaneously inform the concerned Port Authority to take appropriate steps regarding safe handling and storage of hazardous chemicals while off-loading the consignment with the port premises.

(5) Any person importing hazardous chemicals shall maintain the records of the hazardous chemicals imported as specified in Schedule 10 and the records so maintained shall be open for inspection by the concerned authority at the State or the Ministry of Environment and Forests or any officer appointed by them in this behalf.

(6) The importer of the hazardous chemical of a person working on his behalf shall ensure that transport of hazardous chemicals from port of entry to the ultimate destination is in accordance with the Central Motor Vehicles Rules, 1989 framed under the provisions of the Motor Vehicles Act, 1988.

19. Improvement Notices

(1) If the concerned authority is of the opinion that a person has contravened the provisions of these rules, the concerned authority shall serve on him a notice (in this para referred to as "an improvement notice") requiring that person to remedy the contravention or, as the case may be, [12][the matters occasioning it within 45 days.

(2) A notice served under sub-rule (1) shall clearly specify the measures to be taken by the occupier in remedying said contraventions.

20. Power of the Central Government to Modify the Schedule

The Central Government may, at any-time, by notification in the Official Gazette, make suitable changes in the Schedules.

REFERENCE

1. Vide Notification No. S.O. 996(E) dated 27th November, 1989, published in the Gazette of India, Extra, dated 27th November, 1989, Pt. II, sec. 3(ii) and corrected per Notification No. S.O. 115(E), dated 5th February, 1990, published in the Gazette of India, Extra., dated 5th February, 1990, Pt. II, sec. 3(ii).
2. Subs. by MSIIC (Amendment) Rules, 1994 (w.e.f. 22-10-1994).
3. Subs. by MSIIC (Amendment) Rules, 1994 (w.e.f. 22-10-1994).
4. Ins. by MSIIC (Amendment) Rules, 1994 (w.e.f. 22-10-1994).
5. Subs. by MSIIC (Amendment) Rules, 1994 (w.e.f. 22-10-1994).
6. Subs. by MSINC (Amendment) Rules, 1994 (w.e.f. 22-10-1994).
7. Ins. by MSIHC (Amendment) Rules, 1994 (w.e.f. 22-10-1994).
8. Omitted by MSIHC (Amendment) Rules, 1994 (w.e.f. 22-10-1994).
9. Ins. by MSIHC (Amendment) Rules, 1994 (w.e.f. 22-10-1994).
10. Subs by MSIHC (Amendment) Rules, 1994 (w.e.f. 22-10-1994).
11. Subs. by MSIHC (Amendment) Rules, 1994 (w.e.f. 22-10-1994).
12. Subs. by MSIHC (Amendment) Rules, 1994 (w.e.f. 22-10-1994).
13. Subs. by MSIHC (Amendment) Rules, 1994 (w.e.f. 22-10-1994).

APPENDIX—X

RULES FOR THE MANUFACTURE, USE, IMPORT, EXPORT AND STORAGE OF HAZARDOUS MICRO ORGANISMS GENETICALLY ENGINEERED ORGANISMS OR CELLS

(To be notified under the EP Act, 1986)

G.S.R. 1037(E)- In exercise of the powers conferred by sections 6,8 and 25 of the Environment (Protection) Act, 1986 (29 of 1986) and with a view to protecting the environment, nature and health, in connection with the application of genetechnology and micro-organisms, the Central Government hereby makes the following rules, namely:

1. Short Title, Extent and Commencement

(1) These rules may be called the Rules for The Manufacture, Use, Import, Export and Storage of Hazardous micro-organisms Genetically engineered organisms or cells.

(2) These rules shall come into operation on the date to be notified for this purpose in the Official Gazette.

2. Application

(1) These rules are applicable to the manufacture import and storage of micro-organisms and Gene-Technological products.

(2) These shall apply to genetically engineered organisms, micro-organisms and cells and correspondingly to any substances and products and food stuffs, etc. of which such cells, organisms or tissues hereof form part.

(3) These rules shall also apply to new genetechnologies apart from those referred to in clauses (ii) and (iv) of rule 3 and these rules shall apply to organisms/micro-

organisms and cells generated by the utilisation of such other gene-technologies and to substances and products of which such organisms and cells form part.

(4) These rules shall be applicable in the following specific cases:

  (a) sale, offers for sale, storage for the purpose of sales, offers and any kind of handling over with or without a consideration;
  (b) exportation and importation of genetically engineered cells or organisms;
  (c) production, manufacturing, processing, storage, import, drawing off. packaging and repacking of the Genetically Engineered Products;
  (d) Production, manufacture etc., of drugs and pharmaceuticals and food stuffs distilleries and tanneries, etc. which make use of micro-organisms genetically engineered micro-organisms one way or the other.

(5) These rules shall be applicable to the whole of India.

3. Definitions

In these rules unless the context requires,

(i) "Biotechnology" means the application of scientific and engineering principles to the processing of materials by biological agents to produce goods and services;

(ii) "Cell hybridisation" means the formation of live cells with new combinations of genetic material through the fusion of two or more cells by means of methods which do not occur naturally;

(iii) "Gene Technology" means the application of the gene technique called genetic engineering, include self cloning and deletion as well as cell hybridisation;

(iv) "Genetic engineering" means the technique by which heritable material, which does not usually occur or will not occur naturally in the organism or cell concerned, generated outside the organism or the cell is inserted into said cell or organism. It shall also mean the formation of new combinations of genetic material by incorporation of a cell into a host cell, where they occur naturally (self cloning) as well as modification of an organism or in a cell by deletion and removal of parts of the heritable material;

(v) "microorganisms" shall include all the bacteria, viruses, fungi, mycoplasma, cells lines, algae, protodones and nematotes indicated in the schedule and those that have not been presently known to exist in the country or not have been discovered so far".

4. Competent Authorities

1. Recombinant DNA Advisory Committee (RDAC)

This committee shall review developments in Biotechnology at national and international levels and shall recommend suitable and appropriate safely regulations for India in recombinant research, use and applications from lime to time. The committee shall function in the Department of Biotechnology.

2. Review Committee on Genetic Manipulation (RCGM)

This committee shall function in the Department of Biotechnology to monitor the safely related aspect in respect of on-going research projects and activities involving genetically engineered organisms/hazardous microorganisms. The Review Committee on Genetic Manipulation shall include representatives of (a) Department of Biotechnology (b) Indian Council of Medical Research (c) Indian Council of Agricultural Research (d) Council of Scientific and Industrial Research (e) other experts in their individual capacity. Review Committee on Genetic Manipulation may appoint sub groups.

It shall bring out Manuals of guidelines specifying procedure for regulatory process with respect to activities involving genetically engineered organisms in research, use and applications including industry with a view to ensure environmental safety. AII ongoing projects involving high risk category and controlled field experiments shall be reviewed to ensure that adequate precautions and containment conditions are followed as per the guidelines.

The Review Committee on Genetic Manipulation shall lay down procedures restricting or prohibiting production, sale, importation and use of such genetically engineered organisms of cells as are mentioned in the Schedule.

3. Institutional Biosafety Committee (IBSC)

This committee shall be constituted by an occupier or any person including, research institutions handling micro organisms/genetically engineered organisms. The committee shall comprise the Head of the Institution, Scientists engaged in DNA work, a medical expert and a nominee of the Department of Biotechnology. The occupier or any person including research institutions handling microorganisms/ genetically engineered organisms shall prepare with the assistance of the Institutional Biosafety Committee (IBSC) an upto date on-site emergency plan according to the manuals/ guidelines of the RCGM and make available copies to the District Level Committee/State Biotechnology Co-ordinating Committee and the Genetic Engineering Approval Committee.

4. Genetic Engineering Approval Committee (GEAC)

This committee shall function as a body under the Department of Environment, Forests and Wildlife for approval of activities involving large scale use of hazardous microorganisms and recombinants in research and industrial production from the environmental angle. The Committee shall also be responsible for approval of proposals relating to release of genetically engineered organisms and products into the environment including experimental field trials.

The composition of the Committee shall be:

(i) Chairman - Additional Secretary Department of Environment Forests, and Wild life. Co-Chairman - Representative of Department of Bio-technology.

(ii) Members: Representatives of concerned Agencies and Departments, namely Ministry of Industrial Development, Department of Biotechnology and the Department of Atomic Energy.

(iii) Expert members: Director General - Indian Council Research, Director General - Indian Council of Medical Research, Director General -Council of Scientific and Industrial Research, Director General - Health Services, Plant Protection Adviser, Directorate of Plant Protection, Quarantine and storage, Chairman, Central Pollution Control Board and three outside experts in individual capacity.

(iv) Member Secretary: An official of the Department of Environment, Forest and Wildlife.

The Committee may co-opt other members/experts as necessary.

The committee or any person/s authorised by it shall have powers to take actions under the Environment (Protection) Act.

5. *State Biotechnology Co-ordination Committee (SBCC)*

There shall be a State Biotechnology Coordination Committee in the States wherever necessary. It shall have powers to inspect, investigate and take punitive action in case of violations of statutory provisions through the Nodal Department and the State Pollution Control board/Directorate of Health/Medical Services. The Committee shall review periodically the safety and control measures in the various industries/institution handling genetically engineered Organisms/Hazardous microorganisms. The compositions of the Coordination Committee shall be:

(i) Chief Secretary - Chairman

(ii) Secretary, Department of Environment - Member Secretary

(iii) Secretary, Department of Health - Member

(iv) Secretary, Department of Agriculture - Member

(v) Secretary, Department of Industries and Commerce - Member

(vi) Secretary, Department of Forests - Member

(vii) Secretary, Department of Public Works/Chief Engineer, Department of Public Health Engineering - Member

(viii) State Microbiologists and Pathologists - Member

(ix) Chairman of State Pollution Control Board.

The Committee may co-opt other members/experts as necessary.

6. District Level Committee (DLC)

There shall be a District Level Biotechnology Committee (DLC) in the districts wherever necessary under the District Collectors to monitor the safety regulations in installations engaged in the use of genetically modified organisms/hazardous microorganisms and its applications in the environment.

The District Level Committee/or any other person/s authorised in this behalf shall visit the install engaged in activity involving genetically engineered organisms, hazardous microorganisms, form information chart, find out hazards and risks associated with each of these installations and coordinate activities with a view to meeting any emergency. They shall also prepare an off-site emergency plan. District Level Committee shall regularly submit its report to the State Biotechnology Co-ordination Committee/Genetic Engineering Approval Committee.

The District Level Committee shall comprise of:

(i) District Collector
— Chairman

(ii) Factory Inspector
— Member

(iii) A representative of the Pollution Control Board
— Member

(iv) Chief Medical Officer (District Health Officer)
— Member (Convenor)

(v) District Agricultural Officer
— Member

(vi) A representative of the Public Health Engineering Department
— Member

(vii) Distric Microbiologists/Pathologist (technical expert)
— Member

(viii) Commissioner Municipal Corporation
— Member

The committee may co-opt other members/experts as necessary

5. Classification of Micro-Organisms or Genetically Engineered Product

(1) For the purpose of these rules, microorganisms or genetically engineered organisms, products or cells shall be dealt with under two major heads; animal, pathogens and plant pests and these shall be classified in the manner specified in the Schedule.

(2) If any of the microorganisms, genetically engineered organism or cell falls within the limits of more than one risk class as specified in the Schedule, it shall be deemed to belong exclusively to the last in number of such classes.

6. Microorganisms Laid Down in the Schedule are Divided into the Following

(i) Bacterial Agents;

(ii) Fungal Agents;

(iii) Parasitic Agents;

(iv) Viral, Rickettsial and Chlamydial Agents;

(v) Special Category.

7. Approval and Prohibitions, Etc

(1) No person shall import, export, transport, manufacture, process, use or sell any hazardous microorganisms of genetically engineered organisms/substances or cells except with the approval of the Genetic Engineering Approval Committee.

(2) Use of pathogenic microorgnisms or any genetically engineered organisms or cells for the purpose of research shall only be allowed in laboratories or inside laboratory area notified by the Ministry of Environment and Forests for this purpose under the Environment (Protection) Act, 1986.

(3) The Genetic Engineering Approval Committee shall give directions to the occupier to determine or take

measures concerning the discharge of microorganisms/ genetically engineered organisms or cells mentioned in the Schedule from the laboratories, hospitals and other areas including prohibition of such discharges and laying down measures to be taken to prevent such discharges.

(4) Any person operating or using genetically engineered organisms/microogranisms mentioned in the schedule for scale up or pilot operations shall have to obtain licence issued by the Genetic Engineering Approval Committee for any such activity. The possessor shall have to apply for licence in prescribed proform.

(5) Certain experiments for the purpose of education within the field of genetechnology or microorganism may he carried out outside the laboratories and laboratory areas mentioned in sub-rule (2) and will be looked after by the Institutional Bio-safety Committee.

8. Production

Production in which genetically engineered organisms or cells or micro-organisms are generated or used shall not be commenced except with the consent of Genetic Engineering Approval Committee with respect of discharge of genetically engineered organisms or cells into the environment. This shall also apply to production taking place in connection with development, testing and experiments where such production, etc., is not subject to rule 7.

9. Deliberate or Unintentional Release

(1) Deliberate or unintentional release of genetically engineered organisms/hazardous microorganisms or cells, including deliberate release for the purpose of experiment shall not be allowed.

Note: Deliberate release shall mean any intentional transfer of genetically engineered organisms/hazardous, microorganisms or cells to the environment or nature, irrespective of the way in which it is done.

(2) The Genetic/Engineering Approval Committee may in special cases give approval of deliberate release.

10. Permission and Approval for Certain Substances

Substances and products, which contain genetically engineered organisms or cells or microorganisms shall not be produced, sold, imported or used except with the approval of Genetic Engineering Approval Committee.

11. Permission and Approval for Food Stuffs

Food stuffs, ingredients in food stuffs and additives including processing and containing or consisting of genetically engineered organisms or cells, shall not be produced, sold, imported or used except with the approval of the Genetic Engineering Approval Committee.

12. Guidelines

(1) Any person who applies for approval under rules 8-11 shall, as determined by the Genetic Engineering Approval Committee submit information and make examinations or cause examinations to be made to eradicate the case, including examinations according to specific directions and at specific laboratories. He shall also make available an on-site emergency plan to GEAC before obtaining the approval. If the authority makes examination itself, it may order the applicant to delay the expenses incurred by it in so doing.

(2) Any person to whom an approval has been granted under rules 8-11 above shall notify the Genetic Engineering Approval Committee of any change in or addition to the information already submitted.

13. Grant of Approval

(1) In connection with the granting of approval under

rules 8 to 11 above, terms and conditions shall be stipulated, including terms and conditions as to the control to be exercised by the applicant, supervision, restriction on use the layout of the enterprise and as to the submission of information to the State Bio-technology Co-ordination Committee or to the District Level Committee.

(2) All approvals of the Genetic Engineering Approval Committee shall be for a specific period not exceeding four year at the first instance renewable for 2 years at a time. The Genetic Engineering Approval Committee shall have powers to revoke such approval in the following situations:

(a) If there is any new information as to the harmful effects of the genetically engineered organisms or cells.

(b) If the genetically engineered organisms or cells cause such damage to the environment, nature or health as could not be envisaged when the approval was given, or

(c) Non compliance of any condition stipulated by Genetic Engineering Approval Committee.

14. Supervision

(1) The Genetic Engineering Approval Committee may supervise the implementation of the terms and conditions laid down in connection with the approvals accorded by it.

(2) The Genetic Engineering Approval Committee may carry out this supervision through the State Bio-technology Coordination Committee or the State Pollution Control Boards/District Level Committee or through any person authorised in this behalf.

15. Penalties

(1) If an order is not complied with, the District Level Committee or State Biotechnology Co-ordination Committee may take measures at the expense of the person who is responsible.

(2) In case where immediate intervention is required in order to prevent any damage to the environment, nature or health the District Level Committee, or State Biotechnology Co-ordination Committee may take the necessary steps without issuing any order or notice. The expenses incurred for this purpose will he repayable by the person responsible for such damage.

(3) The State Bio-technology Co-ordination Committee/ District Level Committee may take samples for a more detailed examination of organisms and cells.

(4) The State Bio-technology Co-ordination Committee/ District Level Committee shall be competent to ask for assistance from any other government authority to carry out its instructions.

16. Responsibility to Notify Interruptions or Accidents

(1) Any person who under rule 7-11 is responsible for conditions or arrangements shall immediately notify the District Level Committee/State Biotechnology Co-ordination Committee and the state medical officer of any interruption of operations or accidents that may lead to discharges of genetically engineered organisms or cells which may be harmful to the environment, nature or health or involve any danger thereto.

(2) Any notice given under sub-rule (1) above shall not lessen the duty of the person who is responsible to try effectively to minimise or prevent the effects of interruptions of operations or accidents.

17. Preparation of Off-Site Emergency Plan by the DLC

(1) It shall be the duty of the DLC to prepare an off-site emergency plan detailing how emergencies relating to a possible major accident at a site will be dealt with and in preparing the plan, the DLC shall consult the occupier and such other person as it may deem necessary.

(2) For the purpose of enabling the DLC to prepare the emergency plan required under sub-rule (1), the occupier shall provide the DLC with such information relating to the handling of hazardous microorganisms/ genetically engineered organisms under his control as the DLC may required including the nature, extent and likely off-site effects of a possible major accident and the DLC shall provide the occupier with any information from the off-site emergency plan which relates to his duties under rule 16.

18. Inspections and Informations Regarding Finance

(1) The State Biotechnology Co-ordination Committee or the Genetic Engineering Approval Committee/ the DLC or any person with special knowledge duly authorised by the State Bio-technology Co-ordination Committee or the Genetic Engineering Approval Committee or the DLC where it is deemed necessary at any time on due production of identity be admitted to public as well as to private peremises and localities for the purpose of carrying out supervision.

(2) Any person who is responsible for activities subject to rules 7.11 above shall at the request of District Level Committee or State Bio-tehnology Co-ordination Committee or the GEAC submit all such information including information relating to financial conditions and accounts, as is essential to the authority's administration under these rules. He shall also allow supervision or inspection by the authorities or persons indicated in sub-rule (I).

(3) The Genetic Engineering Approval Committee may fix fees to cover, in whole or in part the expenses incurred by the authorities in connection with approvals, examinations, supervisions and control.

19. Appeal

(1) Any person aggrieved by a decision made by Genetic Engineering Approval Committee/ State Biotechnology Co-ordination Committee in pursuance of these rules may within thirty days from the date on which the decision is communicated to him prefer an appeal to such authority as may be appointed by Ministry of Environment and Forests provided that the appellate authority may entertain the appeal after the expiry of the said period of thirty clays if such authority is satisfied that the appellant was prevented by sufficient cause from filing the appeal in time.

20. Exemption

The Ministry of Environment and Forests shall, wherever necessary, exempt an occupier handling a particular microorganism genetically engineered organism from rule 7-11.

Select Bibliography

Abu Sin, M.E. (1991), "Migration from Eastern Gezira into Greater Khartoum - A case study in rural-urban migration and population integration processes." *GeoJournal* 25(1): 73-80.

Agmad, Adil Mustafa (1993), "The neighborhoods of Khartoum: Reflections on their functions, forms and future." *Habitat* 16(4): 27-45.

Aguilar, Adrian Guillermo, Exequiel Ezcurra, Teresa Garcia, Marisa Mazari-Hiriat, and Irene Pisanty (1995), "The basin of Mexico." In Jeanne X. Kasperson, Roger E. Kasperson, and B. L. Turner II (eds.), *Regions at Risk*. Tokyo: United Nations University Press, pp. 304-366.

Alexander, David (1993), *Natural disasters*. New York: Chapman & Hall.

Anderson, Mary B. and Peter J. Woodrow (1991), "Reducing vulnerability to drought and famine: Developmental approaches to relief." *Disasters* 15(1): 43- 54.

Annan, K.A. (1999), Preventing War and Disaster: A Growing Global Challenge, 1999 Annual Report on the Work of the Organization, UN, Department of Public Information, New York, pp. 1-61.

Argyros, Alexander J. (1991), *A blessed rage for order: Deconstruction, evolution, and chaos*. Ann Arbor: University of Michigan Press.

Bakhit, Abdel Hamid (1994), "Availability, affordibility and accessibility of food in Khartoum." *GeoJournal* 34(3): 253-255.

Beanland, G.E., and Duinker, P.N. (1983), An ecological framework for environmental impact assessment, In *RES*, Dalhousie University, Canada.

Berke, Philip R. and Timothy Beatley (1992), *Planning for earthquakes: Risk, politics, and policy.*

Berry, Brian J.L. (1990), "Urbanization." In B. L. Turner II, William C. Clark, Robert W. Kates, John F. Richards, Jessica T. Mathews, and William B. Meyer (eds.), *The earth as transformed by human action: Global and regional changes in the biosphere over the past 300 years.* Cambridge: Cambridge University Press, pp. 103-119.

Blaikie, P. and H. Brookfield (1987), *Land degradation and society.* London: Methuen.

Blaikie, Piers, Terry Cannon, Ian Davis, and Ben Wisner (1994), *At risk: Natural hazards, people's vulnerability and disasters.* London: Routledge.

Bohle, Hans-Georg (1994), "Cities of hunger: Urban food systems in developing countries." *GeoJournal* 34(3): 243-244 (see also additional papers, pp. 245-304).

Boone, Christopher G. (1996), "Language politics and flood control in nineteenth-century Montreal." *Environmental History* 1(3): 70-85.

Bromley, Ray, Peter Hall, Ashok Dutt, Debnath Mookherjee and John E. Benhart (1989), "Regional development and planning." In Gary L. Gaile and Cort J. Willmott (eds.), *Geography in America.* Columbus, OH: Merrill Publishing Company, pp. 351-386.

Browning, Larry D. and Judy C. Shetler (1992), "Communication in crisis, communication in recovery: A postmodern commentary on the Exxon Valdez disaster." *International Journal of Mass Emergencies and Disasters* 10(2).

Brunn, Stanley D. and Jack F. Williams (1993), *Cities of the world: World regional development*, 2nd edn. New York: HarperCollins.

Bryant, E.A. (1991), *Natural hazards*. Cambridge: Cambridge University Press.

Burton, I. (1962), Types of agricultural occupance of flood plains in the United States; University of Chicago, *Department of Geography Research Paper No. 75*.

Burton, I. (1965), Rood damage reduction in Canada; *Geophysical Bulletin* 7, 161-85.

Burton, I. and Kates, R.W. (1964), Perception of natural hazards in resources management; *Natural Resources Journal* 3, 412-41.

Burton, I., Kates, R.W. and Snead, R.E. (1969), The human ecology of coastal flood hazard in megalopolis; *University of Chicago, Department of Geography Research Paper No. 115*.

Burton, I., Kates, R.W. and White, G.F. (1968), The human ecology of extreme geophysical events; *Natural Hazard Research, Working Paper No. 1, Department of Geography, University of Toronto*.

Burton, I., R.W. Kates, and G.F. White, (1993), *The Environment As Hazard*. New York: Guilford.

Cemea, Michael, M. (1988), *Involuntary Resettlement in Development Projects*, World Bank Technical Paper Number 80, Washington: World Bank, 4..

Chandler, Tertius and Gerald Fox (1974), 3000 *years of urban growth*. New York: Academic Press,

Chudacoff, Howard P. and Judith E. Smith (1994), *The evolution of American urban society*. Englewood Cliffs, NJ: Prentice-Hall.

Cohen, D. (1991), *Aftershock: The Psychological and Political Consequences of Disaster*, Paladin.

Cohen, Michael A. and Josef L. Leitmann (1994), "Will the World Bank's real 'New Urban Policy' please stand up?" *Habitat International* 18(4): 117-126.

Commissioner for Scheduled Castes and Scheduled Tribes. *Twenty-Ninth Report of the Commissioner for SC and ST*, New Delhi: The Manager of Publications, Government of India, 245, 1987-89.

Cook, H.L. and White, G.F. (1962), Making wise use of flood plains; In *United Nations Conference on Applications of Science and Technology*, (Government Printing Office, Washington), Vol. 1, 343-59.

Cooke, Ronald U. (1984), *Geomorphological hazards in Los Angeles.* London: Alien & Unwin.

Couch, S. R. (1996), "Environmental contamination, community transformation, and the Centralia mine fire." In James K. Mitchell (ed.), *The long road to recovery: Community responses to industrial disaster.* Tokyo: United Nations University Press, pp. 60-85.

Cronon, William (1991), *Nature's metropolis: Chicago and the Great West.* New York and London: W. W. Norton.

Cuny, F.C. (1983), *Disasters and Development.* New York: Oxford University Press.

Cuny, Frederick C. (1994), "Cities under seige: Problems, priorities and programs." *Disasters* 18(2): 152-159.

Curry, Michael (1988), "Commentary on 'Geographers and nuclear war: Why we lack influence on public policy'." *Annals of the Association of American Geographers* 78(4): 720-724.

Czamanske, D.V. (1967), *Receptivity to Flood Insurance;* (Master's Dissertation, University of Chicago).

Dalby, Simon (1992), "Ecopolitical discourse: 'Environmental security' and political geography." *Progress in Human Geography* 16(4): 503-522.

Dando, W.A. (1994), *Urban famines in a future world of mega-cities: A commentary*. Professional Paper No. 20. Indiana State University, Terre Haute, Department of Geography and Geology, pp. 81-87.

Davis, Mike (1992), *City of quartz: Excavating the future in Los Angeles*. New York: Vintage Books.

Davis, R.K. (1968), *The Range of Choice in Water Management: A Study of Dissolved Oxygen in the Polomac Basin;* (Johns Hopkins Press, Baltimore).

Degg, Martin (1993), "The 1992 'Cairo Earthquake': Causes, effect and response." *Disasters* 17(3): 226-238.

Dow, Kirstin (1992), "Exploring differences in our common future(s): The meaning of vulnerability to global environmental change." *Geoforum* 23(3): 417-436.

Driever, Steven L. and Danny M. Vaughn (1988), "Flood hazard in Kansas City since 1880." *Geographical Review* 78(1): 1-19.

Dunham, A. (1959), Flood control via the police power; *University of Pennsylvania Law Review* 107, 1098-132.

Earthquake Engineering Research Institute (1985), *Proceedings - U.S.-Japan Workshop on Urban Earthquake Hazards Reduction*. Publication No. 85-03. Berkeley: EERI.

Edelstein, M. R. (1988), *Contaminated communities: The social and psychological impacts of residential toxic exposure*. Boulder, CO: Westview Press. El-Bushra,

El-Sayed and Naila B. Hijazi (1995), "Two million squatters in Khartoum urban complex: The dilemma of Sudan's national capital." *GeoJournal* 35(4): 505-514.

Emel, J. and J. R. Peet (1989), "Resource management and natural hazards.' In J.R. Peet and N. Thrift (eds.), *New models in geography: The political-economy perspective.* London: Unwin Hyman.

Ezcurra, Exequiel and Marisa Mazari-Hiriart (1996), "Are megacities viable? A cautionary tale from Mexico City." *Environment* 38(1): 15, 26-35.

Fellmann, Jerome, Arthur Getis, and Judy Getis (1992), *Human geography: Landscapes of human activities.* Dubuque: Wm. C. Brown.

Firman, Tommy and Indira Dharmapatni (1994), "The challenges to sustainable development in Jakarta Metropolitan Region." *Habitat International* 18(3): 74-94.

Fishman, Robert (1987), *Bourgeois Utopias: The rise and fall of suburbia.* New York: Basic Books.

France, Ministere de I'Equipment et du Logement (1968), *Etats-Unis: Recherches Methodologiques sur la Rentabilite Economique des Mesures de la Controle des (rues a L'Etranger;* (Paris, BCEOM).

France, Ministere de I'Equipment et du Logement, *Inventaire des Zones Inondables;* (Paris: BCEOM, n.d.).

Franks, Tom (1991), Institutional Change and Project Rehabilitation, Hardware, Software and Liveware, in Project Rehabilitation in Development Countries, ed. by Colin, Kirkpatrick, London: Routledge 213.

Frater, Alexander (1991), *Chasing the monsoon.* New York: Alfred A. Knopf.

Gaile, Gary L. (1983), "Reanalyses of Chinese spatial inequality." *Professional geographer* 35: 281-283.

Galbraith, John Kenneth (1983), The Anatomy of Power, Boston: Houghton Hifflin.

Gilbert, Alan and Josef Gugler (1992), *Cities, poverty and development: Urbanization in the third world.* Oxford: Oxford University Press.

Gist, M.E. (1987), "Self Efficacy: Implementation for Organization Behaviour and Human Resource Management," Academy of Management Review, July, 472-85.

Glickman, T.S., D. Golding, and E. D. Silverman (1992), "Acts of God and acts of man: Recent trends in natural disasters and major industrial accidents," Center for Risk Management Discussion Paper CRM 92-02, Washington D.C.: Resources for the Future.

Goddard, J.E. (1971), Flood plain management must be ecologically and economically sound; *Civil Engineering* September, 81-5.

Goode, Judith (1996), "On sustainable development in the mega-city." *Current Anthropology* 36(1): 131-133.

Government of Orissa (1968), *Report on the Benefits of Hirakud Irrigation: A Socio-economic Study,* Cuttack: Bureau of Statistics and Economics, Government of Orissa, 13.

Guterbock, Thomas M. (1990), "The effect of snow on urban density patterns in the United States." *Environment and Behavior* 22(3): 358-386.

Hall, Peter (1988), *Cities of tomorrow: An intellectual history of urban planning and design in the twentieth century.* Oxford: Basil Blackwell.

Hansel, G. (1991), "Rural-urban migration and the problem of town planning - The case of Um Badda, Omdurman." *GeoJournal* 25(1): 27-30.

Harvey, D. (1989), *The condition of postmodernity: An enquiry into the origins of cultural change.* Oxford: Blackwell.

Havlick, Spencer W. (1986), "Third world cities at risk: Building for calamity." *Environment* 28(9): 6-11, 41-45.

Hayles, Katherine, ed. (1991), *Chaos and order: Complex dynamics in literature and science.* Chicago: University of Chicago Press.

Hewitt, K. (1969), Probabilistic approaches to discrete natural events: A review and theoretical discussion; *Natural Hazard Research Working Paper No. 8, Department of Geography,* University of Toronto.

Hewitt, Kenneth (1983), *Interpretations of calamity.* Boston: Alien & Unwin. ——— 1992. "Mountain hazards." *GeoJournal* 27(1): 47-60.

Ibrahim, F.N. (1991), "The southern Sudanese migration to Khartoum and the resultant conflicts." *Geo Journal* 25(1): 13-18.

IDNDR (International Decade for Natural Disaster Reduction) (1990), *International Conference 1990 Japan: Toward a less hazardous world in the 21st century: Proceedings.* September 27-October 3,1990, Yokohama and Kagoshima.

Institution of Civil Engineers (1995), *Megacities: Reducing vulnerability to natural disaster.* London: Thomas Telford.

Jairo-Cardenas, J. (1990), "Natural disasters and urban struggle for housing." *Architecture et Comportement/'Architecture and Behaviour* 6(2): 177-191.

Johnson, J.F. (1971), Renovated waste water; *University of Chicago, Department of Geography Research Paper No. 135.*

Jones, Emrys (1990), *Metropolis.* New York: Oxford University Press.

Jones, Gareth A. and Peter M. Ward (1994), "The World Bank's 'new' Urban Management Programme: Paradigm shift or policy continuity?" *Habitat International* 18(3): 33-51.

Kates, R.W. (1962), Hazard and choice perception in flood plain management; *University of Chicago, Department of Geography Research Paper No. 78.*

Kates, R.W. (1964), Variation in flood hazard perception: Implications for rational flood plain use; In *Spatial Organization of Land Uses: The Willamette Valley*, (Oregon State University, Corvallis).

Kates, R.W. (1965), Industrial flood losses: Damage estimation in the Lehigh Valley; *University of Chicago, Department of Geography Research Paper No. 98.*

Kates, R.W. (1971), Natural hazard in human ecological perspective: Hypotheses and models; *Natural Hazard Research Working Paper No. 14,* Department of Geography, University of Toronto.

Kates, R.W. and Wohlwill, J.F. (Eds.) (1966), Man's response to the physical environment; *Journal of Social Issues* 22, 1-140.

Kates, Robert W. (1978), *Risk assessment of environmental hazard.* SCOPE (Scientific Committee on Problems of the Environment) Report No. 8. New York: Wiley.

Kates, Robert W. and Alvin M. Weinberg, eds. (1986), *Hazards: Technology and fairness.* Washington, D.C.: National Academy Press.

Kim, Kwi-Gon (1990), "Risk assessment in urban planning and management: A metropolitan example." *Habitat* 14(1): 177-190.

Kreimer, Alcira and Mohan Munasinghe, eds. (1992), *Environmental management and urban vulnerability.* World Bank Discussion Paper 168. Washington, D.C.: World Bank.

Kreps (1984), Sociological Inquiry and Disaster Research, *Annual Review of Sociology,* 10, pp. 309-312.

Lewis, James (1990), "The vulnerability of small island states: The need for holistic strategies." *Disasters* 14(3): 241-249.

Lewis, Michael (1989), "How a Tokyo earthquake could devastate Wall Street and the world economy." *Manhattan, inc.*, June: 69-79.

Lind, R.C. (1966), *The Nature of Flood Control Benefits and the Economics of Flood Protection;* (Stanford University Institute for Mathematical Studies in the Social Sciences).

Little, Peter D. and Michael M. Horowitz, eds. (1987), *Lands at risk in the Third World: Local level perspectives.* Boulder, CO: Westview Press.

Lowenthal, D. (Ed.) (1967), Environmental perception and behavior; *University of Chicago, Department of Geography Research Paper No. 109.*

MacIver, I. (1970), Urban water supply alternatives: Perception and choice in the Grand Basin, Ontario; *University of Chicago, Department of Geography Rescarch Paper No. 126.*

Main, Hamish and Stephen Wyn Williams, eds. (1994), *Environment and housing in Third World cities.* Chichester: Wiley.

Maskrey, Andrew (1989), *Disaster mitigation: A community based approach.* Development Guidelines No. 3. Oxford: Oxfam.

Masure, P. (1994), "Risk management and preventive planning in mega-cities: A scientific approach for action." *Regional Development Dialogue* 15(2): 183-188.

McHarg, Ian (1969), *Design with nature.* New York: Natural History Press (especially "The City: Health and pathology," pp. 187-195).

McPhee, John (1989), *The control of nature.* New York: Farrar, Straus & Giroux.

Miller, D.H. (1966), Cultural hydrology: A review; *Economic Geography* 42, 85-9.

Miller, Ross (1990), *American apocalypse: The great fire and the myth of Chicago.* Chicago: University of Chicago Press.

Mintzer, Irving M. (1992), *Confronting climate change: Risks, implications and responses.* Cambridge: Cambridge University Press.

Mitchell, J.K., (1989), "Hazards research," in Gary L. Gaile and Cort J. Willmott (Eds.), *Geography in America.* Columbus: Merrill, pp. 410-24.

Mitchell, James K. and Neil Ericksen (1992), "Effects of climate changes on weather-related disasters." In Irving Mintzer (ed.), *Confronting climate change: Risks, implications and responses.* Cambridge: Cambridge University Press, pp. 141-152.

Mitchell, James K., Neal Devine, and Kathleen Jagger (1989), "A contextual model of natural hazard." *Geographical Review* 89(4): 391-409.

Murphy, F.C. (1958), Regulating flood plain development; *University of Chicago, Department of Geography Research Paper No. 56.*

Myers, Mary Fran and Gilbert F. White (1993), "The challenge of the Mississippi flood." *Environment* 35(10): 6-9, 25-35.

National Academy of Sciences Committee on Water (1966), *Alternatives in Water Management;* Publication 1408, (Washington, D.C.).

National Academy of Sciences Committee on Water (1968), *Water and Choice in the Colorado Basin: An Example of Alternatives in Water Management:* Publication 1689, (Washington, D.C.).

National Hazard Research (1970), Suggestions for comparative field observations of natural hazards; *Natural Hazard Research Working Paper No. 16, Department of Geography,* University of Toronto.

O'Riordan, Timothy (1986), "Coping with environmental hazards." In Robert W. Kates and Ian Burton (eds.),

Themes from the work of Gilbert F. White, vol. 2 of *Geography, resources, and environment*. Chicago: University of Chicago Press, pp. 272-309.

Palm, Risa (1990), *Natural hazards: An integrative framework for research and planning*. Baltimore, MD: Johns Hopkins University Press.

Parker, D. J. and J.W. Handmer, eds. (1992), *Hazard management and emergency planning: Perspectives on Britain*. London: James & James.

Parker, Dennis J. and James K. Mitchell (1995), "Disaster vulnerability of mega-cities: An expanding problem that requires rethinking and innovative responses." *GeoJournal* 37(3): 295-301 (see also additional papers, pp. 303-388).

Perlman, Janice E. (1987), "Megacities and innovative technologies." *Cities*, May: 128-136.

Reed, Stuart, Fred Tromp, and Alain Lam (1992), "Major hazards - Thinking the unthinkable." *Environmental Management* 16(6): 715-722.

Revue de Geographic Alpine (1994), "Croissance urbaine et risques naturels dans les montagnes des pays en developpement," No. 4.

Roder, W. (1961), Attitudes and knowledge in the Topeka flood plain; In 'Papers on Flood Problems', *University of Chicago*, Department of Geography Research Paper No. 70.

Rosen, Christine Meisner (1986), *The limits of power: Great fires and the process of city growth in America*. New York: Cambridge University Press.

Rosenau, P.M. (1992), *Post-modernism and the social sciences: Insights, inroads, and intrusions*. Princeton, NJ: Princeton University Press.

Ruppert, Helmut (1991), "The responses of different ethnic

groups in the Sudan to rural-urban migration." *GeoJournal* 25(1): 7-12.

Russell, C.S. (1970), Losses from natural hazards; *Journal of Land Economics*, Vol. 46, p. 38-00.

Saarinen, T.F. (1966), Perception of the drought hazard; *American Geographers, Commission on College Geography*, (Washington, D.C.).

Saarinen. T.F. (1969), Perception of environment; *Association of American Geographers. Commission on College Geography*, (Washington, D.C.).

Sachs, Ignacy (1988), "Vulnerability of giant cities and the life lottery." In Mattei Dogan and John D. Kasarda (eds.), *A world of giant cities*, vol. 1 in *The metropolis era*. Newbury Park, CA: Sage Publications, pp. 337-350.

Schiff, M.R, (1971), Psychological factors relating to the adoption of adjustments for natural hazards in London, Ontario; *Paper presented to Association of American Geographers*, Boston, April 1971.

Sewell, W.R.D. (1965), Water management and floods in the Fraser River Basin; *University of Chicago*, Department of Geography Research Paper No. 100.

Sheaffer, J.R. (1960), Flood proofing: An element in a flood damage reduction program: University of Chieago. Department of Geography Research Paper No. 65,

Sheaffer, J.R. (1964), Economic feasibility and use of flood maps; *Highway Research Record* 58, 44-6.

Sheaffer, J.R. (1967), *Introduction to Flood Proofing: An outline of principles and methods;* (University of Chicago, Center for Urban Studies).

Sims, J. and Saarinen, T.F. (1969), Coping with environmental threat: Great Plains farmers and the sudden storm; *Annals of the Association of American Geographers* 59, 677-86.

Smith, K., (1992), *Environmental Hazards: Assessing Risk and Reducing Disaster*. London: Routledge.

Turner, B.A. and Nick F. Pidgeon (1977), *Man-made Disasters*, Butterworth-Heineman, Oxford.

Turner, B.L., R.E. Kasperson, W.B. Meyer, K.M. Dow, D. Golding, J.X. Kasperson, R.C. Mitchell, and S.J. Ratick, (1990a), "Two types of global environmental change: Definitional and spatial-scale issues in their human dimensions," *Global Environmental Change* 1(1): 14-22.

Turner, B.L., W.C. Clark, R.W. Kates, J.F. Richard, J.T. Mathews, and W.B. Meyer, (1990b), *The Earth as Transformed by Human Action*. Cambridge: Cambridge University Press.

UNEP (United Nations Environment Programme), (1991), *Environmental Data Report*. Oxford: Basil Blackwell.

United States Bureau of Reclamation (1941), *Columbia Basin Joint investigations-Character and Scope;* (Government Printing Office, Washington, D.C.).

United States, Eighty-ninth Congress, Second Session (1966), 4 *Unified National Program for Managing Flood Losses;* House Document 465, (Washington, D.C.).

Wells, C. (1995), *Negotiating Tragedy: Law and Disasters*, Sweet and Maxwell, London.

White, G.F. (1969), *Strategies of American Water Management;* (University of Michigan Press, Ann Arbor).

Index